Published by

GENERAL STORE
PUBLISHING HOUSE

1 Main Street, Burnstown, Ontario, Canada K0J 1G0
1-800-465-6072 or Fax: (613) 432-7184

ISBN 1-896182-15-1
Printed and bound in Canada.

Cover Design and Layout by Tammy L. Anderson

General Store Publishing House gratefully acknowledges the
assistance of the Ontario Arts Council and the Canada Council.

Canadian Cataloguing in Publication Data

Fowler, T. Robert
    Valour in the Victory Campaign: the 3rd Canadian
    Infantry Division, 1995

Includes bibliographical references and index.
ISBN 1-896182-15-1

Cover Photo Credit: THE VICTORIA CROSS
Copyright THE CANADIAN WAR MUSEUM/Photography by William Kent

1. Canada, Canadian Army – Canadian Infantry Division, 3rd – Medals,
badges, decorations, etc. 2. World War, 1939 – 1945–Medals. I. Title.

D796.5.C2F68 1995   940.54'1271   C95-900139-5

First Printing April 1995

What acts of heroism were accomplished in the dark by the unknown soldier! What bravery, what ultimate dedication to face danger. Men like Rochon, Atkinson, Chartrand, Fournier, and so many others that should be named; however, the true soldier looks forward to only one reward and that is the satisfaction of a duty fulfilled. For him, the press releases, the great citations are only a public testimony to his valour, for he only considers two things: Dedication to duty and Honour!

Que d'actes d'héroïsme accomplis dans l'ombre par le soldat inconnu! Que de bravoure, que de dévouement sublime en face du danger! Les Rochon, les Atkinson, les Chartrand, les Fournier et tant-d'autres qu'il faudrait citer, mais le soldat véritable n'attend qu'une récompense et c'est la satisfaction du devoir accompli. Pour lui la publicité, les grandes citations ne sont qu'un témoignage public rendu à sa valeur, car pour lui comptent deux choses: Dévouement et Honneur!

Major J.A. Ross
"La Bataille: l'Attaque sur Hollen"
Fleur de Lys, 1 September 1945

New Year's Morning No. 2. (From a painting by D. K. Anderson Canadian War Museum PL 47038)

CONTENTS

FOREWORD

In 1942 General A. G. L. McNaughton described the Canadian army in Great Britain as a "dagger pointed at the heart of Berlin." These famous words were spoken during the darkest days of the Second World War, when the Allies were on the defensive in virtually every theatre and the Canadian army was an unknown quantity, still waiting to be tested in battle. But McNaughton, a veteran of the First World War, knew the Canadian soldier well. And sure enough, despite the tragedy of Dieppe and the hard slogging in Sicily and Italy, Canadian troops were soon being recognized for their outstanding abilities and fearless tenacity.

If there was ever any doubt on this point, it was laid to rest with the Northwest Europe campaign of 1944-45. Here the Canadians proved their mettle once and for all. Canadian soldiers went toe to toe with the enemy and prevailed each time, whether in the bitter Normandy campaign, the clearing of the Channel ports, or the desperate Battle of the Scheldt. What our men lacked in experience they made up for in sheer determination, and though some hard lessons had to be learned along the way, by the end of 1944 the Canadian army was a force to be reckoned with.

By the beginning of 1945 it was no secret that the German army in the west was close to collapse. The Ardennes offensive, a last futile attempt to halt the Allied advance, had fallen short. Preparations were now underway for a final push into the Third Reich. But the German army, even on its last legs, was not to be taken lightly, especially with its back to the wall. Several months of hard work lay ahead. Indeed, this last phase of the war was to produce some of the most vicious fighting yet encountered by the Canadians.

This is made brutally clear in Valour in the Victory Campaign. Robert Fowler has reproduced the citations for the gallantry decorations awarded in 1945 to the men of the 3rd Division which, along with the 2nd and 4th Divisions, led the Canadian thrust into Germany and Holland. No award is passed over–from the Victoria Cross and the Distinguished Service Order to the Military Cross, the Distinguished Conduct Medal and the Military Medal. Even foreign orders, decorations and medals are included.

These citations offer the reader a fascinating glimpse into the individual heroism and courage of the Canadian soldier during the Battle of the Rhineland and the liberation of Holland. Fighting as members of some of Canada's most famous regiments–including my own, the North Shore (New Brunswick) Regiment–these men, as the following accounts attest, let no obstacle stand in the way of reaching their objectives. Again and again, the reader is exposed to tremendous acts of daring and sacrifice in the face of mortal danger. One can only react with awe, for example, at the performance of the men of the 3rd Division, dubbed the Water Rats, as they struggled during the Battle of the Rhineland to overcome appalling weather conditions in addition to the spirited defence of the German opposition. Allied casualties were heavy, but the Germans were shoved back, setting the stage for the crossing of the Rhine and the eventual push by the Canadians into Holland and northern Germany.

The skill, bravery, and perseverance of the Canadian soldier in the dying months of the war leap off these pages. Mr. Fowler has performed a valuable service in confirming once again the proud military tradition enjoyed by Canada. But as a veteran of the Northwest Europe campaign, I caution to add that there were many others not mentioned in this book who made a contribution to victory in the Second World War. Their sacrifice, while perhaps not always meriting official recognition, was nevertheless critical. Fifty years later, they too should be remembered.

Colonel, the Honourable Jack Marshall, CD
Senator, retired

PREFACE

Over the past two years, while carrying out a research project on the Canadian Army in the Second World War, I became aware that little had been written about the gallantry decorations awarded to men of the Canadian forces in that struggle. As a result, I began to assemble a collection of citations for these awards for the formation about which I was studying at the time—the 3rd Canadian Infantry Division. In reviewing these, I became very impressed by the dramatic examples they provided of Canadians who had risked their lives in an era which was fading into history, but about which the Canadian public was unaware.

I therefore used the 50th Anniversary of the landing in Normandy as an opportunity to produce a book on the gallantry decorations for the 6th of June 1944 which, as one reviewer wrote, finally paid attention to the soldiers who actually landed on those beaches rather than the generals and politicians who planned the landings.

Perhaps I should have left it at that. Some veterans have criticized the system of awarding decorations—for example, many men did not receive a deserved decoration because no one observed their act of gallantry. In addition, because decorations were awarded according to a quota system, recommendations for awards in a particularly fierce battle could be turned down if the quota was used up. Some men even questioned why they received an award when they felt others around them deserved it even more. Finally, the wording used in the citations is stylized and, at times, appears grandiose.

But the system of awarding decorations, despite its flaws, has left the only clear record for giving today's generation some idea of what happened to many men in the war. Overall, the flaws in the system should not take away from the broader picture. A veteran who served with the 3rd Division put it well when he wrote: "It is thought (and said), by some who remember, that decorations are a reflection on the Unit and this is a admirable conclusion."

And of all the periods of the campaign in Northwest Europe, the last few months seemed to be more unknown to the Canadian public than the more dramatic periods of 1944. As the 50th Commemoration of V-E Day approached, I felt it was only appropriate that the stories of those men who had continued to risk—and lose—their lives needed to be known. Because of the effort required to assemble the citations, I continued to focus on the 3rd Division and the 2nd Canadian Armoured Brigade even though I realized that all units of the Canadian forces deserve credit. It also made some sense to describe the final miles travelled by these units on the path which had begun at Juno Beach on the 6th of June 1944.

I have chosen to leave the wording of each citation as close as possible to the original. Minor changes have been made only for style and grammar, or to provide a reasonable continuity with the preceding text. However, every effort has been made to preserve the original text since I felt this wording best conveys the emotions of what happened during those days, fifty years ago.

Unfortunately, no single complete source is available to identify all the decorations awarded. I have tried to examine all possible sources, but realize that some men have been left out. I apologize for those who have been omitted.

In addition, the book is designed to concentrate on the immediate awards—that is, those decorations awarded for an act of gallantry performed on a single date. Some periodic awards are also included but, unless such awards focused on particular actions in 1945, they have been omitted because of limits on the size of this book. I must also apologize to these individuals.

This book is not a military history but a record of what happened to a number of Canadian soldiers in the spring of 1945. In the end, it is an imperfect collection, but I believe the story that remains will impress, and even surprise, most readers.

I would like to thank all the people who assisted in the preparation of this book, including Honorary Lieutenant-Colonel G. D. Corry of The Canadian Scottish Regiment (Princess Mary's), Captain John Fotheringham of The Queen's Own Rifles of Canada, Brereton Greenhous, Sergeant (retired) Leo Major DCM of Le Régiment de la Chaudière, Lieutenant-Colonel (retired) Frederick F. Moar of The North Shore (New Brunswick) Regiment, Major (retired) J. Armand Ross DSO of Le Régiment de la Chaudière, and Morley Verdier. In particular, Cliff Chadderton of The War Amps provided strong moral support through his belief that this is a book that should be written.

T. Robert Fowler
Ottawa, 1995

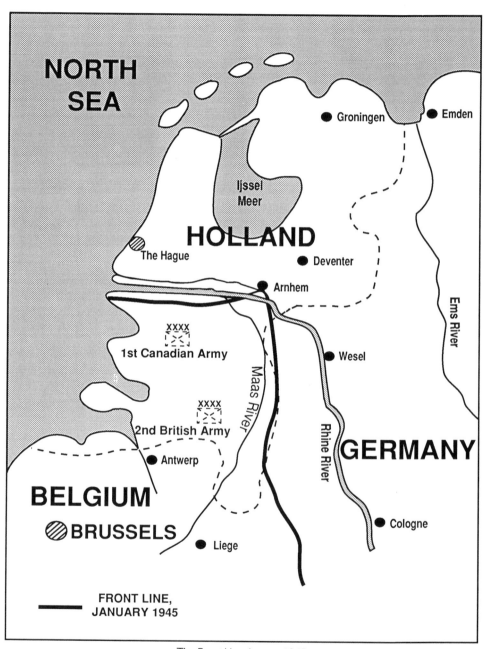

The Front Line, January 1945.

INTRODUCTION

Midnight, the 1st of January 1945. As the hands of the clocks clicked into the new year, the blackness of night on the border between Germany and the Netherlands was shattered by the artillery of the First Canadian Army. It was their way of saying Happy New Year, Hitler!

The New Year also marked the fifth year of the Second World War. With the world becoming weary of this devastating war, there was hope in the eyes of the Allied armies as they stood on the frontier of Germany. The despair of the dark months of 1942, when Nazi Germany stood as the invincible conqueror from the English Channel to the Caspian Sea, was now long past. The Western Allies had carefully mustered their strength and finally launched their armies against Hitler's Atlantic Wall on the 6th of June 1944. The Supreme Allied Commander, General Dwight Eisenhower, told his troops that, on landing on the coast of France, they were beginning the "great crusade."

The battles in Normandy over the next three months were long and bloody but resulted in a victory in which the German Armies on the Western Front received devastating losses. In September, as the remnants of the German forces fled towards their own borders, the Allied commanders felt that war was all but over. However, they did not appreciate the determination of Hitler and the efficiency of the German military organization. They found that the old defensive positions of the Siegfried Line, prepared before the war had begun, allowed them to finally make a stand and stop the pursuing Allied forces. With the onset of winter, the battle line stabilized and General Eisenhower had to form new plans for defeating Germany in the spring.

The Allied forces were organized into three army groups, the British 21st Army Group in the north, the US 12th Army Group in the centre, and the 6th Army Group in the south. Field-Marshal Bernard Montgomery, commanding the northern group, was convinced that the Allies should concentrate the bulk of their forces in a powerful thrust from the north to seize the industrial area of the Ruhr. In his sector, the banks of the lower Rhine River could more easily be crossed than in the south and Allied mobility could best be exploited on the flat plains of northern Germany for a rapid advance directly on Berlin. The three armies under Montgomery, the First Canadian, Second British and Ninth US Armies, thus began massing their strength for an offensive to begin as soon as the weather permitted.

Within the First Canadian Army, the 3rd Canadian Infantry Division would play an important role. This division had been one of the five Allied divisions chosen for the assault on D-Day. In the desperate fighting in the Normandy campaign, it had unfortunately suffered the most losses of any division but had become battle-hardened. It had enjoyed the brief period of exhilaration in pursuit of the retreating Germans through northern France, but had been involved in the final battles of the year as the Germans held on stubbornly in the Channel ports and to the mouth of the Scheldt River.

As in all the Canadian army divisions, consideration had been given to ensuring appropriate representation from all regions of the country. This can be recognized in the make-up of the division's three infantry brigades. The 7th Brigade was the "Western Brigade"–The Royal Winnipeg Rifles, The Regina Rifles and 1st Battalion, The Canadian Scottish Regiment (from British Columbia). The 8th Brigade included The Queen's Own Rifles of Canada (from Toronto), Le Régiment de la Chaudière (from the heart of Quebec), and The North Shore (New Brunswick) Regiment. The 9th Brigade was the "Highland Brigade," consisting of The Highland Light Infantry of Canada (from central Ontario), The Stormont, Dundas and Glengarry Highlanders (from eastern Ontario), and The North Nova Scotia Highlanders. The machine-gun battalion was The Cameron Highlanders of Ottawa and the reconnaissance regiment was the 7th Reconnaissance (17th Duke of York's Royal Canadian Hussars, from Montreal).

The vital tank support for the battles through France and Belgium was provided by the 2nd Canadian Armoured Brigade. As with the other major Canadian formations, its component units also reflected the various regions of the country: the 6th Canadian Armoured Regiment (1st Hussars) from London, Ontario; the 10th Canadian Armoured Regiment (The Fort Garry Horse) from Winnipeg, Manitoba; and the 27th Canadian Armoured Regiment (The Sherbrooke Fusiliers) from Quebec.

The 3rd Division and 2nd Brigade had come ashore together on 6 June 1944, at a time when the outcome of the struggle against Nazi Germany still seemed to hang in the balance. Now, at the start of 1945, victory appeared close at hand. However, Germany still was resisting with all the vigour it could muster and many desperate battles still lay ahead before this could be achieved. It would require many more acts of gallantry by all the men of the First Canadian Army and many men would still die in this cause.

This is the story of those men of two of the formations of the Canadian Army, the 3rd Canadian Infantry Division and 2nd Canadian Armoured Brigade, which in the closing months of the war carried out acts of gallantry which were above the call of duty.

-I-
Winter Warfare

Oh, the old Wyler Meer,
Where dangers were plenty but the boys showed no fear;
The weather was cold — it rained all the time,
Five days in wet dugouts, just holding the line.

Now Platoon Sergeant Johnson went out on patrol
To recce* the Jerry by daylight, so bold.
But soon he was spotted and bullets whined near,
His patrol had to swim 'cross the old Wyler Meer.

Our Major and Captain are two of the best,
On the old Wyler Meer they stood guard with the rest.
Saying "Boys, it's no fun in a trench when it's cold,
But the job must be done and the line we must hold."[1]

Ditty composed by men of "D" Company,
North Nova Scotia Highlanders

The main German defences in the West were based on two major obstacles—the Siegfried Line and the Rhine River. In the closing weeks of 1944, the Allies had hoped to break through these defences and advance into Germany to end the war. While these hopes had not been fulfilled, the Siegfried Line had been breached in the south where an American offensive had penetrated the Siegfried Line in front of the Roer River at Aachen. In the north, General Montgomery had attempted to outflank the Seigfried Line by dropping airborne forces into Holland to capture Nijmegen and the bridge over the Waal River. This audacious strategy had not been decisive, however, as the Germans held onto the last bridge at Arnhem. As winter descended, no further offensive action could be taken and both sides settled in for a period of stationary warfare.

* Colloquial term for "making a reconnaissance."

Following its battles in October to clear south-western Holland of the enemy, the First Canadian Army was given the task of holding the eastern flank of the Nijmegen salient in the area of the village of Groesbeek. Here, the salient's lines extended for about 15 km across a narrow neck of land between the River Maas in the south and to the Rhine in the north. The terrain was generally flat, but varied from the low-lying flood plain of the Rhine in the north, dyked in polders to prevent flooding in the spring, to the Reichswald on higher ground in the southern part. The Reichswald was a German state forest made up of coniferous trees mixed with oak, planted about four metres apart. It covered an area about 13 km long by 6.5 km wide, cut into rectangles by tracks, with poor visibility within its confines. With the coming of snow, the dark mass of the Reichswald stood out in gloomy contrast. Here, the German 84th Division had established its forward defences, using a continuous line of well-dug trenches of the 1914-18 type.

While no major offensives would be undertaken during the winter, both sides were very active in sending out patrols every night to gather information as to the location of enemy weapons, to capture prisoners, and to generally keep the other side off balance. Charles Martin described the tension that can come with a period of static warfare: "The need for complete silence was so great and the stress so overpowering that a man could sweat out five or six pounds. A patrol was as tough as or tougher than any regular attack. The tension didn't let up for a second."[2]

Some men seemed to be suited for this type of warfare more than others. The long dark nights required exceptional skills of moving stealthily, of braving individual encounters with the enemy, far from one's own lines, cut off from help if one got into trouble. It was a deadly game where enemy patrols also roamed silently in no man's land, waiting to spring their own ambush. Charles Martin later wrote about this type of patrol action:

> We learned that speed, timing, teamwork and sometimes physical strength were important. The ability to work together in silence was vital . . . A strange thing about patrols was that they produced men from all ranks who had a natural instinct for the work. Some could move like a ghost — one moment he'd be there; next moment, gone.[3]

Sergeant Joseph Antoine Ouellet came to the North Nova Scotia Highlanders in July 1944 and fought as a Platoon Sergeant in "D" Company through the Falaise period. On the formation of the scout platoon in August, Sergeant Ouellet was transferred and became scout sergeant. In this rather hazardous job this sergeant excelled. He took out patrols continually, at great personal risk, and he went through the enemy positions time after time. Two scout officers were killed in this first month, but Sergeant Ouellet still carried on until January 1945, at which time this sergeant while on a particularly dangerous patrol had the misfortune of having his leg blown off, near Nijmegen, Holland.

Sergeant Ouellet excelled himself in the Nijmegen salient. Here this sergeant did a series of extremely dangerous patrols to find out enemy dispositions. One position in particular, always referred to as "Little Tobruk"* was a very strong enemy outpost bordering the Wyler Meer southeast of Nijmegen. This position had been attacked unsuccessfully by two other battalions as it was decided to send Sergeant Ouellet and two men in to investigate. There was only one approach, along a dyke, the rest of the ground was a sheet of ice—but Sergeant Ouellet penetrated into the heart of the position, discovered the dispositions but was himself spotted and came under direct automatic fire. He was grazed in three places but managed to escape. Two nights later, this sergeant's patrol again returned to this position, this time with two engineers. It was a bright moonlit night with snow on the ground so the whole patrol had to be covered by a smoke screen. Sergeant Ouellet and four men covered the engineers while they removed the mines, and he and one other again personally investigated the position. He was able this time to report the strength quite accurately, but was again intercepted and had to fight his way out. This time he killed two Germans and was slightly wounded himself. As a result of these patrols, the battalion was able to successfully cope with this position.

Sergeant Ouellet continued his patrols several times a week in the Nijmegen area and brought back much valuable information until the night of January 4 when he stepped on a Schu-mine** and lost a leg, which afterward resulted in the loss of both legs. This sergeant's heroic devotion to duty and fearless courage on all occasions was a wonderful example to his men. His contribution to the success of the battalion during the winter in Holland was very great.

For these actions, Sergeant Ouellet received the Netherlands Bronze Lion.

On the 4th of January 1945, Lance/Corporal Allen Plumb MacMaster was a section commander in "C" Company, the Highland Light Infantry of Canada. His section had been detailed as part of a forty-man fighting patrol, to probe the enemy defences on the Quer Damm near Nijmegen.

It was an extremely black night, making movement very difficult. The patrol penetrated approximately 500 yards into enemy territory when it came under heavy machine-gun fire. Lance/Corporal MacMaster was wounded in the right arm and had to be sent back for medical attention.

While passing through a section of men, Lance/Corporal MacMaster stepped on a German Schu-mine and heard the click of the mechanism. He shouted "Schu mine—take cover!" and remained standing on the mine until it exploded, blowing off his foot. The section of infantry meanwhile dropped to the ground and one of them was injured.

---

*   A German strongpoint at the end of the Quer Damm, near Zyfflich; given this nickname because of its strong firepower.

**   A German mine designed not to kill a man but to blow off his foot.

Lance/Corporal MacMaster, already wounded, accepted serious injury to himself, thereby preventing serious and certain casualties to his fellow soldiers. This non-commissioned officer's great presence of mind, self-sacrifice and courage set a magnificent example to his comrades at arms.

For this action, Lance/Corporal MacMaster received the Military Medal.

In the Nijmegen salient on the night of 11/12 January 1945, Private Edward Davis Scott, "A" Company, Stormont Dundas and Glengarry Highlanders, conducted himself with great skill and gallantry thereby saving his outpost, personally killing one German officer and a corporal, wounding one other rank and taking him prisoner.

It was a dark, moonless night and snowing heavily. At 0544 hours, Private Scott perceived an enemy patrol in snow suits creeping up the ditch towards him. He warned his companion and held his fire until the enemy were thirty feet away. The German officer put his head up to observe and was killed instantly by a bullet fired by Private Scott. The German patrol then fired Panzerfausts and machine guns at Private Scott and his comrade who returned the fire and held to their posts.

The enemy soldier who fired the Panzerfaust was defiladed and could not be hit. Private Scott, without a snow suit and showing complete disregard for his personal safety, left his position and, under covering fire from his companion, went forward and killed the enemy soldier, a non-commissioned officer, in a hand-to-hand fight.

Riflemen of The Queen's Own Rifles of Canada on patrol
near the Reichswald,Germany, January 1945
B. J. Gloster, NAC, PA-114073

As a result of Private Scott's coolness and courage in ambushing the patrol, followed by his bold attack on them, the enemy patrol abandoned their weapons and withdrew. This soldier then volunteered to follow up the enemy, which he did, enabling the recovery of two enemy dead and one seriously wounded, who provided much needed identification and information.

For this action, Private Scott was awarded the Military Medal.

On the night of 13 January 1945, Private Ernest Morris Miller and another soldier of the Stormont Dundas and Glengarry Highlanders were standing guard in their platoon location in the Nijmegen area. At approximately 2350 hours, Private Miller saw some figures crossing a dyke about 100 yards to his front. Knowing that none of our patrols were out, he as senior private, sent his companion back to warn the outpost, remaining himself to observe.

Private Miller allowed the eight dark figures to approach within sixty feet. At this point, he heard low remarks made in German. He appreciated that he must put up a show of strength until reinforced. Being in a partly destroyed building, he was allowed a certain freedom of movement so, immediately after opening fire with a Sten gun, he rushed, showing utter contempt to the returned fire, to a further point of vantage to engage the enemy with a light machine-gun. Moving to a third point, Private Miller tossed a 36 Grenade to further mislead the enemy. At this moment, reinforcements arrived.

There followed a thirty–minute fight, during which time Private Miller was in the forefront calmly pointing out the enemy to his companions and engaging them with fire. In the morning, large patches of blood were seen about fifty feet in front of the position that Private Miller occupied. A German Machine-Gun 42, two Panzerfaust, four stick grenades, and a large amount of small arms ammunition were abandoned by the enemy.

Private Miller's coolness, fortitude, and initiative were the highest order. This soldier has consistently displayed courage in battle and was a source of real inspiration to all about him.

For this action, Private Miller was awarded the Military Medal.

Acting Captain Robert Bryant Menzies served with the Highland Light Infantry of Canada from 10 October until 8 May 1945. At all times he displayed personal courage and leadership of a high order and his initiative and persistence as scout officer were frequently responsible for securing information of great value to the success of subsequent operations.

During the period in the Nijmegen salient, from 12 November 1944 to 8 February 1945, Captain Menzies personally led twenty patrols over the open polders and dykes of that sector.

On 28 December 1944, Captain Menzies led a patrol to take prisoners and make identification along the Quer Dam. As the patrol approached what was believed to be the advance German positions, it was fired on from a previously undisclosed enemy position on the flank. The patrol was subjected to intense small arms fire and several casualties were caused. Although the situation was confused, Captain Menzies personally rallied the patrol and led them in a charge at the enemy position, where the necessary identifications were made. He then organized the withdrawal of the patrol and personally remained behind until the entire patrol and wounded were safely away.

On 1 February 1945, Captain Menzies led a small reconnaissance patrol to determine the extent of a break in the Rhine dyke well inside the German positions. Although it was a bright moonlit night, this officer set out with two scouts over the open ground. To reach his objective, he had to cross two enemy minefields, marking a safe route as he went. As the patrol neared their objective, they spotted a strong German patrol coming up the same dyke. Captain Menzies ordered the two scouts to withdraw while he remained with a Bren Gun and grenades to keep the German patrol off. By sporadic fire and grenades from different positions, Captain Menzies enabled the patrol to get safely away, before he withdrew to our forward positions. He then quickly organized a stronger force and led them back out through the minefields in an effort to ambush the German patrol.

The unceasing devotion to duty and meritorious service rendered by this officer was reflected in the amount of valuable information accumulated during this period—information which had a marked effect on the later offensive operations in this area.

For these actions, Captain Menzies was awarded the Netherlands Bronze Lion.

Despite patrols through December and early January, the 3rd Division still had not a satisfactory picture of the enemy defences. Headquarters felt it was urgent that they get a prisoner who they could question in detail. Because the German defences here were in the form of a continuous line of trenches, such as had been used in 1914-18, it was more difficult for small patrols to grab a defender. It was therefore decided that the only way to get a prisoner was to plan a large–scale raid to drive deeply into the enemy forward defence line, take what prisoners they could, and retire quickly. A point was chosen near the German village of Wyler where the continuous line of trenches came to an end on the high ground which dropped away very steeply to the small lake called the Wyler Meer. The North Shore Regiment was chosen to carry out "Operation PLUM."[4]

Sergeant Horace Boulay, Support Company, North Shore (New Brunswick) Regiment, came to France with the carrier platoon as a private on 13 June 1944. Since that time he has continually taken a major part in all battles in which the carriers have been involved. His deeds of valour and exploits have become a tradition in the unit. On many occasions he had accomplished dangerous and special tasks with great personal risk but through his skilful and courageous actions, he was able to accomplish the tasks and bring his section back safely. [His first commendable action took place at Boulogne in September 1944.]

At Wyler Germany on 8 January 1945, Sergeant Boulay led the assault made by "D" Company, with a section of flame throwers. They came under heavy shell fire and ran into a minefield. Sergeant Boulay's carrier was the only one that was not destroyed yet he continued to his objective, burned out the enemy position, which was holding up the company attack, and then on his own initiative picked up all the casualties. This required several trips under heavy enemy shelling. His gallant action enable all the wounded to be given immediate medical treatment.

See page 66 for continuation of Sergeant Boulay's citation.

On 4 February 1945, Corporal Sherman Walter Erison, a section leader in 7 Platoon, "A" Company, The Highland Light Infantry of Canada, displayed outstanding courage and devotion to duty.

Number 7 Platoon was given the task of occupying Eindjeshof, a large group of farm buildings in enemy territory, at night, in order to provide a firm base from which to launch a first–light attack.

At 0330 hours, February 5, while approaching Eindjeshof, Number 7 Platoon encountered a thick anti-personnel mine field, suffering two casualties. The platoon commander detailed Corporal Erison to return to the start line for stretcher bearers. Corporal Erison led the stretcher bearers into the minefield to the casualties. A stretcher bearer stepped on a mine and Corporal Erison was painfully wounded about the face and eyes by the explosion. Despite his own wounds, he assisted and directed the evacuation of casualties from the mine field.

When it became evident that the launching of the first–light attack was imperilled by the delay in the mine field, Corporal Erison refused evacuation and guided the attacking force quickly and safely through the minefield. He then rejoined his section and remained on duty until the operation was complete.

Corporal Erison's devotion to duty and courageous disregard for his own safety were directly responsible for the success of the operation.

For this action, Corporal Erison received the Military Medal.

NOTES

1. Will R. Bird, *No Retreating Footsteps* (Kentville: Kentville Publishing Co.), p. 295.

2. Charles Cromwell Martin, *Battle Diary* (Toronto: Dundurn Press, 1994), p.30.

3. Martin, pp. 31-34.

4. Public Archives of Canada, RG 24, Vol 14143, North Shore Regiment War Diary, January, 1945.

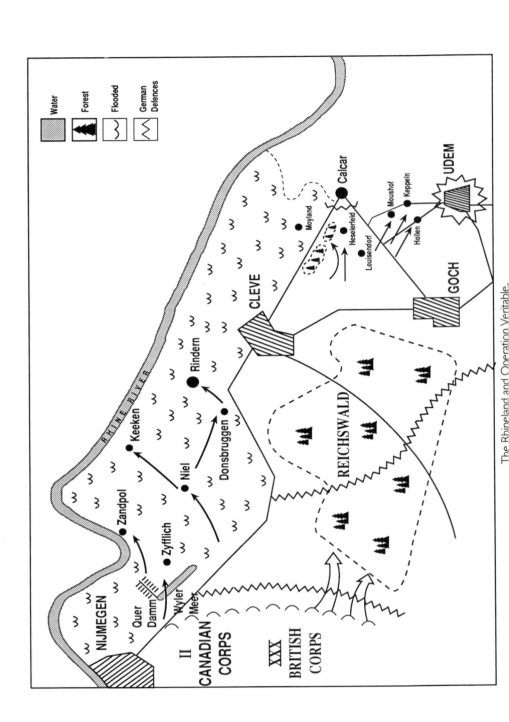

The Rhineland and Operation Veritable.

-2-
VERITABLE — THE "WATER RATS"

Message to the men of the 21st Army Group

In 21 Army Group we stand ready for the last round. There are many of us who have fought through the previous rounds: we have won every previous round on points; we now come to the last and final round; and will want, and will go for, the knockout blow.

The rules of the last round will be that we continue fighting till the final count; we must expect him to fight hard to stave off defeat possibly in the vain hope that we may crack before he does. But we shall not crack; we shall see this thing through to the very end. The last round may be long and difficult, and the fighting hard; but we now fight on German soil; we have got our opponent where we want him; and he is going to receive the knockout blow . . .

Field-Marshal Bernard L. Montgomery
GOC-in-C[1]

In January 1945, the final strategy for the Allied spring offensive was approved. Eisenhower decided that his forces should close up to the Rhine River along its entire length, but the main effort would be made by Montgomery in the north, reinforced by the US Ninth Army under his command. The fortifications of the Siegfried Line still presented an obstacle, but the two penetrations, at Aachen and Nijmegen, could be used as levers to break through. Montgomery would use the First Canadian Army to attack southwards through the corridor formed between the Maas and Rhine Rivers (Operation VERITABLE), while the US Ninth Army would cross the Roer River and drive northwards (Operation GRENADE). As the two forces converged on the city of Wesel, they would crush the defending forces between them.

Once through the initial German positions, Montgomery expected a rapid advance over the flat terrain to bring the operation to a quick conclusion. However, this would only happen if the ground remained dry or hard; if this condition was not satisfied, he told his commanders, "then a slower and more methodical progress may be forced upon us."[2] General Eisenhower ordered VERITABLE to begin no later than February 8, in the hope that the ground would remain frozen, and GRENADE no later than February 10.

For the operation, Montgomery reorganized his 21st Army Group, building up the First Canadian Army into a powerful offensive force to make the quick breakthrough he anticipated: thirteen divisions, three armoured brigades, and five heavy artillery groups[3] under the XXX British and II Canadian Corps.

The Germans, however, had been busy improving their defences in the north. Three defensive belts, each between five hundred and a thousand yards wide, had been constructed in the corridor between the Maas and the Rhine using the German state forests in the area to their advantage:

> The first was an outpost position to the main Siegfried defences—a double series of trenches covered in front of the Reichswald by an anti-tank ditch. All the villages and farmhouses had been converted into strongpoints . . . Three miles to the rear of the outpost system was the north end of the Siegfried Line, the main belt of which traversed the Reichswald from north to south, then skirted the south edge as far as the town of Goch . . . The third defended zone, some 11 miles further south and known as the Hochwald Layback, was a series of entrenched systems with anti-tank ditches about a mile deep and protected by a continuous belt of wire. All the towns and villages were designed to provide individual islands of resistance.[4]

As the day of attack approached, ominous signs appeared regarding the conditions which were so necessary to the plan's success. An early thaw began to show on February 4; rain began on February 6; the Germans blew open the dykes along the Rhine on February 7; and General Alfred Schlemm, commanding the German First Parachute Army, sent in one of his first-class parachute regiments to bolster the left flank of his Reichswald defences.

Operation VERITABLE began as planned on February 8. Following a massive artillery barrage by a thousand guns, the British divisions of XXX Corps easily reached their objectives for the first day. However, the Germans rushed up reinforcements and fanatically resisted any attempt by the British to make any further advances. To make matters worse, all routes began to disappear under continuing rain and heavy traffic. Vehicles constantly became bogged down and getting supplies forward was an exhausting task.

During this first phase of the battle, the 3rd Canadian Infantry Division orders were to clear the northern flank—the area between the Nijmegen-Cleve road and the Rhine River. In this area, however, the floodwaters from the broken dykes on the Rhine were rising on the day of the attack at the rate of a foot per hour, disrupting all the battle plans. The division quickly made arrangements for the use of amphibious vehicles, Buffaloes and DUKWs,* to get the units onto their objectives. For the next week, a strange amphibious war took place on this flank, with some isolated villages falling easily while others were defended vigorously. Here,

> the 3rd Canadian Division developed a form of "naval" warfare piloted by British crews in ungainly Buffaloes, Weasels and amphibious jeeps. Navigating with land maps, taking bearings on steeples, and constantly attempting to avoid the elaborate wire and minefields of the hidden defences, the Buffaloes, buffeted by the waves, taking in water across their blunt bows, moved steadily upon their objectives, answering bursts of Spandau fire from windmills and roof tops with bursts from their Brownings and Brens.[5]

Personnel of The North Shore Regiment boarding Buffalo amphibious vehicles
for the attack on Zyfflich, Germany
Colin Campbell McDougall, NAC, PA-145769.

---

* The "Buffalo" was the British term for the American LTV, a tracked armoured amphibious vehicle which could carry 30 men. It had been used extensively for amphibious operations in the Scheldt and the South Pacific. The DUKW was a US Army 2-1/2 ton amphibious truck usually called a "Duck."

On the left flank, the North Shore regiment led the attack with a quick move late in the day by two companies carried in Buffaloes to capture the dyke and village of Zandpol. The failing winter light made the German machine-gun fire inaccurate, as the men climbed from the vehicles into waist-deep water, only to find they were in a minefield.

On 8 February 1945, Private Russell Georald Munro, runner for the Commander of "B" Company of the North Shore Regiment, landed on the Zandpol dyke with the company commander whose Buffalo had, due to navigational difficulties, landed before the assault platoons. He at once fought his way to a commanding position on top of the dyke where he kept the enemy at bay, thus allowing Company Headquarters to get established. There, under heavy machine-gun fire, he made contact with "A" Company and, as a result, a continuous and coordinated front was established between the two assault companies.

Subsequently, "B" Company advanced along the dyke and the leading platoon with Company Headquarters following was held up by a minefield and machine-gun fire. Casualties were suffered in the minefield and the remainder of the platoon pinned down on the dyke by machine-gun fire. Private Munro repeatedly entered the minefield and rescued wounded and stunned men. Then, on his own initiative, taking a PIAT,* occupied an exposed position on top of the dyke and, while himself under heavy fire, blasted the machine-gun position into submission, thus allowing his company to proceed to its final objective. The courage, determination and endurance shown by this private soldier was definitely a battle-winning factor in the success of the battalion plan. His gallantry, initiative and disregard for his own personal safety far exceeded his duty, rank and orders.

For this action, Private Russell Georald Munro was awarded the Military Medal.

In Holland, on 8 February 1945, Sapper Alexander McCullagh of the 16th Canadian Field Company RCE, was a member of a sapper party accompanying the assault wave of 8th Canadian Infantry Brigade [the North Shore Regiment] during the amphibious attack on Zandpol dyke. His duty was to act as a runner between the platoon officer working behind the leading infantry and the wireless set located at the landing ramp. Due to the presence of Schu-mines on the slopes of the dyke, the only route possible was along the exposed road on top of the dyke. Once the enemy had been cleared off the dyke, this road was subjected to heavy concentrations of mortar fire and continually swept by their machine-gun fire. It was not practical in the dark to move the wireless jeep forward along the dyke road.

For several hours, Sapper McCullagh carried, back and forth along this fire-swept road, messages containing information about the condition of roads inside the polder. This information proved to be of utmost value to the brigade commander,

---

*   Acronym for the Projector Infantry Anti-Tank, a hand-held anti-tank weapon. (See Glossary.)

enabling him to determine the type and number of vehicles he could dispatch to support this attack.

Sapper McCullagh performed this hazardous task with utter disregard of personal danger, displaying a high sense of responsibility and unflinching devotion to duty. His action and conduct was a source of inspiration and confidence to his officers and men alike and contributed materially to the success of the attack.

For this action, Sapper Alexander McCullagh was awarded the Military Medal.

To the south of Zandpol, the Regina Rifle Regiment also moved off at dusk toward the Quer Damm and the village of Zyfflich which had not yet been cut off by the floodwaters. "D" Company quickly seized the enemy defence post at the southern end of the Quer Damm and a night attack was then launched on the village with the aid of "artificial moonlight" (powerful searchlight beams reflected off the clouds to illuminate the objective). By 2200 hours, "C" Company was moving through "B" Company to capture the last half of the village.[6]

Major Donald Gordon Brown was in command of "D" Company, 1st Battalion, The Regina Rifle Regiment, in the push out from Nijmegen to Zyfflich. His company was water-borne during the attack and, although coming under enemy fire, this officer led his men with such efficiency and daring that the enemy positions in and around his objective were completely overrun with a few casualties to themselves, and the result that a large number of prisoners were taken and the company objectives captured.

For this action and actions later at Wehl and Deventer, Holland, Major Donald Gordon Brown was awarded the Netherlands Bronze Lion.

Corporal (Lance Sergeant) Gerald Royce Langton, on the night of 8/9 February 1945 as a section commander, 14 Platoon, "C" Company, 1st Battalion, Regina Rifle Regiment, was ordered to clear a large cheese factory in the eastern part of the town of Zyfflich Germany.

While Lance Sergeant Langton was leading his section towards the factory, it came under heavy small arms fire and several were wounded, including himself. But with complete disregard for his wound and personal safety, this NCO continued forward into the building alone and engaged the enemy in close quarter fighting, during which he killed two and wounded several others. Such was the fury of his attack that he succeeded in driving the enemy into the cellar. Bringing the rest of his section forward, they successfully took the remainder, fifteen in all, prisoner.

Lance Sergeant Langton then reported to his company commander who ordered him to go to the Regimental Aid Post. He asked, and was granted permission, to stay with his section until the action was completed. On his return he led his section in the clearing of several more houses that yielded another eighteen prisoners of war. Only after consolidating on his final position would this NCO consent to being evacuated.

The leadership, courage and offensive zeal displayed by Lance Sergeant Langton inspired the whole section to press forward and capture a very dominating feature at a critical stage in the battle, thereby assisting his company to carry out the task.

For this action, Lance Sergeant Gerald Royce Langton was awarded the Military Medal.

Meanwhile, the 1st Battalion, The Canadian Scottish Regiment, launched a two-pronged attack: one company against "Little Tobruk" at the far end of the Quer Damm, and two companies carried by Buffaloes against the town of Niel, in the floodwaters to the east of Zyfflich. Unfortunately, the latter force went off course, landing at a village a mile-and-a-half from their objective. No word of the situation of these companies was received by the battalion commander, Lieutenant-Colonel Crofton. When questioned by his brigadier, Lieutenant-Colonel Crofton was therefore unable to provide any information as to progress of this force.

> Since D-Day, Crofton had been noted for his aggressiveness and general desire to be as close to the forward positions as possible. In fact, in Normandy, as a company commander, Crofton had to be ordered not to go on patrols into No-Man's Land. As a Commanding Officer, however, he realized his place was a position where he could control the entire battalion . . . The circumstances were such, however, that he was given no alternative. Shortly after midnight, therefore, Crofton and his group clambered aboard two "Buffaloes" and the craft waddled down the muddy road . . . and headed for the appointed rendezvous at Niel.[7]

As a result, just before daylight, Lieutenant-Colonel Crofton's craft churned into the edge of the village of Niel, while it was still in enemy hands.

The 1st Battalion, The Canadian Scottish Regiment, under Lieutenant-Colonel Desmond Gerald Crofton took its full share of patrolling and gathering of information in the Nijmegen salient from November to early February. The commanding officer, by his personal interest and aggressive spirit in junior leaders' patrols, successfully kept morale at a high level.

Lieutenant-Colonel Crofton prepared and briefed the battalion for its role in the big push of 8 February 1945. This operation "VERITABLE" was extremely difficult, being chiefly water borne; nevertheless all sub-units got away successfully. During the night 8/9 February 1945, Battalion Headquarters (TAC) had no information from forward elements, so Lt-Col Crofton went forward to investigate. At approximately 0400 hours, the colonel's party had reached the town of Niel and made no contact with our companies. Realizing that daylight approached, he decided to move into shelter of a group of buildings with his staff. On reaching these buildings, enemy fire poured on his small party, wounding the commanding officer, intelligence officer and several of the staff. Although seriously wounded, Colonel Crofton continued in his endeavour to reach his men and to control his small party. Unfortunately, his wounds were so severe that he had to drag himself to the shelter of a small building, instructing the others to gain our own lines. Lt-Col Crofton remained seriously wounded in this exposed position twelve hours, when he was finally evacuated by our Medical Officer. Throughout these actions in Holland, Lt-Col Crofton's fearless leadership, gallantry and devotion to duty were an inspiration to all ranks and in no small measure influenced the tide of battle. His splendid part in the liberation of Holland was in keeping with the highest traditions of the Canadian Army and of the Regiment he so faithfully commanded.

For this action, and other actions on the Leopold Canal and in the Breskens Pocket, Lieutenant-Colonel Desmond Gerald Crofton was awarded the Netherlands Bronze Lion.

The next day, the Royal Winnipeg Rifles attacked the village of Keeken, at the far northern flank of the flooded area.

Sergeant Cecil James Brown showed outstanding leadership and gallantry in a company attack out onto the low ground west of Nijmegen, Holland on 9 February 1945. In a company attack on the village of Keeken, he personally led his platoon in an assault on a group of farm buildings across an anti-tank ditch and into the outer defences of the Siegfried Line. All throughout the fighting, Sergeant Brown showed outstanding leadership and disregard for personal safety, and it was largely due to the success of Sergeant Brown's platoon that the company was able to secure its objective.

Lt-Col Desmond Gerald Crofton, Commanding Officer, the 1st Battalion, The Canadian Scottish Regiment, was awarded the Netherlands' Bronze Lion for his actions on the Leopold Canal, in the Breskens Pocket, and at Niel.
NAC, PA-180341

For his action, Sergeant Cecil James Brown was awarded the Netherlands Bronze Cross. Sergeant Brown was later wounded in action on 21 February at Moyland Wood.

The 9th Canadian Infantry Brigade was to come into action on February 10 to complete the clearing of the flood plain. However, by now the waters had risen so much that the artillery could not get forward to provide the planned support. Despite this, the two assaulting battalions started their attack by moving off in Buffaloes late in the afternoon. Donsbruggen was soon taken by the Stormont, Dundas and Glengarry Highlanders, but the advance was held up east of the town until aggressive action by Corporal Baker of "C" Company cleared the way. Pushing on in the fading light, the Glens found that "considerable opposition was met in Rindern from a system of trenches and fortified houses. The battalion was counter-attacked here by paratroops" and fighting continued until daylight.[8]

On the night of February 10/11, at Donsbruggen Germany, Corporal Ernest William Baker, section leader, "C" Company, Stormont, Dundas and Glengarry Highlanders, unassisted cleared the enemy from four houses where they were holding up the Regiment's advance. He killed five Germans and captured sixteen.

On the road from Donsbruggen to Cleve, about 200 yards east of Donsbruggen, the enemy held four houses which covered the main road to Cleve with fire. Corporal Baker quickly appreciated the situation and ordered his section to give him covering fire. He dashed to the first house with complete disregard for his personal safety, killing all the enemy, then systematically cleared the other three houses single-handedly. This aggressive action resulted in the death of five Germans and the capture of sixteen.

Corporal Baker's leadership, initiative and courage was of the highest order and set an example to the rest of "C" Company who quickly followed this success and captured their objective.

For this action, Corporal Ernest William Baker received the Military Medal. Corporal Baker was later killed in action on 4 April during the advance into Holland.

On the night of 10/11 February 1945, Major Gordon Emerson Clarke, "C" Company of the Stormont, Dundas and Glengarry Highlanders, fought his company with great gallantry, determination and superb leadership, in the hand-to-hand fighting which resulted in the capture of the battalion objective, Rindern Germany.

Major Clarke led his company 1000 yards from the Start Line over the most difficult flooded country, and cleared the intermediate objective of Donsbruggen. The outer trench system of the Siegfried Line and the German headquarters position of Chateau Guandanthal were then attacked with speed and determination. Major Clarke then assaulted the southern half of the village of Rindern. Due to the flooding and darkness, "C" Company was entirely unsupported and the artillery forward observation officer could not be used to advantage. By careful manoeuvring, Major Clarke was able to gain almost complete tactical surprise. This assault carried his company into the centre of the enemy position where close hand-to-hand fighting of the bitterest nature ensued. At approximately 0945 hours, *Major Clarke's position at the south end of Rindern was counter attacked by German paratroops. This attack was successfully beaten off.*

During the fierce fighting, Major Clarke was to be found leading his troops, organising and directing assaults on stubborn enemy strong points. His company overcame all obstacles, inflicting severe casualties on the enemy. The success of this operation formed a firm base for the rest of the Brigade which then secured crossing over the Spoy Canal. This company only established a firm base after fierce fighting, and by the inspiring and magnificent leadership of its commander.

For this action, Major Gordon Emerson Clarke received the Distinguished Service Order. Major Clarke was later wounded in action on 28 April during the attack on Leer Germany.

The weather continued to be miserable—cloudy with intermittent heavy showers—while the floodwaters of the Rhine poured into the polders. The few roads above water began to deteriorate and transportation problems continued to be serious as vehicles either bogged down or broke down.

Corporal Alfred Harold Stroud was a motor mechanic with "B" Company, Cameron Highlanders of Ottawa (MG). This NCO was mainly responsible for maintaining the mobility of his machine-gun company during the long journey through Holland. Many of these vehicles landed in Normandy on D-Day. On 9 February 1945, Corporal Stroud was acting as a driver mechanic with 7 Platoon of "B" Company in support of the 8th Canadian Infantry Brigade during the advance to the Rhine over the flooded area east of Nijmegen. Two carriers became stuck in a muddy, water-soaked minefield. Although under heavy small arms fire and working under great difficulties, Corporal Stroud, showing a cool disregard for his own safety, was successful in extricating the vehicles from the flooded minefield, thereby enabling the platoon to advance at full strength to regain contact with the enemy, and to support and assist the Queen's Own Rifles of Canada in pressing home their attack to a successful conclusion.

During the difficult period, and working under the most adverse conditions, Corporal Stroud displayed courage, leadership and devotion to duty to a marked degree.

For his action, Corporal Alfred Harold Stroud received the Netherlands Bronze Cross.

With the continuing miserable weather, the hoped–for breakthrough and rapid advance by the armour did not occur. It appeared that VERITABLE would deteriorate into a bitter infantry battle.

Message to the men of the 3rd Division

The Army Commander, Commander 30 British Corps, Commander 2 Canadian Corps are all extremely pleased with the excellent work done by the Division in Operation VERITA-

BLE. In view of operations SWITCHBACK and VERITABLE, Commander 2 Canadian Corps now refers to us as "THE WATER RATS." I have accepted our new nickname and I am sure that all ranks will agree.

Good luck, God bless, and keep splashing!

(DC Spry) Maj-Gen
GOC 3 Cdn Inf Div[9]

NOTES

1.   H. Essame, *The Battle for Germany* (New York: Charles Scribner's Sons, 1969), p. 144.

2.   Terry Copp and Robert Vogel, *Maple Leaf Route: Victory* (Alma: Maple Leaf Route, 1988), p. 22.

3.   R. W. Thompson, *Battle for the Rhine* (New York: Ballantine Books, 1959), p. 123.

4.   Essame, p. 140.

5.   Thompson, p. 147.

6.   Eric Luxton, *1st Battalion The Regina Rifle Regiment 1939-1946* (The Regina Rifle Association, 1946), p. 56.

7.   R. H. Roy, *Ready for the Fray* (Vancouver: The Canadian Scottish Regiment, 1958), p. 368.

8.   National Archives of Canada Record Group (RG) 24, Vol 15123, North Novas Scotia Highlanders War Diary, April 1945, "Operation Veritable Report Prepared by Hist Offr" dated 17March 1945.

9.   Jeffery Williams, *The Long Left Flank* (Toronto: Stoddart Publishing Co. Ltd., 1988), p. 206.

Edge of the Reichswald Forest (From a painting by D. K. Anderson, Canadian War Museum, PL 47030)

-3-
VERITABLE AND THE
GOCH-CALCAR ROAD

As soon as the German High Command realized the Allied spring offensive had begun, they reacted quickly. Recognizing the threat posed by the US Ninth Army to the south, the valves in the Roer dams were blown to flood the Roer River valley. This blocked any move by the American forces, and Operation GRENADE could not start as planned. In addition, Hitler ordered that no fortified area or town was to be evacuated without his permission and he directed Army Group H's strategic reserve, the 116th Panzer and 15th Panzer Grenadier Divisions, to launch an immediate counter-attack against the British XXX Corps.

This was carried out on February 12 but was immediately checked with heavy losses. General Schlemm had no choice but to pull back his forces, concentrating them in a defensive line covering the vital Goch-Calcar road. The northern flank of this line was anchored on a series of wooded knolls called the "Moyland Wood." Here, a strong German battlegroup built around the II Battalion of the 60th Panzer Grenadier Regiment, 116th Panzer Division, and part of the 346th Fusilier Battalion dug in so firmly that all attempts by the 15th (Scottish) Division failed to drive them out.

On February 15th, II Canadian Corps under Lieutenant General Guy Simonds took over the left flank of the front, planning to use the 3rd Division to cut the Goch-Calcar road with an attack two days later. However, it soon became apparent that the exhausted Scottish troops could not capture the intermediate objectives and it was decided to launch the 7th Canadian Infantry Brigade a day earlier to assist in this task.

On February 16th, the attack began with the Royal Winnipeg Rifles on the right, supported by two squadrons of the 3rd (Armoured) Battalion Scots Guards, making a dash in armoured personnel carriers through heavy shell fire to take the high ground near Louisendorf, three miles south of Moyland.[1]

On 16 February 1945 Lieutenant Harry Haultain Badger was commanding Number 9 Platoon which led "A" Company's assault on the fortified village of Louisendorf, Germany. The attack was made in Kangaroos, troop-carrying tanks, and in the advance two of the tanks were knocked out leaving only the platoon commander and 10 men to make the attack.

About 50 yards from the objective, Lieutenant Badger and his men dismounted under extremely heavy shell fire as well as machine-gun fire from a group of buildings nearby. Undeterred, the platoon commander quickly rallied his men and pressed home his attack with such vigour that the enemy's resistance collapsed. They were then fired on by the enemy in a blockhouse to the right. Realizing that, with his small party, he could not hope to clear the blockhouse, he dashed out of the building across a field that was being swept by machine-gun fire to a troop of tanks that were supporting the company attack and obtained one from the troop commander to support his attack. Gathering up his men on the return trip, the small party rushed the blockhouse with such zeal that the enemy, 50 in all, surrendered. This attack was carried out with such daring that the group only suffered two casualties.

By his courage, determination, offensive spirit and coolness under fire, Lieutenant Badger was able to demoralize the enemy, break into the defences and seize his objective.

For his action, Lieutenant Harry Haultain Badger was awarded the Military Cross. Lieutenant Badger was wounded in action at Moyland Wood two days later, on 21 February.

Lieutenant Harry Haultain Badger of The Royal Winnipeg Rifles, on the right, at Buckingham Palace after receiving the Military Cross for his actions at Louisendorf Germany

NAC, PA-192259

During the next two days, with the regiment consolidating on its objective, some aggressive patrols were sent out.

At Louisendorf Germany, on 17 February 1945, Sergeant James Ivan McIvor and one man went out and captured thirteen of the enemy. The next day and evening, Sergeant McIvor went out again, this time with seven men, taking fifty-seven prisoners.

In all these patrols which Sergeant McIvor carried out with such great success, he displayed unusual gallantry. He went on extremely hazardous missions, without thought of his own safety, and handled the men in his patrols so expertly that, for the successes achieved, casualties suffered were almost negligible. He was absolutely dependable and would not hesitate even in the greatest danger and thereby inspired the men who worked with him.

For these actions, and those previously described in the salient east of Nijmegen, Sergeant James Ivan McIvor was awarded the Distinguished Conduct Medal.

Sergeant Thomas William Todd, 12th Canadian Field Regiment, came to France on D-Day as a Lance Bombardier in charge of an artillery line maintenance vehicle. During the battle for the bridgehead, he displayed great bravery and fortitude in keeping communications open across exposed ground to the forward observation officers with the infantry. He was promoted to Lance Sergeant in charge of troop signals when his sergeant was killed at Carpiquet on 6 July 1944 and, since that time, he served faithfully through every engagement in which the Regiment has taken part.

On 16 February 1945, after the capture of Louisendorf Germany by the 7th Canadian Infantry Brigade, the battalions were defensively disposed pending the passing through of the 2nd Canadian Infantry Division, which did not take place until 18 February. The 11th Canadian Field Battery Observation Post was established under cover of fog in the area of "C" Company, Royal Winnipeg Rifles, in an exposed position only some five hundred yards from the enemy lines. To reach it from battalion headquarters necessitated traversing more than a mile of open high ground which was under direct German observation, where any movement immediately drew down heavy fire from enemy guns and mortars. Over this ground, Sergeant Todd, as NCO in charge of line maintenance, continually crossed and recrossed in order to maintain line communications—in the initial stages directing his crew and, finally, when the going had become too precarious, alone on foot. Owing to the continuous enemy shelling and mortar fire, the line at no time remained uncut for longer than one hour, but orders had been given that the line must be maintained at all costs. To carry this out, Sergeant Todd never once hesitated to expose himself by day or night, despite not only the shelling, but also the activities of snipers still at large along the route between the company areas. For three days and nights, neither Sergeant Todd nor his crew had any opportunity for sleep and his devotion to duty and bravery was not only a great inspiration to his own men but won the praise and admiration of all the infantrymen in "C" Company, Royal Winnipeg Rifles.

Throughout the entire campaign, Sergeant Todd has done an outstanding job. His bravery, great devotion to duty and efficiency in maintaining communications in forward positions under the most difficult circumstances have contributed in no small degree to the support given the 7th Canadian Infantry Brigade by the 12th Canadian Field Regiment.

For these actions, Sergeant Thomas William Todd received the Military Medal.

On 18/19 February 1945, Bombardier James Ninnes, 12th Canadian Field Artillery Regiment, Royal Canadian Artillery, was in charge of a cable party operating between the guns and an observation post with The Royal Winnipeg Rifles.

This battalion had the task of taking the high ground at Louisendorf Germany, since it dominated the area from which the larger operation for the capture of the Hochwald defences could start.

It was essential to the success of the attack that the forward observation officer should have good communications with battalion headquarters and the guns. Throughout the thirty-six hours of the attack and consolidation of the objective, the area was subjected to intense enemy machine-gun and mortar fire which not only frequently cut the cable but made the repair of it extremely hazardous.

During the period, Bombardier Ninnes showed great bravery and leadership. On several occasions during heavy mortar fire, he went out alone along the line to make the necessary repairs. His actions and tenacity of purpose were an example to his men, resulting in the communications seldom being out for long. The artillery support, so necessary during the critical stages of the battle, was thus always available.

For his actions, Bombardier James Ninnes was awarded the Military Medal.

At the eastern end of Moyland Wood, Germany, Sergeant Lorne George Sandy Blue of The Royal Winnipeg Rifles, with eight men, took up a defensive position for an observation post in front of the forward company. While in this position, twenty enemy paratroopers attacked them, but they held their fire until the enemy were almost on top of them, and then wiped them out.

For this action, and others north of Nijmegen in December and in central Holland in April, Sergeant Lorne George Sandy Blue was awarded the Military Medal.

Moyland Wood

Meanwhile, on the left flank of the 7th Brigade's attack, the Regina Rifles began a battle for Moyland Wood that would turn out to be one of the bitterest actions of the campaign. As described by Denis Whitaker, Moyland Wood was:

> a series of pine-covered knolls, just over two miles long and one-third of a mile wide, extending southeast from Bedburg (below Cleve) towards Calcar. From the crests of these knolls, the Germans blocked all Allied attempts to advance south.[2]

The troops of 15th Scottish Division, which had been attempting to push forward during the night of 15/16 February, had not yet cleared the Forming Up Place (FUP) for the Reginas to prepare their assault. Consequently, the Canadians had to fight their way into this area, with only "C" Company managing to work its way further forward to the high ground of the Wood. The Germans, however, infiltrated around the forward company, forcing it to withdraw under heavy fire to its former position. All units were continuously shelled, mortared and rocketed during the day and night.[3]

On the 16th of February 1945, "C" Company of the 1st Battalion The Regina Rifle Regiment was the right-hand company of a two-company attack, with the object of clearing the woods south of Moyland Germany. In this attack, Sergeant Edward Stanley Tenklei was platoon sergeant of Number 13 Platoon.

The advance was made under extremely intense fire and less than half-way to the objective, the platoon commander was wounded and could not continue. Sergeant Tenklei immediately took over and continued the advance. Three times his platoon was forced to ground by heavy machine-gun and light automatic fire, and three times this NCO organized and led the charge which overwhelmed the positions, inflicting heavy casualties on the enemy.

It was chiefly the superb leadership, courage and example of Sergeant Tenklei that inspired his men to advance and take their platoon objective. His actions on this day were worthy of the highest traditions of this regiment and the Canadian Army.

For his action, Sergeant Edward Stanley Tenklei was awarded the Military Medal. Sergeant Tenklei later died of wounds, on 5 April.

On February 17, the Reginas attacked again, but made no progress against heavy fire. Casualties now had become so bad that "C" Company had to be pulled out and placed in reserve.

Higher headquarters were frustrated that the Reginas were not making more progress, since they estimated that the woods were held by only about 200 men.[4] However, unknown to the Canadians, the battlegroup of the 116th Panzer Division holding the Wood was relieved on February 18 by a fresh battalion of an even more determined unit–the 6th Parachute Division. This force, just arriving from Holland, was thoroughly indoctrinated in the Nazi cause and of their supposed superiority over the Allied troops. It was against this strength that the Reginas were ordered to attack again, with a slight drizzle falling, at midday on February 18. This time, with the assistance of Wasp flamethrowers, the Canadians managed to gain a foothold in the woods before they were halted by determined counter-attacks. One platoon finally managed to seize the highest crest and, for five hours, held out against repeated counter-attacks. The continuous machine-gun fire and shelling were so heavy that the number of casualties became alarming. The regimental historian later wrote, "Afterwards, company commanders agreed that the shelling was as bad as anything encountered in the Normandy beachhead."⁵

On the afternoon of the 18th of February 1945, "B" Company of the 1st Battalion The Regina Rifle Regiment was the leading company in a battalion attack on the woods south of Moyland Germany. Number 10 Platoon was the right forward platoon, commanded by Sergeant William James Shaw.

As soon as the platoon crossed the start line, they came under extremely heavy shelling, mortar and small arms fire. Seeing that the heaviest part of the barrage was ahead, Sergeant Shaw went to the head of the platoon and led them into the woods. Here, after hand-to-hand fighting with German paratroopers, they gained their objective.

At this point, Sergeant Shaw was seriously wounded but, notwithstanding, he organized the consolidation of his position and moved from post to post, supervising the digging and siting of defences. All this time, his position was being heavily shelled and it was only when his company commander arrived and gave Sergeant Shaw a direct order that he would consent to go to the Regimental Aid Post.

The superb leadership, bravery and fortitude displayed by Sergeant Shaw was the example which inspired his platoon to achieve their objective and hold it.

For his action, Sergeant William James Shaw was awarded the Military Medal.

Corporal Milton Eugene Adolph was a crew commander in Number 2 Section (WASP) of the carrier platoon when, on the afternoon of the 18th February 1945, it was supporting the attack on the woods south of Moyland.

Under extremely hazardous conditions, Number 2 Section advanced with the leading elements of the first company and gave them close support until their fuel was exhausted. When returning to re-fuel, the section was forced to cross a stretch of open country under direct observation and fire of the enemy. Corporal Adolph was leading with his section commander following and, about half-way across, the section commander's carrier struck a mine, overturned and burst into flames.

Without hesitation, Corporal Adolph stopped his carrier, jumped out and, with a fire extinguisher, ran back to the burning carrier. He found the driver dead, the gunner seriously wounded and the section commander suffering from shock and blast; and all were pinned beneath the machine. With the enemy dropping mortar bombs about him and with aimed small arms fire directed at him, he got the fire under control. With the assistance of his crew, he then succeeded in extricating the gunner. When they could not release the section commander, Corporal Adolph very quickly dug the earth out from under him using his hands, and dragged him free of the fire.

Corporal Adolph loaded the two men on his carrier and took them to the Regimental Aid Post. Then, taking command of the remainder of the section, he refuelled and returned through an area he knew to be mined, and supported the follow-up companies with fire until his fuel was again exhausted and his section put out of action by the difficult terrain on the edge of the objective.

Corporal Adolph's quick action and superb heroism under fire undoubtedly saved the two men from burning to death and his return to the area was instrumental in the taking of the final objective.

For this action, Corporal Milton Eugene Adolph received the Military Medal.

Infantry of The Regina Rifles preparing to attack Moyland Wood, Germany
Colin McDougall, NAC, PA-177577

On the 18th February 1945, at approximately 1330 hours, "D" Company of the 1st Battalion The Regina Rifle Regiment moved off in an attack through "B" Company into the woods south of Moyland Germany. Lieutenant Warren Lincoln Keating was in command of Number 16 Platoon which was to take a portion of the high ground in the centre of the woods.

The Company met with extremely heavy resistance and the flame throwers which were to support the attack were knocked out, but Lieutenant Keating led his platoon through intense machine-gun and mortar fire directly to their objective, driving the Germans from their slit trenches. On consolidation, Lieutenant Keating found he had only twelve men left and on his left were eight men of Number 17 Platoon. The remainder of the company were unable to advance, so Lieutenant Keating organized this little group and for five hours drove off repeated counter-attacks, all the while completely cut off from his company and battalion. Several times the Germans penetrated within his defences, but each time the enemy were repulsed in hand-to-hand combat.

During this period, Lieutenant Keating was reinforced by the remainder of "D" Company and for a further period of twenty-four hours, the position was repeatedly counter-attacked and each time these counter-attacks were beaten off. Throughout the entire bitter action, the enemy poured heavy machine-gun and mortar fire into the position.

The magnificent leadership and courage displayed by Lieutenant Keating was directly responsible for the taking of this important height and, although weary from days without sleep, he so inspired and cheered his men that they held it under most adverse conditions.

For this action, Lieutenant Warren Lincoln Keating received the Military Cross.

Prior to and during the attack on the 19 February 1945 on the wood covering the approaches to Calcar [Moyland Wood], Corporal Ernest Augustine Stanley was in charge of the line detachment of "J" Section, 3rd Canadian Infantry Division Signals. The tactical disposition of the units required that the line communications be laid along a road which was in full view of the enemy and which ran parallel to the wood. The plan to capture this wood was intricate and, to effect success, it was of paramount importance that line communications be maintained to all units under command at all times. For forty-eight hours prior to the operation, this road was under continuous mortar and heavy artillery fire and all during this time, without pause for rest or food, with members of his detachment being killed or wounded about him, Corporal Stanley laboured to build this line. He succeeded just prior to zero hour in completing an air line, thirty feet above the ground, and it withstood all mortaring and shelling throughout the operation, thus contributing materially to the success of the operation.

This non-commissioned officer's matchless courage, determination and devotion to duty was an example and inspiration to all ranks of "J" Section, and his actions are worthy of the highest traditions of the Signal Corps.

For this action, Corporal Ernest Augustine Stanley received the Military Medal.

Despite the gains made by The Regina Rifles attack on February 18, the Germans were still holding the main part of Moyland Wood, posing a threat to the further advance of the 2nd Canadian Infantry Division against the Goch-Calcar road. General Simonds was displeased with the delay in taking the woods and ordered that "Moyland Wood was to be cleaned up promptly."[6]

The 3rd Division, from reports from prisoners, now finally realized that they were facing a far stronger opponent than originally believed. Consequently, a more thorough plan was prepared:

A very carefully coordinated attack by The Royal Winnipeg Rifles was planned for February 21. The whole wooded area east of the Moyland lateral road was divided into belts 300 yards wide, each to be successively saturated from west to east by a timed programme of fire from divisional artillery and mortars, while from the southern flank the battalions' anti-tank guns and medium machine-guns of the Cameron Highlanders of Ottawa provided close support over open sights.[7]

Acting Major Lesmere Forrest Kirkpatrick, 12th Canadian Field Regiment, acted as forward observation officer with The Royal Winnipeg Rifles during the operations in France, Belgium and Holland, from June 1944 to February 1945. This officer then acted as his commanding officer's representative to The Regina Rifles Regiment during the operations designed to pierce the Siegfried Line and across the River Rhine until the final capitulation of the enemy on 5 May 1945.

Such was the organizing ability, the careful planning and intelligent anticipation of Major Kirkpatrick that never at any time was the infantry that he supported without the necessary artillery support.

Major Kirkpatrick's extreme devotion to duty can not be better illustrated than by his actions in the attack on Moyland Germany. The taking of the woods near Moyland required a most comprehensive fire plan. This involved the use of not only the field guns but also anti-tank guns, machine-guns, 4.2-inch mortars and all the three-inch mortars of the brigade. The plan as conceived by him undoubtedly played a great part in the successful conclusion of this operation. Never for one minute of the action, which lasted throughout the entire day, were the infantry without intimate fire support. This officer prepared the fire plan from a forward observation post which, at that time, was under constant enemy shell and mortar fire.

Major Kirkpatrick has pursued his duties with the utmost energy, devotion and efficiency even to the complete disregard of his own personal safety, with a result that the infantry whom he supported never entered into operations without the utmost confidence in their ultimate success and in the supporting artillery fire. Thus were the best traditions of the Royal Canadian Artillery exemplified by the actions of this officer.

For these actions, Acting Major Lesmere Forrest Kirkpatrick was awarded the Distinguished Service Order.

At 1015 hours on February 21, the attack by The Royal Winnipeg Rifles went in, supported by tanks of the Sherbrooke Fusiliers, flame-throwing Wasps and, with clear weather, rocket-firing Typhoon aircraft. Fighting continued to be bitter, with mounting casualties from heavy German machine-gun fire and shells bursting in the treetops. All companies of the Winnipegs suffered such heavy losses ("A" Company had no officers and only twenty-five men left) that a reserve company of the Reginas had to be called forward, allowing "D" Company of the Winnipegs to push on to finally clear the tip of the woods. The Germans launched two counter-attacks during the night, but these were repelled with casualties on both sides. Thus ended the battle for Moyland Wood.[8]

On the 21st of February 1945, "D" Company of The Winnipeg Rifles, commanded by Captain (Acting Major) Latimer Hugh Denison was ordered to cap-

ture the high ground which is thickly wooded and overlooks Moyland Germany to the north-east. This attack was quickly pushed home despite the heavy defensive fire put down by the enemy and the few enemy that were left alive withdrew.

Later in the day, "D" Company was ordered to pass through "C" Company to seize the high ground at the eastern tip of the wood. This required a 1000-yard advance through an extremely thick wood which was being subjected to the full weight of the enemy's fire. Casualties amongst Major Denison's men were heavy but, ceaselessly moving from platoon to platoon, he kept control of his company and, by his own personal courage, inspired his men to go on. Machine-gun fire from prepared positions on the hill feature was intense but, by skilfully manoeuvring his men, he got his now depleted company into an assaulting position and stormed the hill top with he himself leading.

During the consolidation phase, they were counter-attacked twice by the enemy, both of these were successfully beaten off with heavy casualties to the Germans. When the enemy were seen forming up for a third attack, Major Denison, from the crest of the hill and in full view of the enemy, personally sited and directed the fire of a troop of tanks which had come up in the meantime. The defensive fire brought down by the company and the tanks quickly broke up the enemy attack and they withdrew.

By his initiative, leadership, courage and offensive spirit, Major Denison was able to inspire his men to hold their hard-won objective, thus securing the left flank of the brigade.

For this action, Acting Major Latimer Hugh Denison was awarded the Distinguished Service Order. Major Denison was later killed in action on 30 March in the Rhine bridgehead.

On the 21st of February 1945, Lieutenant George Galt Aldous was commanding 16 Platoon, Royal Winnipeg Rifles. The battalion had been ordered to capture a

Major Latimer Hugh Denison of The Royal Winnipeg Rifles was awarded the Distinguished Service Order for his actions at Moyland Wood, Germany.
NAC, PA-192252

large wood southeast of Moyland Germany, this area being held by a large number of fanatical young paratroopers who had resisted all previous attempts to dislodge them.

Number 16 Platoon was the leading platoon of "D" Company and, throughout the 1000 yard advance through the woods to their objective, was under heavy machine-gun and shell fire. The courage, leadership and coolness displayed by Lieutenant Aldous quickly carried his men to their objective. He personally accounted for one machine-gun post en route, which was firing on his platoon from a flank.

While the platoon was consolidating, the enemy counter-attacked and overran his forward section. Gathering up his reserve section, Lieutenant Aldous rushed forward and, inflicting heavy casualties on them, drove the enemy off. During this, he was wounded and temporarily blinded by an egg grenade. This did not deter him, however, and he reorganized his platoon under heavy machine-gun and mortar fire in time to beat back a second counter-attack, thereby restoring the situation.

Had this counter-attack been successful, it would have jeopardized the battalion position and it was only through Lieutenant Aldous' bravery, coolness and quick thinking that the men of his platoon were kept together and so prevented this flank from being penetrated.

For this action, Lieutenant George Galt Aldous was awarded the Military Cross.

On 21 February 1945, in the attack of The Royal Winnipeg Rifles on the woods south-east of Moyland Germany, Rifleman Mervin Frank Milson displayed exemplary courage and devotion to duty.

"D" Company, Royal Winnipeg Rifles, to which Rifleman Milson was attached as a stretcher bearer, had the task of securing the eastern tip of the woods, which contained a number of enemy paratroopers. During the fierce fighting that followed, Rifleman Milson noticed two of his comrades lying wounded in a clearing that was being swept by machine-gun fire and exploding rifle grenades. He immediately ran out to their assistance and was himself struck by a bullet which passed through his helmet and creased his scalp. Just then, the enemy launched a counter-attack but, undeterred, this soldier ran on and, seizing the men by their collars, succeeded in dragging them back into our positions where he dressed their wounds. Rifleman Milson was then ordered to the Regimental Aid Post for treatment. He refused to be evacuated and returned to his company where he continued to succour his wounded comrades.

His gallant action undoubtedly saved the lives of two wounded men and his courage was an inspiration to all ranks of the battalion and was worthy of the highest traditions of this Regiment and the Canadian Army.

For this action, Rifleman Mervin Frank Milson was awarded the Military Medal.

Heselerfeld

While two battalions of the 7th Canadian Infantry Brigade were struggling to seize Moyland Wood, the third battalion—the 1st Battalion, The Canadian Scottish Regiment—became engaged in an equally desperate battle a short distance to the southeast. Here, when the Royal Winnipeg Rifles had advanced to Louisendorf, the Canadian Scottish had moved up behind them in reserve. However, when the Regina Rifles were repulsed in their first attacks on Moyland Wood, the Canadian Scottish was ordered to send two companies forward to occupy a position on the right flank of the Reginas—to Heselerfeld, a small hill in a farm area a half mile south of the Woods. The purpose was presumably to be prepared to give support to the Reginas. But the Scottish became involved in a fight for their existence.

On February 17, "A" and "D" Companies of the Scottish moved off and reached their first objectives without much trouble. However, mortaring and rocket fire increased to such an intensity that they could not advance down the forward face of the hill. With the Reginas still unable to make progress to the west, these companies were now out on a limb, exposed to fire from both the front and rear.

The next day, the forward companies attempted to attack again, but were immediately met with a hail of fire. Company Sergeant Major James Nimmo of "B" Company later reported that:

> When we moved off we were under heavy shell and mortar fire . . . Enemy machine-gun and mortar fire was hellish. In no time at all, we had lost half our lead platoon and the attack threatened to bog down . . . The ground was literally covered by a mass of singing lead . . . At 1700 hours, Major English made the decision that we had better get going as we couldn't stay where we were.[9]

Number 10 Platoon under Sergeant Lloyd Cummings managed to occupy a fortified farmhouse which they immediately converted into a strongpoint. This became a key point in anchoring the position. German paratroops, as desperate to overrun the attackers as the Canadians were to hang on to their gains, launched a series of counter-attacks. Attack followed counter-attack, and artillery and mortar fire continued to sweep the hill for the next three days.

In "B" Company, Major E. G. English and CSM Nimmo played key roles in ensuring that a coherent defence was sustained—getting food up, reorganizing the battered platoons, and getting ammunition to the platoon virtually cut off in the blockhouse. It was impossible to contact Sergeant Cummings' group during the day because of the intensity of machine-gun fire sweeping the area, and only the continuing fire of the Cummings' Bren gun told the others that the little garrison was still hanging on.

The Scottish threw in all their reserves as the three forward companies were reduced to only 130 men and "C" Company virtually wiped out in a disastrous attack. On February 21, with dead and wounded Germans lying around the fortified farmhouse, CSM Nimmo wrote, "There was a steady drum of noise as the shells hummed overhead in both directions. At this point, none of us figured on coming out alive!"[10]

On the 17th of February 1945, during the battle for possession of the high ground (Heselerfeld) at the approaches to Calcar, Corporal Philip Peter Katchanoski of the 1st Battalion The Canadian Scottish Regiment showed courage and leadership above and beyond the call of duty. During the reorganization on the objective, his platoon officer and platoon sergeant became casualties. Corporal Katchanoski then took charge of the remainder of Number 8 Platoon and personally sited fire positions, and saw that his men were dug in. This was in the face of terrific mortar and machine-gun fire. When darkness came, acting under orders from his company commander, this NCO gathered his platoon and moved them into a new position on the exposed flank. There he again saw that his men were properly sited and dug in.

In the next five days, three of which he was in command, his platoon successfully beat off counter-attack after counter-attack. During this time, Corporal Katchanoski seemed, by continually visiting his men's positions, to be everywhere at once, lending encouragement to his platoon and by his actions inspiring them to deeds of heroism. Though sniped at from all directions and intermittently mortared unmercifully, he was completely oblivious of his own personal safety.

His actions are in keeping with the highest traditions of the regiment and of the Canadian Army.

For his actions, Corporal Philip Peter Katchanoski was awarded the Distinguished Conduct Medal.

Warrant Officer II (CSM) James Little Nimmo of "B" Company, 1st Battalion The Canadian Scottish Regiment, has consistently performed his duties with outstanding courage and shown excellent leadership in the face of heavy enemy opposition.

On the night of 18/19 February 1945 during the taking and holding of the high ground (Heselerfeld) at the approaches to Calcar Germany, in the face of strong enemy resistance, CSM Nimmo showed extreme bravery and coolness in reorganizing his company, and beating off four determined enemy counter-attacks.

In the early evening, his company commander was called to attend an Orders Group and, owing to the enemy's harassing fire and the difficult terrain, was unable to rejoin the company until just before first light. All platoon commanders had become casualties during the day's bitter fighting and CSM Nimmo took over command. It was his energy and utter disregard for his own personal safety that inspired the men to fight through the long night. When dawn came it was discovered that the enemy had dug in about one hundred yards in front of the company position. It was estimated that they were about eighty strong and the company strength at this time was fifty-three men, of which twenty-four were holding a blockhouse 300 yards away. This left twenty-nine men opposing the enemy.

The company commander appreciated that reinforcements were needed to meet this new threat and that the battalion headquarters must be advised of the situation. CSM Nimmo volunteered to try and get back to the battalion command post. To do this, he had to cross 300 yards of flat ground, in full view of the enemy, before he came to any cover. He made it, although it seemed incredible that anyone could live through the hail of machine-gun and rifle fire that the enemy laid down. The information which the sergeant major brought back enabled the battalion commander to re-group his forces to meet the new threat and to supply the badly needed reinforcements to "B" Company. Company Sergeant Major Nimmo with the reinforcements again made the hazardous journey and arrived at the company without the loss of a single man. His actions this day were worthy of the highest tradition of this Regiment and the Canadian Army.

For these actions, Company Sergeant Major James Little Nimmo was awarded the Distinguished Conduct Medal.

During the night of 18/19 February 1945, in the taking and holding of the high ground (Heselerfeld) at the approaches to Calcar, Sergeant Lloyd Cummings of the 1st Battalion The Canadian Scottish Regiment showed coolness and courage of the highest standard. His platoon commander having been hit earlier in the engagement, Sergeant Cummings took command of Number 10 Platoon and led them into an assault on a vital blockhouse, a part of the Siegfried defences, which was held by thirty Germans.

To accomplish this, the platoon had to cross 250 yards of flat open ground through a storm of mortar and machine-gun fire. An entry into the blockhouse was effected and Sergeant Cummings, with the remnants of his platoon (fifteen men), successfully beat off five strong counter-attacks during the next six hours. A total of twenty-seven prisoners were taken and at least seventeen enemy dead were counted after this engagement. Sergeant Cummings suffered a slight but painful wound on his hand, but he refused to leave his platoon. By his leadership and his bravery, he inspired his men to fight on for another forty-eight hours, at which time reinforcements arrived to augment the few still alive in the blockhouse. His actions are in keeping with the highest traditions of this regiment and of the Canadian Army.

For this action, Sergeant Lloyd Cummings was awarded the Military Medal.

During the attack on Heselerfeld on 18/19 February 1945, Private Wallace Malcolm Hazlewood of the 1st Battalion The Canadian Scottish Regiment displayed extreme bravery in the performance of his duties as stretcher bearer. At the time the company was consolidating its position on the objective, mortar fire, artillery and machine-gun fire was so intense that casualties were very heavy despite the protection of the slit trenches. Private Hazlewood, completely disregarding his own personal safety, walked about the position ministering to the wounded. Machine-guns and snipers on both flanks were deliberately attempting to shoot him but, with a coolness that was an inspiration to all, he continued to succour the wounded. At one point, when shelling was so intense that it was impossible to evacuate a wounded man, Private Hazlewood dug a shallow slit trench and gave the wounded man cover at the risk of his own life.

During the ensuing four days of bitter and costly fighting, Private Hazlewood showed the same high standard of bravery. His fearlessness in going about his work was largely responsible for saving the lives of many wounded comrades.

His actions are in keeping with the highest traditions of this regiment and of the Canadian Army.

For his actions, Private Wallace Malcolm Hazlewood was awarded the Military Medal.

On the 17th of February 1945, Captain William Patrick Hair of the 12th Canadian Field Regiment RCA was acting as a forward observation officer with "A" Company, 1st Battalion The Canadian Scottish Regiment in the attack on Heselerfeld near Calcar Germany.

During the attack, the platoon commander and sergeant of a forward platoon became casualties and the platoon began to falter. Seeing this, Captain Hair, with complete disregard for his own safety, took over command, reorganized the platoon on its objective, and completed the consolidation. In the ensuing grim and bitter fighting, he not only carried out his artillery duties, but fought the badly depleted platoon as well.

Later he took over the duties of the artillery representative at battalion headquarters, his predecessor having been killed, and in the performance of which his advice was invaluable to the Commanding Officer. On three occasions, despite savage enemy counter-attacks, he made trips up to the forward defended localities to satisfy himself that the defensive fire tasks adequately covered all possible lines of approach by the enemy.

His presence on these occasions was a source of great inspiration and an example to the now battle-weary men. Captain Hair displayed a personal courage and a devotion to duty on this day that was above and beyond the normal call, and his actions were worthy of the highest traditions of the Royal Canadian Artillery and the Canadian Army.

For his actions, Captain William Patrick Hair was awarded the Military Cross.

During the attack on Heselerfeld on 19 February 1945, Lance Corporal Roy Wilfred Conrad of the 1st Battalion Canadian Scottish Regiment was attached to "D" Company as a signaller. Despite the terrific difficulties, not the least of which was intense shelling and machine-gun fire, Lance Corporal Conrad maintained communications with supporting arms and higher formations without which many more casualties would have been sustained. His reactions in promptly anticipating the requirements of the situation were at all times an assis-

tance to the company commander. Finally, his tireless and unceasing devotion to duty contributed in no small way to the success of the operation as well as being an inspiration to those about him.[11]

For his actions, Lance Corporal Roy Wilfred Conrad was Mentioned in Despatches.

Late on February 21, with the key positions at Moyland Wood and the town of Goch taken by the First Canadian Army, the Germans abandoned the defence of the Goch-Calcar road. The agony of the Canadian Scottish was over as, late on the evening of February 22, the battalion was relieved. As they marched back to a rest camp along the dimly lit German roads, each company was met by a lone piper. As described by Reginald Roy:

> The shrill, triumphant sound of the pipes gave something to the men that nothing else could. Almost automatically, the bone-weary soldiers began to march in step . . . Swinging into the rest area, the companies were met by the pipes and drums of the whole battalion. It was an electrifying moment . . . a message of praise and admiration for a job well done. No battle had been tougher and none had exacted such a heavy toll in dead and wounded as had "Slaughter Hill."[12]

Action on the front quieted down to only small-unit actions as preparations were made for renewing the offensive. The 9th Canadian Infantry Brigade moved up to take over a section of the front held previously by the 2nd Canadian Infantry Division, allowing the II Corps forces to regroup for the next phase. However, during this period, several more awards were made:

> On 23 February 1945, Captain John Douglas MacFarlane of the 14th Canadian Field Regiment, Royal Canadian Artillery, was attached to "A" Company, The Highland Light Infantry of Canada, as forward observation officer for the attack on Ebben Germany. Before first light, February 24, after "A" Company had taken its objective, Captain MacFarlane went forward and established an observation post in the forward platoon locality.

> At first light, Captain MacFarlane's observation post was engaged by an enemy self-propelled gun firing at about 600-yard range. The first shot was a direct hit, killing Captain MacFarlane's signaller and wounding Captain MacFarlane about the face and eyes. Five more shots were fired into the building in rapid succession and the whole area was subjected to concentrated shelling and mortar fire, destroying Captain MacFarlane's line, his only remaining means of communication.

> In spite of his wounds, Captain MacFarlane ignored the enemy fire and traced his line until he had found and repaired all breaks. He then returned to his observation post, which was still being mortared, and registered the area of the self-propelled gun as a target. His action enabled him to bring down an artillery concentration which silenced the gun.

Enemy mortars were still active and Captain MacFarlane remained at his post all that day directing artillery fire on many active enemy positions and troop movements.

Captain MacFarlane, by his courageous action and devotion to duty, dealt the enemy a heavy blow by registering accurate artillery shoots and preventing the enemy from counter-attacking "A" Company's position.

For his action, Captain John Douglas MacFarlane was awarded the Military Cross.

Preparations now began for the next phase of the offensive, to be called Operation BLOCKBUSTER. Considerable regrouping of the front-line positions was carried out to get the 2nd and 3rd Canadian Infantry Divisions in place.

At Keppeln on the afternoon of 24 February 1945, an enemy shell hit an ammunition lorry that was being unloaded on a gun position in preparation for operation BLOCKBUSTER. The lorry was set on fire, one man was killed and two wounded. Acting Bombardier John Riley Stromquist of the 13th Canadian Field Regiment RCA, although seriously wounded in the neck, called for a stretcher to evacuate the other wounded case. He jumped into the truck and, by throwing out cartridge cases and beating down the flames, he was able to put out the fire.

This action prevented the explosion of many rounds of ammunition with the almost certain result of more casualties on the troop position. During the whole time, the enemy continued to harass the gun position with artillery shelling.

When the fire was put out, Acting Bombardier Stromquist collapsed and was then found to be seriously wounded. By his initiative and courage, he ensured that this troop was able to provide artillery support in the opening of Operation BLOCKBUSTER. He was an example of a high fighting spirit to all ranks of the Regiment.

For this action, Acting Bombardier John Riley Stromquist was awarded the Military Medal.

In the early hours of February 26, German paratroopers made an unexpected attack against the right flank of the 2nd Division. Here, in heavy fighting, The Royal Hamilton Light Infantry managed to hang on to their critical positions which were the Start Line for BLOCKBUSTER. The Highland Light Infantry of Canada were ordered to launch a counter-attack to relieve the pressure.

Major Erwin Frank Klugman displayed unusual courage and leadership throughout the entire campaign in Holland and Northwest Germany. His initiative and drive played a major part in the success achieved by the Highland Light Infantry of Canada during these operations.

During the bitter fighting in the Calcar area, the Essex Scottish Regiment and the Royal Hamilton Light Infantry were heavily counter-attacked on numerous occasions. On the 25 February 1945 the Germans were applying strong pressure on the Royal Hamilton Light Infantry. Major Klugman was ordered to attack Eben Farm and relieve some of the pressure. He led his men across 200 yards of open ground and captured his objective after bitter fighting. The Germans attempted three counter-attacks with infantry supported by tanks. Major Klugman, by personal example, inspired his men and succeeded in beating off these attacks with great loss to the enemy.

For his action here and later east of the Hochwald Forest, Major Erwin Frank Klugman was awarded the Distinguished Service Order.

NOTES

1.   Col C. P. Stacey, *The Victory Campaign* (Ottawa: The Queen's Printer, 1966), p. 482.

2.   W. Denis Whitaker and Shelagh Whitaker, *Rhineland* (Toronto: Stoddart Publishing Co. Ltd., 1989), p. 116.

3.   National Archives of Canada Record Group (RG) 24, Vol. 14132, 7th Canadian Infantry Brigade War Diary, 16 August 1945.

4.   Ibid.

5.   Captain Eric Luxton, *1st Battalion The Regina Rifle Regiment 1939 - 1946* (Regina: The Regina Rifle Assoc., 1946), p. 57.

6.   Terry Copp and Robert Vogel, *Maple Leaf Route: Victory* (Alma: Maple Leaf Route, 1988), p. 42.

7.   Stacey, p. 486.

8.   Stacey, p. 486; RG 24, Vol 14132, 7 CIB W.D., February 21, 1945.

9.   RG 24, Vol 15041, 1 BN, The Canadian Scottish War Deary, February 19, 1945, "'B' Company's Narrative of Heseler Field."

10.   Ibid.

11.   RG 24, Vol 15041, 1 C Scot W.D., February 1945.

12.   R. H. Roy, *Ready for the Fray* (Vancouver: The Canadian Scottish Regiment, 1958), p. 389.

-4-
THE VICTORIA CROSS AT MOOSHOF

Message from
the German Commander in Chief West

Soldiers of the Western Front:

The enemy is launching a general offensive towards the Rhine and the Ruhr. He will use all means in his power to smash into the west of the Reich and bring the industrial Ruhr district under his control. Following the loss of Silesia, you know what that would mean—the Wehrmacht without weapons, the Homeland without coal.

My soldiers, you have beaten the enemy in the great Autumn and Winter battles. Now you must protect the Homeland which works for you steadfastly: protect our women and children from foreign despotism. Protect the rear of our heavily engaged troops on the Eastern Front, so that they can smash the Bolshevik onslaught and liberate Eastern Germany.

My gallant comrades-in-arms! The coming battle will be very hard, but put all you've got into them and your resolution will shatter the enemy's offensive. With unshakable confidence we look to our Fuehrer to save Volk and Reich from a dastardly fate.

(signed) von Rundstedt
Field Marshal
C-in-C West[1]

On February 22, General Schlemm pulled his German First Parachute Army back from the Siegfried Line towards the third and last defensive zone in the Rhineland which they called the "Schlieffen Position." However, instead of concentrating in the already prepared defences on the west edge of the Hochwald, they occupied an advanced zone of resistance on the high ground to the southwest and south of Calcar and hurriedly continued to improve its defence works. Here, the flat open farmland was under clear observation from the Calcar-Udem ridge. On this plateau, the Germans had turned all the isolated farmhouses into strongpoints, reinforcing their stone walls and digging trenches around them. In particular, both Calcar and Udem were prepared as all-round centres of resistance, surrounded by trench systems and anti-tank ditches with flak positions.

Units of the 2nd Parachute, 6th Parachute, and 116th Panzer Divisions manned this line and were still the best fighting forces the Germans had available on the Western Front. Although the Germans had already suffered severe losses in infantry, they hoped that, by using this screen, they would inflict heavy damage on the Canadian and British armour before these reached the Schlieffen Position proper.[2]

On February 23, the Allied outlook improved significantly as forces of the US Ninth Army finally launched Operation GRENADE. The Germans were unable to hold a coherent line before the Americans for long because all their reserves had been drawn into the battles to the north. Consequently, by February 25, American units were racing towards the Rhine.

General Harry Crerar, anticipating that the Germans might now be prepared to retire from their line in the Hochwald if pressed strongly enough, prepared plans for the second phase of VERITABLE: a new set-piece attack called Operation BLOCKBUSTER, designed to break through towards the Rhine at Xanten. Crerar felt that "if everything broke in our favour . . . I would not be surprised if armour . . . reached the Geldern-Xanten line in a few days. On the other hand, if conditions are against us . . . the battle may well last three weeks."[3] Since British and Canadian infantry casualties had already been heavy and there were insufficient replacements, he therefore indicated that if, by D+1 a breakthrough did not appear imminent, "a partial BLOCKBUSTER will terminate the operation . . . securing the high ground east of the Calcar-Udem road."[4]

BLOCKBUSTER was to begin in the early hours of February 26 with II Canadian Corps attacking on the left and XXX British Corps on the right. Following a powerful artillery program from 700 guns, the 2nd Canadian Infantry Division would seize the north end of the Calcar-Udem ridge, after which battlegroups of the 4th Canadian Armoured Division would thrust southwards along the ridge and then turn east with the hope of making a quick breakthrough in the Hochwald Layback.

The 3rd Canadian Infantry Division would attack on the right of the Corps' front, protecting the 4th Division's advance by seizing the Germans' southern anchor at Udem. This would also open up the way for the British 11th Armoured Division to sweep south of Udem and join the 4th Canadian Armoured Division in breaking through the Hochwald. For this attack, the 8th Canadian Infantry Brigade would first have to capture the intermediate defences in the area of the village of Keppeln early on February 26.

The 8th Brigade's plan called for successive attacks by each of its three battalions to secure the central area between Calcar and Udem.

The terrain was flat and without cover for 1800 yards in all directions, except for scattered stone farmhouses around which the enemy had dug in. Because the entire area was under enemy observation, the initial attack would be made well before sunrise on February 26 by the Queen's Own Rifles on the left. Le Régiment de la Chaudière would next attack on the right at 0800 hours and, after it had seized its objective, the North Shore Regiment was to attack Keppeln in the centre, protected by the fire of its sister regiments on its flanks.[5]

The Queen's Own Rifles' War Diary describes the mood as the men prepared for what they knew would be a difficult battle:

> Those who slept, slept fitfully. At 0330 hours, the men were roused to hot coffee or rum, and sandwiches. Equipment was donned, final instructions given, and at 0400 the barrage began.
>
> For us, there had been no precedent to this. As the lead companies, Charlie and Dog, moving in extended line formation to the start line, the night was alive with light and noises. AA guns pumped incessantly long, whipping lines of tracer overhead; machine-guns hammered and criss-crossed out into the darkness; behind them the sky was silver with the glare of searchlights, trees and buildings stark against it; out forward in the blackness, the lines of the enemy flared on their length like typewriter keys under the pounding fingers of shelling.
>
> The forward companies, each with a troop of tanks in their rear, followed white tapes that had been laid down the evening before. And then there was no more tape. Our artillery was falling just a few yards ahead. It lifted. The hour was 0435. The attack began, Charlie right, Dog left.[6]

"D" Company of The Queen's Own Rifles quickly captured its first objective, the hamlet of Mooshof. But the Germans immediately brought down a heavy artillery bombardment and violently counter-attacked. The company commander, Major Ben Dunkelman, reported that "all hell has broken loose. Every minute more men are hit." Number 16 Platoon was severely disrupted when, in attempting to counterattack, it was struck by German artillery bombardment which killed the platoon commander and wiped out one section of men. The survivors moved to join forces with the other forward platoon but, in doing so, allowed the Germans to reoccupy one of the farmhouses. At this point, "D" Company's lead troops were in a very vulnerable position as the Germans prepared to move in on them from the flank.

It was at this point that Sergeant Aubrey Cosens, the surviving NCO in 16 Platoon, took the heroic action that turned around the direction of the battle. Sergeant Cosens was born at Latchford, Ontario in 1921 and was raised in Porquis Junction, near Iroquois Falls. He joined the

Canadian Army in November 1940 at the age of eighteen and was assigned to the Queen's Own Rifles of Canada in Normandy on August 1, 1944 as a corporal. Three months later he was the platoon sergeant of Number 16 Platoon, "D" Company. He was described as:

> quiet, wonderfully-built, firm-featured, a fine soldier and a great NCO. "He was the sort of chap you naturally want to have around to be your next CSM [Company Sergeant Major]," said [Major Ben] Dunkelman.
>
> He loved sports. A few days before the action, he organized a company athletic meet. The boys knew they were going into something grim and he wanted to do something to take their minds off it. Then he proceeded to win almost every event.[7]

On the night of February 25/26, The Queen's Own Rifles of Canada launched an attack to secure ground, the possession of which was essential for the large-scale operations in the immediate future.

The first phase of the attack was made by "D" Company with two platoons up. Sergeant Aubrey Cosens was sergeant of Number 16 Platoon which had, under command, two tanks of the 6th Canadian Armoured Regiment, with orders to capture the hamlet of Mooshof. The platoon was to cross its start line, which was about half a mile from the objective, at 0430 hours. Before reaching the start line, it came under heavy enemy shell fire, but the attack went in on time and was pressed home through the darkness in the face of intense artillery, mortar and small arms fire.

Sergeant Aubrey Cosens of The Queen's Own Rifles of Canada was awarded the Victoria Cross posthumously for his valour at Mooshof, Germany.
Printed with permission of The Queen's Own Rifles of Canada.

On reaching Mooshof, the enemy was found to have prepared positions throughout the area and to have strongpoints in three farm buildings. The pla-

*toon attacked these buildings twice but, on each occasion, was beaten back by fa-
natical enemy resistance.*

*The enemy then counter-attacked in strength. In the darkness, and aided by
his knowledge of the ground, the Germans succeeded in infiltrating into the position which Number 16 platoon had hastily taken up. In bitter and confused
fighting, this counter-attack was beaten off, but not until the platoon had suffered
heavy casualties, including the platoon commander.*

*Sergeant Cosens at once assumed command of the platoon. To a lesser spirit,
the situation would have seemed hopeless as the enemy was obviously present in
force, and he was able to find only four survivors of his platoon. In addition, one
of his two tanks had become separated from the infantry during the fighting and
the area was being swept from all sides by intense enemy fire.*

*Not daunted, and determined to carry on with the attack notwithstanding the
odds, Sergeant Cosens organized his four men in a covering fire position and himself ran across twenty-five yards of open, flat, bullet-swept ground to his one available
tank. Here, with magnificent contempt for the very great danger, he took up an exposed position on the tank, sitting in front of the turret and, with great daring,
calmly directed the fire of the tank against enemy positions which had been pin-
pointed in the previous fighting or which disclosed themselves by their fire.*

*Once again, the enemy counter-attacked savagely in force. Remaining on the
tank and completely disregarding the enemy's superiority in numbers and the
withering fire, Sergeant Aubrey Cosens led and inspired the defence. He plunged
the tank, in the blackness, into the middle of the attackers. His bold tactics resulted in the complete disorganization of the enemy force, which broke and fled after sustaining many casualties.*

*Turning promptly and with great courage to the offensive, and notwithstand-
ing the sustained enemy fire from all directions and the obvious risks in the darkness from concealed enemy posts and from snipers, Sergeant Cosens determined to
clear the three buildings. To do so, he ordered his four men to follow the tank on
which he was riding. He ordered the tank to ram the first building, a one-storey
farmhouse and, when it had done so, aided by the covering fire of his men, he entered
the building entirely alone, killed several of the defenders, and took the rest prisoner.*

*Sergeant Cosens then pressed relentlessly on and directed the tank, under con-
tinuous heavy fire, towards the second building. En route, he saw in the flash of
shell fire, the body of one of his comrades who had been killed in one of the first
abortive attacks on his position, lying in the path of the tank. Calmly he halted
the tank and removed the body. Continuing, he had the tank fire into this building and then he entered it alone to find that the occupants had fled.*

*With splendid persistence, he then advanced to the third building which was a
two-storey farmhouse and strongly held by the enemy. Under cover from the tank
and from his little band of four men, he again made a one-man entry into this
building and personally killed or captured its occupants.*

The hard core of the German resistance in the immediate area was thus broken. Sergeant Cosens promptly gave his small force orders for the consolidation of the position and started off to report to his company commander. He had not travelled more than twenty-five feet when he was shot through the head by an enemy sniper. He died almost instantly. The German force in the Mooshof area had by this time become so completely battered and dispirited, however, that there was no further counter-attack against this position. The Queen's Own Rifles of Canada was able to pass through to its next objective and the other attacks were able to proceed according to plan.

Throughout this action, Sergeant Aubrey Cosens displayed unsurpassed leadership, initiative and devotion to duty. He was faced by an enemy force which was numerically, and in firepower, far superior to his own and was composed of resolute men who had every possible advantage of ground cover. Never for a moment, however, did he hesitate and he fought his tiny force under the most difficult conditions with the utmost skill and determination, absolutely refusing to consider the possibility of defeat. In the actual fighting, his personal gallantry was of the highest order. He was always to the forefront of the battle and, in the course of the operation, he personally killed at least twenty of the enemy and took an equal number of prisoners.

Sergeant Aubrey Cosens' heroism and his brilliant conduct of this successful action have been an inspiration to his regiment and will remain for all time a glorious example to the Canadian Army.[8]

For his action, Sergeant Aubrey Cosens was posthumously awarded the Victoria Cross.

The riflemen who supported Sergeant Cosens were A. W. Ferrell, G. W. Parsons (later killed in action around Weiner in North Friesland) and G. Dosser, along with Corporal H. F. Cough. Corporal Cough later added some further detail to the description of the action:

After our platoon commander, Lt L. C. McKay, was wounded, Sergeant Cosens took over. He asked me to gather up the men who were not wounded. There were only four of us left. He used us to give covering fire while he made a dash to find a tank. He appeared on the top of the tank and directed fire which broke up the German counter-attack. The Germans ran for their building in disorderly fashion. They started to open fire on us from there with automatic weapons. As he could not stop the withering fire, he crouched on the tank and had it ram the first building. With his pistol in hand, he wounded one German. After clearing the first building, he had the tank moved towards the building along side. Before reaching the building, he jumped off the tank to remove Lance Corporal Fraser's body from the path of the tank . . .[10]

The commander of the tank which supported Sergeant Cosens so effectively was Sergeant C. R. Anderson of "C" Squadron of the 6th Canadian Armoured Regiment (1st Hussars) whose support in general proved to be very important for the infantry.

In the attack south of Cleve which was designed to drive the Germans from the west bank of the Rhine, II Canadian Corps' plan called for the 4th Canadian Armoured and the 11th British Armoured Divisions to pass around Udem and on to the Hochwald Forest. This operation could not commence until the village of Keppeln had fallen into our hands. Keppeln was very heavily defended and was the core of the enemy's defence. The 8th Canadian Infantry Brigade, with the 6th Canadian Armoured Regiment in support, were allotted this task. The brigade plan was to have the Queen's Own Rifles of Canada capture the high ground north of Keppeln and the Régiment de la Chaudière to capture Hollen on the right. When this attack was successfully under way, the North Shore Regiment was to pass through the corridor and take Keppeln supported by the units on the high ground to either flank.

"C" Squadron of the 6th Canadian Armoured Regiment, commanded by Major J. W. Powell MC, was in support of the Queen's Own Rifles of Canada. H hour for their attack was 0430 hours, 26 February 1945. In order to ensure complete co-operation between the tanks and infantry, Major Powell moved his squadron into position the evening of the 25th of February. After discussing the plan of attack with the Commanding Officer, Queen's Own Rifles of Canada, he returned to his squadron where he passed on the details to his troop leaders. Instead of resting during the night, he walked from tank to tank, talking to all ranks, infecting them with his determination to make the attack a success.

At 0430 hours, tanks and infantry moved forward in the dark. However, the attack did not progress as quickly as anticipated due to heavy enemy small arms, machine-gun and mortar fire. The tanks found it extremely difficult to manoeuvre due to the darkness, boggy ground, minefields and Panzerfausts.* During this time, Major Powell, moving with the forward elements, directed his squadron ahead and, although his squadron was suffering casualties, gave effective support.

By first light, it appeared that the attack would bog down due to the infantry being pinned to the ground by very heavy enemy fire. Realizing that the situation was becoming critical, Major Powell dismounted from his tanks and, disregarding the hail of murderous fire, contacted the infantry. Wherever and whenever the attack was held up, this officer directed his tanks in support and, although progress was slow, momentum was maintained. In many instances, his utter disregard for personal safety was an inspiration to all ranks and his grim determination to push on in the face of such fanatical resistance overcame many a crucial situation.

For this action, and for actions later in the day at Keppeln with the North Shore Regiment, Major John Wilson Powell MC was awarded the Distinguished Service Order.

Lieutenant McKay was also decorated for his role in the opening phase of the attack.

---

*   A hand-held German anti-tank weapon (see Glossary)

In the attack on Mooshof, Lieutenant Lloyd Carlton McKay commanded 18 Platoon of "D" Company, 1st Battalion The Queen's Own Rifles of Canada, on 26 February 1945. This platoon, upon reaching its objective, came under extremely heavy mortar and shell fire, and the platoon was immediately counter-attacked by strong enemy forces.

Without regard for his personal safety, Lieutenant McKay refused to take cover and directed the fire of his platoon under the most hazardous conditions. He then personally led three attacks against enemy counter-blows, completely disorganizing the attacking enemy forces.

At this point, Lieutenant McKay was seriously wounded through the chest and legs. Despite his wounds, he climbed on to the top of a supporting tank and, although still under intense enemy fire, directed the tanks into the buildings held by the enemy. In these buildings, Lieutenant McKay killed ten Germans and took twelve prisoners.

Through his supreme courage and magnificent leadership, the company was able to consolidate its position and hold off all enemy attempts to retake it. Lieutenant McKay's extreme bravery and coolness in action was an inspiration to all ranks and is an example of the highest standards of a Canadian Army officer.

For his actions, Lieutenant Lloyd Carlton McKay received the Military Cross.

Meanwhile, "C" Company, advancing on the left, was also facing heavy resistance and coming under fire from other small groups of buildings. While a large part of the company was pinned down, some sections managed to infiltrate forward to attack the enemy from the rear and thus fight their way towards the objective. But casualties were severe, including most of the platoon commanders.

On the morning of 26 February 1945, Major Orson Allen Nickson, commanding "C" Company, 1st Battalion The Queen's Own Rifles of Canada, having successfully completed the assault on the company objective near Tuenbauenshof, was ordered to press forward and seize the buildings near Tackenhof. Reorganizing his company, Major Nickson decided that a bold plan of attack was vital to the success of this operation.

With utmost disregard for his personal safety and, showing great leadership, Major Nickson led his company across the flat country, through very heavy enemy fire, and assaulted the enemy positions. Fierce hand-to-hand fighting followed and, through the inspiring actions and extreme courage displayed by Major Nickson, the company was successful in killing large numbers of the enemy, taking many prisoners, and completely breaking the backbone of enemy resistance.

This action was the deciding factor which enabled the breakthrough of the main body of our troops. This performance by Major Nickson was an example to the regiment, and his coolness in action, personal courage, and bravery was an inspiration to all ranks under his command. Major Nickson landed on D-Day, 6 June 1944, with this battalion, and has commanded a company in action ever since that date, with the exception of the period 8 September 1944 until 18 November 1944 when he was recovering from wounds received in action.

The is just one example of the many instances when Major Nickson inspired his men by his own courage and daring in the face of the enemy. His coolness under fire in all of the actions in which he has taken part has been a great credit to the Canadian Army and he has, in no small way, by his deeds, contributed to the success achieved by the 1st Battalion, The Queen's Own Rifles of Canada in all of their actions in this theatre of warfare.

For his actions, Major Orson Allen Nickson was awarded the Distinguished Service Order.

Sherman tanks of the 6th Canadian Armoured Regiment (1st Hussars) refuelling and replenishing their ammunition early on the morning of February 26 in preparation for the attack on Keppeln, Germany.
NAC, PA-192254

"A" Company's role was to pass though the forward companies, after they had seized their objectives, and carry out the second phase of the attack. Even in this initial reserve role, they began to suffer casualties from the enemy artillery. Upon advancing, they managed to seize a foothold on their first objective but came under fire from a German self-propelled gun, which inflicted many casualties and drove off the supporting tanks. By dawn, the company had suffered so many losses that it had to be reorganized on a two-platoon basis and await reinforcements. All platoon commanders and platoon sergeants had been wounded or killed. However, the survivors resumed the attack at midday and, with the assistance of flame-throwing Wasps, finally captured their final objective, the village of Steeg.

On the morning of 26 February 1945, at 0730 hours, "A" Company, 1st Battalion The Queen's Own Rifles of Canada, under command of Major Richard Dillon Medland, was ordered to attack the buildings at Lockerhof. Having taken this objective, Major Medland was ordered to press forward and clear out a large number of Germans located in the buildings in the path of the advance. This particular enemy stronghold was impeding the general advance of the unit. Major Medland, fully appreciative of the importance attached to the operation and realizing that speed was vital, decided that too much valuable time would be lost in bringing to bear an artillery fire program.

With complete disregard for his own personal safety, and showing magnificent leadership, Major Medland led his company into the attack in the face of withering small arms fire from the enemy-held buildings. So awe-inspiring was the example set by Major Medland, showing his coolness under fire, supreme courage and devotion to duty, that although suffering from heavy casualties, "A" Company completely overran the enemy positions. The enemy, after having severe losses inflicted on them, became completely disorganized and those surviving fled.

The success of this bold attack won for Major Medland the undying respect and admiration of the unit, and made possible the advance of the unit and the taking of the final objective.

For his actions, Major Richard Dillon Medland received the Distinguished Service Order. Major Medland was later badly wounded on 3 March when he stepped on a Schu-mine in the fighting for the Balberger Wald.

In the early morning of 26 February 1945, Number 7 Platoon, "A" Company, 1st Battalion The Queen's Own Rifles of Canada attacked a strongly held locality in the vicinity of Steeg. While advancing over open ground against three enemy machine-gun positions, a large percentage of Number 7 Platoon, including the platoon officer and the platoon sergeant, were killed or wounded. Rifleman James Matthew Watson, one of the members of the platoon, received a bullet wound in the leg, but continued to advance, firing a Bren gun from the hip at the known enemy positions. He was again wounded, this time in two places by shrapnel, but refused to leave the field of action. Rifleman Watson continued to advance until all of the enemy were killed, wounded or captured. All during this performance, he displayed absolute fearlessness in the face of the enemy, and his bravery and aggressiveness, which carried him far beyond the call of duty, was a determining factor in enabling the platoon to capture the objective.

For this action, Rifleman James Matthew Watson received the Military Medal.

On 26 February 1945, Number 7 Platoon, "A" Company, 1st Battalion The Queen's Own Rifles of Canada, attacked a strongly held enemy position over flat open ground near Lockerhof. The platoon suffered heavy casualties, including the platoon commander and the platoon sergeant. Rifleman Charles Nahwegezhik was seriously wounded in the head but kept advancing.

The platoon eventually had to withdraw. Rifleman Nahwegezhik refused to go back and stayed behind with his Bren gun to cover the withdrawal. His accurate and determined fire enabled the balance of his Platoon to pull back and reorganize for a further successful attack.

Rifleman Nahwegezhik was too weak from shock and loss of blood to move back himself, so he hid until the second attack went in. At this time, he again opened fire on the enemy, enabling his platoon to take its objective.

In displaying this supreme courage and devotion to duty, Rifleman Nahwegezhik was, in a large measure, responsible for the capture of the platoon objective.

For his actions, Rifleman Charles Nahwegezhik was awarded the Military Medal. Rifleman Nahwegezhik died of his wounds two days later, on 28 February.

By the end of the day, the Queen's Own Rifles had successfully captured all their objectives in Operation BLOCKBUSTER in the bitterest fighting they had experienced. Their losses had been severe, but they in turn had left the fields littered with bodies of fanatical German paratroops. Major Ben Dunkelman of "D" Company described the cost that was necessary for this victory:

> The price was dreadful. At the end of that gruesome day, there were only 36 fighting men left in my company, out of the 115 who had crossed the start line. I was the only officer to come through unwounded along with only one NCO . . . I was exhausted: sick in body, and even sicker in spirit. Never in my life, either before or since, have I found a body of men who were closer or dearer to me that the young soldiers of D Company.[11]

NOTES

1.   National Archives of Canada, Record Group (RG) 24, Vol. 14144, 8th Canadian Infantry Brigade War Diary, February 1945.

2.   NAC, RG 24, Vol. 14144, 8th CIB W.D., February 1945, "3rd Canadian Infantry Division Intelligence Reports" for 20, 22 and 24 February 1945; Col C. P. Stacey, *The Victory Campaign* (Ottawa: The Queen's Printer, 1966), p. 495.

3.   Terry Copp and Robert Vogel, *Maple Leaf Route: Victory* (Alma: Maple Leaf Route, 1988), p. 54.

4.   Copp, p. 54.

5.   RG 24, Vol. 15170, Queen's Own Rifles War Diary, February 1945, "Operation BLOCKBUSTER - Lessons Learned," dated 13 March 1945.

6.   RG 24, Vol. 15170, QOR W.D., February 1945, Appendix 39, "Operation BLOCKBUSTER, 1 Bn, QOR."

7.   RG 24, Vol 15170, QOR W.D., May 1945, "Two Canadians Win the Victoria Cross, " *The Maple Leaf* dated May 23,1945.

8.   RG 24, Vol. 10572, Honours and Awards, 2 Canadian Corps, File 215C1 (D88). This citation contains the original wording submitted with the recom-

mendation for the Victoria Cross. The citation finally published in the London Gazette was edited for space limitations.

9.   Lt H. K. MacDonald, "The Legend of Aubrey Cosens, V.C.," *The Legionary*, February 1964.

10.   RG 24, Vol. 12738, CMHQ, Recommendations for Awards.

11.   Ben Dunkelman, *Dual Allegiance* (Toronto: MacMillan of Canada, 1976),p. 135.

-5-
HELL'S CORNERS
AT HOLLEN AND KEPPELN

As daylight broke on February 26, and the Queen's Own Rifles were locked in battle to the north, the other two battalions of the 8th Canadian Infantry Brigade launched their attacks against the determined defenders of the Calcar-Udem line. As with the QOR, they too had to advance over a thousand yards of flat farmland, devoid of cover, before coming to grips with the units of the German 6th Parachute Division who were waiting in their fortified buildings. However, with daylight, the enemy could clearly see the Canadians, and were ready to open fire when they were the most vulnerable.

Hollen

> Et l'avance continue pied par pied, de trous d'obus en trous d'obus. Le ciel s'assombrit, des nuages de poussière embrouillent l'atmosphère, des explosions grondent et font jaillir des colonnes de fumée noire . . . les blessés demandent du secours dans un murmure sinistre . . . d'autres gisent à demi brûlé dans un trou trop petit. D'autres ne peuvent pas parler, et dans un effort désespéré ils élèvent une main toute sanglante vers un brancardier . . . et l'avance continue toujours.[1]
>
> Major J. Armand Ross
> Le Régiment de la Chaudière

At 0830 hours, "A" and "B" Companies of Le Régiment de la Chaudière were the first to step out, with support coming from "B" Squadron of the 1st Hussars. Moving across the open terrain, they soon came under German artillery fire, but continued to advance so close to our own barrage that they received a few casualties from our own shells. The leading elements of "B" Company were onto the German positions so quickly that the enemy had not time to man their machine-guns. As the Chaudière War Diary described, "Quite a few [Germans] were hit by Bren or Sten fire while on the run to their weapons or trenches." The first positions in the hamlet of Felmanshof were captured by 1000 hours.

The two reserve companies then passed through to attempt to move onto the final objective at Hollen. However, they came under heavy fire from their flank from the Germans in Keppeln and were counter-attacked by enemy infantry supported by three Panther tanks. Supporting tanks could not come forward as an 88-mm gun destroyed the first to try. Communications with battalion headquarters were lost as the available wireless sets were damaged. Both companies received heavy casualties and had to withdraw to their previous positions where they remained under enemy fire.[2]

On 26 February 1945, Le Régiment de la Chaudière was attacking a series of enemy strongpoints at Hollen Germany. During this fierce action against enemy paratroopers, Company Sergeant Major Guy Nadeau displayed a very high standard of devotion to duty and exemplary personal bravery.

The attack started early in the morning and, from the outset, the enemy reacted violently, bringing down intense concentrations of fire from all types of weapons. For two hours, the company advanced very slowly, crawling from cover to cover. Early during this advance, the wireless set was damaged and two of the three runners wounded. Constantly exposing himself, this warrant officer, with entire disregard for his personal safety and in full view of the enemy, maintained contact with the platoons, at the same time encouraging the men and boosting their morale. Supporting tanks were attracting the bulk of the fire; nevertheless, Company Sergeant Major Nadeau contacted them often, directing their fire on enemy positions.

When the attack was launched, he was the first one up and, disregarding enemy fire, encouraged the men forward. Leading the company, he was the first to reach the objective, where he personally accounted for five of the enemy paratroopers. Inspired by this superb display of personal bravery, his men rushed forward and flushed the enemy out of their positions in very quick time. In this action fifteen of the enemy were killed or wounded and fifty taken prisoner.

The brilliant leadership of this warrant officer, his disregard of danger, personal bravery, utmost gallantry and outstanding courage were instrumental in winning the day, allowing other troops to get through and capture Udem the same evening.

During the entire period that Company Sergeant Major Nadeau had been a member of Le Régiment de la Chaudière, he has displayed outstanding ability and has been an inspiration to all who have served with him.

For these actions, Company Sergeant Major Guy Nadeau received the Distinguished Conduct Medal. Company Sergeant Major Nadeau was later wounded in action on 28 April near Leer Germany.

On 26 February 1945, "D" Company of Le Régiment de la Chaudière assaulted a very strong enemy position, a farm near Keppeln, held by heavy machine-gun fire supported by 88-mm guns and a troop of heavy tanks.

Lance Corporal Emile Desjardins' section became disorganized by very heavy machine-gun and 88-mm fire. Although wounded and with no cover available, Lance Corporal Desjardins regrouped his section in an open field. Disregarding his wounds, and crawling with the help of only one leg, he kept advancing and led his section to its final objective. His action drew most of the enemy fire upon him-self, but this did not deter him from his intention to reach the objective at all costs.

Lance Corporal Desjardins' coolness and utter disregard for his personal safety was an inspiration to his section and to the remainder of the platoon. This action was responsible mainly for the company attaining its objective.

For his action, Lance Corporal Emile Desjardins received the Military Medal. Lance Corporal Desjardins was later wounded in action on 31 March.

Keppeln

> There's a "Hell's Corner" around every bend in Europe. Every unit went through one. Keppeln was ours.[3]
>
> Rev. R. Myles Hickey, Padre
> The North Shore Regiment

At 0900 hours, the third battalion of the brigade, the North Shore Regiment, began its advance toward the hamlet of Keppeln. Unlike their sister regiments, however, they had no tank support because all available armour had been assigned to other attacking units. The well-concealed enemy defenders held their fire until the North Shore men were only 150 yards away.

The padre of the North Shore Regiment, the Reverend R. Myles Hickey, later wrote that:

> An open space of about a thousand yards was the trap. All went well till we were half-way across, then all the hell in "Hell's Corner" opened up on us. Frantically we tried to dig in. Major Parker and Lieutenant Don McPherson were instantly killed. Lieutenants Power, Degrace, Quinn, Staples and Sutton went down wounded. For a while the situation looked hope-less. Everywhere men were falling dead or wounded. Right there heroes were made. Colonel Rowley ran out across the field, ordered the men to follow him — and they did.[4]

The North Shore (New Brunswick) Regiment was ordered to attack and take the town of Keppeln on 26 February 1945. The attack got under way as sched-uled but was held up many hundred yards from the town by heavy mortar and shell fire, and many casualties were suffered. Ten enemy dug-in tanks in the area of the church and machine-gun fire made further advances not only prohibitive in cost of lives but impossible.

Lieutenant-Colonel John William Horsley Rowley, commanding the North Shore Regiment, re-organized the attack. Under extremely heavy enemy shell and machine-gun fire, he personally led the first wave of the attack over 1800 yards of flat open country, calmly moving directly across country toward the objective.

Lieutenant-Colonel Rowley's gallant action, the apparent lack of fear, and calm determination, inspired his men and was instrumental in the complete success of the battalion and the brigade plan.

For his actions, Lieutenant-Colonel John William Horsley Rowley was awarded the Distinguished Service Order. Lieutenant-Colonel Rowley was killed in action at Millingen in the Rhine bridgehead on 24 March.

With the enemy still holding out in Steeg and Hollen, the North Shore men were exposed on both flanks. Facing German armour in Keppeln, as well as heavy machine-gun and artillery fire, the Canadians attacked three times but could not reach the village. They were pinned down about 800 yards from the outskirts.

Wasp flame-throwing carriers supporting the attacking companies attempted to move up to assist, but only one, driven by Sergeant Boulay, managed to get through.

Sergeant Horace Boulay, Support Company, North Shore (New Brunswick) Regiment, came to France with the carrier platoon on 13 June 1944 and subsequently took part in actions at Boulogne and Wyler, which were mentioned in his citation.

Lt-Col John William Rowley, commanding officer, the North Shore (New Brunswick) Regiment, was awarded the Distinguished Service Order for his actions at Keppeln, Germany *NAC, PA-192251.*

During the attack on Keppeln Germany on 26 February 1945, it was Sergeant Boulay's dauntless leadership that destroyed an enemy outpost which included two enemy self-propelled guns, one half-track, several machine-guns and thirty enemy troops. This enabled the two companies which were pinned down to continue their attack on the town. This non-commissioned officer led the attack against directed and constant enemy fire. His carrier was the only one to return.

Sergeant Boulay immediately had his flame thrower refuelled, reported back, and asked for another task.

Sergeant Boulay, by his enthusiasm, his cheerful personality and continuous determination, had been an inspiration to his whole platoon. His example and leadership has been responsible for the high morale of the carrier platoon, in spite of the severe losses which it has sustained. Many successes of the battalion can be directly attributed to the outstanding courage of this non-commissioned officer who, without thought for his own personal safety, volunteered for many operational tasks beyond the call of duty.

For his actions at Keppeln, as well as at Boulogne and Wyler, Sergeant Horace Boulay was awarded the Military Medal.

Brigadier J.A. Roberts, commanding the 8th Canadian Infantry Brigade, realized that the brigade was facing more difficult resistance than anticipated and the attack on Keppeln was in danger of failing. All battalions were struggling to gain ground and no reserves were available. The North Shores had to have armoured support to overcome the dug-in tanks and could only hang on in the exposed position until help arrived.

Just after dawn, Lieutenant-Colonel White, commanding officer of the 6th Canadian Armoured Regiment, met with Brigadier Roberts who proposed sending armoured support to help the North Shores. Lieutenat-Colonel White indicated that sending tanks down a bare forward slope of 1500 yards, with enemy armour waiting for them in covered positions, would likely fail. Roberts agreed but, as no better alternative seemed possible, they would have to take this risk.

Accordingly, White immediately ordered Major J. W. Powell to extricate his "C" Squadron from supporting the Queen's Own Rifles and proceed towards Keppeln where the North Shores were struggling. Upon arrival at the North Shores Headquarters, Powell worked out a bold plan with the North Shore's commanding officer, Lieutenant-Colonel John Rowley. Under cover of an artillery barrage, the tanks would rush the village, carrying infantry PIAT crews, to engage the enemy armour.[5]

As described in the previous chapter, "C" Squadron, 6th Canadian Armoured Regiment, commanded by Major J. W. Powell MC, had been initially assigned to support the Queen's Own Rifles of Canada.

At 1030 hours, the North Shore Regiment commenced their attack, although the Queen's Own Rifles had not yet reached their objective. After proceeding about five hundred yards, they were pinned to the ground and unable to proceed. At this time, the Queen's Own Rifles were ordered to consolidate and "C" Squadron was ordered to withdraw, replenish their ammunition and petrol, and prepare to support the North Shore Regiment. Powell and the commanding officer of this battalion met to formulate a plan. It was obvious that the North Shore Regiment could not proceed without tank support and it was also obvious that it was very unlikely that tanks could reach the village of Keppeln since they would be required to cross 1800 yards of open ground which was heavily mined and very boggy.

Not only did this make the tank attack extremely hazardous, but the enemy were bringing heavy fire of all types to bear whenever any sign of an attack appeared. From information obtained, it was known that there were ten self-propelled guns in the village and four tanks in the outskirts. Major Powell decided that the only possible chance of success lay in mounting infantry on his remaining tanks and charging at full speed across the ground.

It was a suicidal task, but not once did Major Powell hesitate. In fact, when questioned by his commanding officer as to the possible success of this plan, he stated, "I don't think it's on, sir, but we'll do our best and will at least cause a diversion to enable the infantry to get forward." Several other of the tank crews remarked that they had "had it," but Major Powell's cheerfulness and determination was so noticeable, that all ranks were prepared to follow him to an almost certain death.

At approximately 1320 hours, they crossed the start line with Major Powell immediately behind the leading troop. They charged at full speed with all guns blazing. At the time, it looked as if this attack might also be a failure as tank after tank bogged down, blew up on mines, or was hit by enemy SP (self-propelled gun) fire. An extremely heavy mortar barrage was brought down by the Germans but, without faltering, the remaining tanks with the infantry charged on. All this time, Major Powell was firing and directing the attack and not once did he pause or hesitate. Four tanks managed to reach the outskirts of the village where the infantry dismounted. One tank managed to enter the town and sweep through it. Major Powell's tank bogged down in a shell hole and became useless. One of the remaining tanks was destroyed, and the fourth bogged down. Major Powell refused to evacuate his tank, although it was a sitting target for the enemy armoured fighting vehicles and Panther tanks. He continued to direct and control the battle by wireless, insisting that the attack be pressed home.

At this time, the regimental headquarters troop was sent to reinforce the depleted squadron which consisted of one mechanically fit tank. Major Powell saw their approach and, realizing that they too would be destroyed by hidden enemy tanks, climbed out of his own and, although enemy infantry completely surrounded him, crossed the open ground to warn them off. Unfortunately, he was not able to attract their attention and all but one of this troop was destroyed. Refusing to return to safety, he returned to his own tank where he continued to give all the support he possibly could, and fought off many enemy infantry who tried to close and destroy him. Fifteen dead Germans, subsequently found beside his tank, bear witness to this officer's great courage and drive.

Three hours later, a recovery tank arrived and managed to pull out the bogged-down tank. Major Powell immediately proceeded into the village to support the hard-pressed infantry, seeking out and destroying the enemy wherever they could be found. As dusk drew down, enemy dead littered the streets. Four enemy armoured fighting vehicles had been destroyed just outside, and three enemy armoured fighting vehicles so badly damaged that they were not able to proceed more than six hundred yards before being abandoned by their crews.

As Keppeln was of such vital importance to the enemy defence in this area, an immediate counter-attack was expected. As two more tanks had been recovered, Major Powell now had at his disposal four of his original squadron of nineteen. Without thought of retiring, despite a shortage of ammunition, he immediately took up a defensive position although subjected to terrific enemy mortar and artillery fire. He visited the infantry positions from time to time throughout the night, enquiring of their needs and inspiring them with his confidence and unwavering determination. For forty-eight hours, this officer had no rest, but not once in the long vigil of the night did he slacken or waver in his untiring effort to instill determination to hold the village at all costs. His utter disregard of the shelling and mortaring throughout the night was an inspiration to all.

During all this time, the main divisional objective, Udem, remained an constant threat, and yet so speedy and decisive was the taking of Keppeln that the whole corps plan was successfully effected. It allowed the 9th Canadian Infantry Brigade to pass through and enter Udem against minor resistance and, of even greater importance, it allowed immediately the 4th Canadian Armoured and 11th British Armoured Divisions to sweep past to the Hochwald Forest.

At 0800 on 27 February 1945, Major Powell was ordered to retire with his three remaining tanks. There is no doubt that without tanks, this attack would have failed and the speed and daring of the tank charge resulted directly in the successful completion of this operation. Major Powell's utter disregard for danger and steady determination made possible the success of a seemingly hopeless task, and his encouragement to the exhausted troops set an example which can never be surpassed. There is no praise too high for the action of the very gallant officer.

Major John Wilson Powell, 6th Canadian Armoured Regiment (1st Hussars), was awarded the Distinguished Service Order for his actions at Mooshof and Keppeln, Germany. NAC, PA-192247

For his actions this day, at both Mooshof and Keppeln, Major John Wilson Powell MC was awarded the Distinguished Service Order.*

For the North Shore infantry who rode into Keppeln in that wild charge, the experience must have been daunting. The commander of the platoon selected, Lieutenant Harry Nutter, later wrote:

> To say I was scared to death does not describe my condition at all . . . We went tearing across the start line . . . the enemy immediately laid down a curtain of shell and mortar fire which we went through at all the speed the tanks could muster . . . A German tank dug in behind the church began picking off the first tanks and I could see my men jumping off as the tanks were hit.[6]

On 26 February 1945, the North Shore (New Brunswick) Regiment attacked and gained possession of the town of Keppeln Germany. Sergeant John Alexander Tree at that time was a Lance Sergeant and in charge of a section of Number 2 Platoon, "A" Company. When the attack slowed down, the platoon was carried up to the town on tanks, thus forming a base for the following companies to enter and clear the town.

The platoon suffered heavy casualties when several of the tanks were knocked out by enemy guns and mines. The platoon became scattered and Sergeant Tree with bold initiative organized his section, placed them in firing positions, and brought fire on the enemy. Sergeant Tree was under heavy mortar, tank and small arms fire during the period, and his Sten gun was shot out of his hands.

Seeing that the situation was becoming very precarious, Sergeant Tree, at the head of his section, assaulted the enemy on his own initiative, thus allowing the following companies to close with the enemy. Accompanied by one man, he entered the town in search of elements of his platoon which were still scattered. This non-commissioned officer took twenty-three enemy prisoners and returned with several members of his platoon.

The ultimate success of the operation was made possible to a great degree by the courage, initiative, coolness and clear thinking of Sergeant Tree, and the decisive action he took saved a great number of lives in the following attacking companies.

Sergeant Tree's conduct alone inspired the men of his section in the assault on the enemy positions and his personal disregard of danger under heavy concentrated fire was an inspiration to his men.

---

*   The Commander-in-Chief of the First Canadian Army, in his original submission, recommended that Major Powell be awarded the Victoria Cross for this action. However, this was not approved by Field-Marshal Montgomery. As usual, Montgomery gave no reason for this change.

For his actions, Sergeant John Alexander Tree was awarded the Military Medal.

Company Sergeant Major Joseph Edward Bernard, on 26 February 1945, during the assault on the village of Keppeln when "B" Company of The North Shore (New Brunswick) Regiment were pinned down in the open under intense machine-gun, mortar and artillery fire, evacuated several of the wounded and gave encouragement to the remaining men.

The advance was resumed after some artillery fire had partially neutralized the enemy fire. A machine-gun position again pinned down the Company. Company Sergeant Major Bernard, with utter disregard for his own personal safety, rushed forward and wiped out this enemy position single-handedly, killing three and taking the remainder prisoner, thus allowing the Company to proceed. In the further advance of the company, the company commander was killed and all three platoon commanders became casualties. Company Sergeant Major Bernard immediately took command and led the Company into the village, clearing the company's objective. He then assumed command of the complete company and re-organized it. The company made firm the bridgehead obtained in the village, allowing the remainder of the battalion to pass through. The bridgehead enabled the battalion to complete its task and seize the battalion objective, the village of Keppeln.

For his action, Company Sergeant Major Joseph Edward Bernard was awarded the Distinguished Conduct Medal.

On 26 February 1945, at 0430 hours, "C" Squadron of the 6th Canadian Armoured Regiment was in support of The Queen's Own Rifles. Lieutenant David George Carnegie Eggo, a troop leader in the squadron, was heavily engaged with his troop in the van of the attack, although when the enemy brought down a heavy concentration of artillery and mortar fire, one tank was lost from his troop.

At 1030 hours, the squadron was ordered to disengage, refill with ammunition and petrol, and assemble to assist the North Shore Regiment which had two companies pinned down by enemy fire in its attack on Keppeln. The main core of resistance came from ten known enemy tanks situated in and around the town. The squadron attacked Keppeln immediately but, by the time Lieutenant Eggo had reached the town itself, he had lost the remainder of his troop and was out of communication with his squadron. Although alone, he decided to enter the town from the east, but was immediately met by a hail of fire from enemy infantry, artillery, Panzerfaust and armoured fighting vehicles. So determined, however, was his advance that the enemy were forced to withdraw, leaving behind many dead and wounded. Having fought his way through the town, he returned to the North Shores and supported them in mopping up enemy strongpoints. Again, without hesitation, he attacked where resistance was the heaviest, finally taking up an anti-tank role until Keppeln was cleared.

Lieutenant Eggo's grim determination to close with and kill the enemy, without regard for his own personal safety or the odds against him, was outstanding in a brilliantly successful squadron attack.

For his actions, Lieutenant David George Carnegie Eggo was awarded the Military Cross. Lieutenant Eggo was later wounded in action on 5 March.

On 26 February 1945, Sergeant Lewis John Campbell was commanding a reconnaissance tank attached to the Regimental Headquarters Troop of the 6th Canadian Armoured regiment. Due to the severe losses sustained by "C" Squadron of the Regiment in their attack on Keppeln, this troop was ordered to proceed to that area to reinforce them.

Approaching the town, they were suddenly attacked by enemy tanks and self-propelled guns which were hull-down on the high ground to the east. Sergeant Campbell's tank was hit immediately and two of his crew killed. The remaining tanks of the troop also engaged were destroyed, with one exception, by the enemy fire. The survivors from these crews were under intense mortar and machine-gun fire from an enemy strongpoint three hundred yards to their left. Finding that his turret was still functioning, this NCO, with absolute disregard for his own personal safety and with the hope of drawing fire from his comrades onto himself, courageously engaged the enemy tanks and self-propelled guns with his 37-mm gun. His tank was hit again and his turret jammed. Unable to fight back, Sergeant Campbell now went to the assistance of the wounded and succeeded in carrying two back to cover.

Returning to the area just before last light, he discovered two more wounded. Unable to move them both, he climbed back into his tank and, after considerable effort, managed to repair it sufficiently to make it run. He then placed the two wounded men on the rear deck and drove them to safety. All this was accomplished under intense machine-gun, mortar and shell fire. This non-commissioned officer's actions were an unequalled example of courage, determination and devotion to duty.

For these actions, Sergeant Lewis John Campbell received the Military Medal. Sergeant Campbell died on 27 June 1945.

Hollen

Late in the day, with the North Shores finally making progress in capturing Keppeln, Le Régiment de la Chaudière was ordered to resume its advance. By now, "Hollen had become a 'scene from an inferno.' The sky was black with the thick smoke from crashing shells . . ." However, the forward companies moved so quickly that they surprised the defenders and were able to capture a vehicle and some large guns. Well-supported by tanks and artillery, "A" Company reached the hamlet of Hollen at 1600 hours. Some hand-to-hand fighting was still needed, with "the enemy having to be flushed out of every cellar and dug out by tank fire, grenade and sten gun." "C" Company then moved forward but became pinned down by enemy mortars and machine-guns. Well-coordinated fire from tanks, artillery, and supporting platoons allowed

Sergeant Chartrand's platoon to dash forward and clear the final objective by 1845 hours.

With fifteen men dead and fifty-five wounded on this day, the regimental war diary remarked that "to the veterans of D-Day, there was no doubt that this had been the toughest action yet."[8]

On 26 February 1945, during a battalion attack on a series of enemy strongpoints at Hollen near Keppeln Germany, Captain Robert Rochon, commanded "A" Company of Le Régiment de la Chaudière. His task was to capture two enemy strongpoints held by paratroopers. Advancing over open country against unusually heavy enemy defensive fire from artillery, mortars and machine-guns, Captain Rochon took the lead of his company, many men of which were going into the attack for the first time. By his skilful use of artillery and tank support, he got on his first objective and led his men in hand-to-hand fighting. Inspired by this display of leadership, his men made short work of cleaning out the enemy position, capturing many prisoners.

Captain Rochon could not proceed on to his second objective until an enemy position on his left had been captured by a flanking battalion. So he was ordered to consolidate on the spot, which he did. The work was slow, due to enemy fire. He went around the position, exhorting his men on, though this necessitated exposing himself continually. The display of leadership and disregard of danger inspired his men, who held their position despite intense and accurate fire from enemy artillery.

This officer's coolness and fine example inspired his men to carry on to take the second objective, capturing one 88-mm gun and two 50-mm guns and numerous machine-guns. This important gain eased the pressure considerably and was instrumental in winning the day. It was executed so quickly that an enemy half-tracked vehicle had no time to retire and was captured intact. The unusually high standard of leadership and bravery, and the entire disregard of this officer for his personal safety, was largely responsible for the success of his company and of his battalion.

For his actions this day, Captain Robert Rochon was awarded the Military Cross. Captain Rochon was later killed in action on 24 April as the Chaudières advanced into Germany.

On 26 February 1945, during a battalion attack on a series of enemy strongpoints at Hollen, near Keppeln Germany, Captain William Atkinson was commander of "B" Company, Le Régiment de la Chaudière. He displayed unusual qualities of leadership and coolness.

Under extremely heavy enemy defensive fire, disdaining to take cover, he personally led his men. To ensure success, he had correctly appreciated that he had to follow our own artillery fire very closely. The men were lagging behind, but Captain Atkinson went forward and, by his personal example, encouraged his men to do the same. It is to his credit that none of his men faltered and they kept moving until the objective was reached. Many prisoners were taken before they could come out from cover. Later on, "D" Company went through and were pinned down, once again. Captain Atkinson showed initiative and quick thinking by bringing all his available firepower to bear to extricate this unfortunate company. Because of the depleted state of "D" Company after its rescue, Captain Atkinson to take on the task of this company to maintain the momentum of the attack, though he and his men were just getting over a hard battle against a very tough opponent, the 12th Reconnaissance Battalion of the German 6th Parachute Division. Once again, by his leadership and outstanding courage, he captured the objective which was vital to the enemy. The Germans fought extremely hard to keep their position, but to no avail, due to the inspiration which Acting Captain Atkinson infused in his men.

Le Régiment de la Chaudière's successful attainment of its objective was due in a great measure to the fine example set by this officer whose cool bearing and gallant example was an inspiration to his company in the excellent action they fought.

For his actions, Captain William Atkinson was awarded the Military Cross.

On 26 February 1945, Le Régiment de la Chaudière was given the task of attacking and taking a series of very heavily defended strongpoints at Hollen near Keppeln Germany. During the heavy and fierce fighting against enemy paratroops, Sergeant Roger Chartrand, commanding a platoon of "C" Company, distinguished himself by his leadership and personal bravery.

From the start of the attack, the enemy fought tenaciously and kept our troops under constant and heavy shell fire. The leading company was delayed in taking its objective and, for three hours, "C" Company had to wait on open ground. During these hours, this non-commissioned officer constantly exposed himself, visiting each section in turn, encouraging the men, keeping their morale up.

The first part of "C" Company's attack went very well. This NCO led his platoon himself, succeeded after fierce hand-to-hand fighting to gain its objective, though some casualties were suffered.

The reserve platoon went through and were, early on, pinned down by accurate and heavy machine-gun fire and by the fire of snipers. Tanks and artillery support were increased but to no avail. Realizing the situation and, knowing it was vital to the whole plan that this final objective should be taken, Sergeant Chartrand volunteered with his platoon to take this last strongpoint. In a magnificent dash, this NCO, leading the platoon, raced across yards of open ground where he led his platoon in hand-to-hand fighting, killing several enemy and capturing more. This success completed the battalion task, allowing another brigade to go through to capture Udem.

This superb display of gallantry, exceptional personal bravery, and entire disregard of danger on the part of this NCO was largely instrumental in the regiment completing its task and the subsequent success of the brigade plan. Throughout his service, Sergeant Chartrand, by his bravery, determination and initiative, has set an outstanding example to all ranks and made a considerable contribution to the success of many actions.

For his actions, Sergeant Roger Chartrand received the Distinguished Conduct Medal.

On 26 February 1945, "B" Squadron, 6th Canadian Armoured Regiment, was supporting Le Régiment de la Chaudière in an attack on the high ground at Hollen Germany. Corporal John Charles Pritchard was a crew commander and this his first time in action.

Just prior to crossing the start line, his tank developed mechanical trouble which reduced its speed to about two miles per hour. He was ordered by his troop leader to remain where he was and attempt to repair the trouble. This proved to be impossible and this NCO, with great determination and courage, decided to fight his tank in its crippled condition. He pushed forward into the battle area which, at the time, was dominated by enemy guns. The sight of one more tank of the battlefield was of inestimable value because the squadron had been reduced to nine tanks. Although his tank was an easy target for enemy guns, Lance Corporal Pritchard, by careful use of ground, frustrated every attempt to destroy him. The enemy however did not escape so lightly for, by well-directed fire, he inflicted numerous casualties on enemy riflemen and others with Panzerfausts hidden in ditches and slit trenches. Throughout the day, he continued to fight in an inspired manner and, although subjected to more than normal punishment from enemy fire due to his inability to manoeuvre, not once did this NCO lose his determination to destroy the enemy.

He remained with the squadron until they were released at the completion of the attack. His courage and persistence were an inspiration to the remainder of the squadron throughout the course of the battle.

For his actions, Corporal John Charles Pritchard was awarded the Military Medal.

On 26 February 1945, Lance Sergeant Donald Gustave Campbell was a crew commander in 4 Troop, "B" Squadron, 6th Canadian Armoured Regiment. His troop was in support of "A" Company, Le Régiment de la Chaudière whose objective was Hollen Germany.

The attack went in at 0830 hours but the infantry immediately came under very heavy shell fire and were forced to go to ground. Number 4 Troop proceeded forward to the objective and, in close fighting, in which crew commanders used grenades and even pistols, succeeded in subduing fierce enemy resistance. While occupying positions covering the infantry forward, an enemy anti-tank gun opened up from close range and destroyed one of the troop's tanks. While two of the tanks took cover, Lance Sergeant Campbell manoeuvred his tank into a position of observation from which he was able to see the anti-tank gun in a hedge about 75 yards away. Despite the fact that it was pointing directly at him, he decided to attack it. With complete disregard for his own safety, he left his cover and managed to fire a round before the crew of the enemy gun could lay on to this tank. The one shot killed or wounded all the crew and destroyed the gun itself. While getting off this one shot, he saw the blast of another anti-tank gun on his right flank. Realizing that this gun was a dangerous threat to Number 3 Troop of his squadron and, disregarding the danger involved, he charged his tank forward through a hail of enemy mortar, artillery and machine-gun fire and, with four rounds, knocked out the gun.

Lance Sergeant Campbell's quiet courage and determination has always been an inspiration to his squadron and, in this instance, his coolness and quick action restored the momentum of the attack when it appeared to be bogging down. There is no doubt that Lance Sergeant Campbell's destruction of these two guns was a deciding factor in the success of the whole attack.

For this action, Lance Sergeant Donald Gustave Campbell received the Military Medal. Lance Sergeant Campbell was later wounded on 12 April in central Holland.

During Operation BLOCKBUSTER on 26 February 1945, Lance Bombardier Robert Donald Kerr, of the 13th Field Regiment, was one of the artillery signallers responsible for maintaining line communications to a forward observation officer with Le Régiment de la Chaudière.

At 1500 hours, Le Régiment de la Chaudière, after seven hours of bitter fighting, were held up short of their last objective. All communications to the left forward company had broken down. It was essential that this objective be taken before Phase II of Operation BLOCKBUSTER could be launched. To do this, communication had to be opened to this forward company and a new fire plan prepared. Lance Bombardier Kerr, on foot, crossed a field swept by enemy machine-gun and mortar fire to lay a line to the company which he established just twenty-five minutes before the zero hour set for the attack.

At times, during this daring action, his jacket was pierced in several places by shrapnel. However, with utter disregard for his own safety, Lance Bombardier Kerr continued on foot and established all the essential communications.

Due to his gallant action, the artillery plan involving two field regiments, one medium battery and two heavy batteries was co-ordinated with the infantry attack, the final objective taken, enabling Phase II of the operation to be launched.

For his actions, Lance Bombardier Robert Donald Kerr received the Military Medal.

Udem

With the 8th Canadian Infantry Brigade's capture of its objectives on the high ground between Calcar and Udem, a secure area had been obtained from which the 9th Brigade could launch its attack on Udem itself to complete Phase III of BLOCKBUSTER. Udem, the southern anchor of the German defence line, was heavily fortified as a centre of resistance. The attack began after dark on February 26, with the Highland Light Infantry of Canada on the left and the Stormont, Dundas and Glengarry Highlanders on the right. Their routes were illuminated by artificial moonlight from searchlights as well as burning farmhouses.

Progress was surprisingly good and the advance troops quickly crossed the anti-tank ditch to come to grips with the garrison from the German 7th Parachute Regiment. Fighting continued through the night, but resistance had pretty well been overcome by 0400 hours the next morning.

Infantry of The Stormont, Dundas and Glengarry Highlanders, near Keppeln, passing through units of the 8th Canadian Infantry Brigade to attack Udem, Germany.
NAC, PA-192253

At Udem Germany on the night of 26/27 February 1945, Private David Harold Snyder, Bren gunner in "A" Company of the Stormont, Dundas and Glengarry Highlanders, dispersed two enemy counter-attacks, one after having been wounded. This daring action was instrumental in saving his company position from being overrun.

"A" Company had attacked and captured its allotted area in Udem under cover of darkness and immediately consolidated. Private Snyder was detailed to cover one of the approaches to "A" Company's position. Unable to find suitable cover to permit a good field of fire, he built a parapet on the sidewalk of a road leading to "A" Company's position. An enemy counter-attack developed and Private Snyder, alone, maintained such steady and accurate fire that he forced the enemy to withdraw after inflicting casualties of three killed and six wounded.

The enemy then fired Panzerfausts at Private Snyder's position, destroyed his parapet, and wounded him. The enemy immediately followed up their success with an attack by approximately thirty men. Private Snyder did not withdraw but courageously opened fire with such telling effect that the enemy were again forced to withdraw, this time leaving two dead and three wounded. After ascertaining that the attacks were dispersed, Private Snyder then allowed himself to be relieved at his post.

The repulse of the enemy counter-attack and the heavy casualties inflicted on the enemy were entirely due to Private Snyder's personal courage, tenacity, and daring action which went beyond the call of duty. This action enabled "A" Company of The Stormont, Dundas and Glengarry Highlanders to hold its position in Udem Germany.

For his action, Private David Harold Snyder was awarded the Military Medal. Private Snyder was later wounded in action on 24 March during the attack on Greitherbusch in the Rhine bridgehead.

One of the oldest non-commissioned officers in point of combatant service with The Highland Light Infantry of Canada, Sergeant Thomas Alexander Hopkins, landed on D-Day in Normandy, serving as scout platoon sergeant. During the operations in France, he served continuously with forward companies and invariably commanded reconnaissance patrols personally. His devotion to duty and fearless disregard of personal safety were repeatedly noted both by the troops he commanded and the commanders under whom he served . . .

On 27 February 1945, Sergeant Hopkins commanded a platoon of "A" Company during the attack on Udem. The attack was launched at night and, in the darkness of the town, the situation became confused. Sergeant Hopkins showed great leadership and personal bravery in leading his platoon in the task of clearing German snipers from the dark and shattered buildings in order to reach his objective on the eastern edge of the town. Before first light, the enemy paratroops infiltrated into the town, which necessitated a hazardous mopping up operation at first light. Although he and his troops were extremely fatigued, having fought for three days with no rest, Sergeant Hopkins immediately organized his platoon for the mopping up operation and, by his own sterling example and leadership in the face of the heavy sniper fire, inspired his men to mop up the eastern section of the town. Sergeant Hopkins, during this mopping up action, located a dug-in German armoured fighting vehicle on the outskirts of the town and personally led a self-propelled gun to a position from where the enemy gun could be successfully engaged.

For this action, and others described in his citation in the Scheldt and east of the Hochwald Forest, Sergeant Thomas Alexander Hopkins was awarded the Military Medal.

With the fall of Udem, the way was open for the 11th British Armoured Division to move south of the Calcar-Udem ridge. For the next two days, the brunt of the fighting against the German Hochwald defences was taken by this division and the 4th Canadian Armoured Division. The 3rd Canadian Infantry Division did not have an immediate role in this advance, but battle and death were still not far away.

At 1700 hours, 28 February 1945, just south of Udem, an enemy shell made a direct hit on a fully loaded ammunition lorry which was parked a few feet from the gun tractor of which Gunner Floyd Marshall Tufts, 4th Light Anti-Aircraft Regiment RCA, was the driver. The ammunition lorry and a nearby car immediately burst into flames and the 17-pounder ammunition burned and exploded to the great danger of all personnel in the vicinity. All the personnel nearby took cover, with the exception of Gunner Tufts who, with great coolness and utter disregard for his personal safety, ran over to his vehicle, started it up and drove it to a place of safety. His truck carried ammunition, petrol and the kits belonging to the men in his detachment and, by his action, all these were saved as well as his vehicle.

During all this, the enemy continued to shell the point and the action of Gunner Tufts was a source of inspiration to his comrades whose morale was greatly heightened by it.

For his action, Gunner Floyd Marshall Tufts was awarded the Military Medal.

On February 28, Padre Hickey of The North Shore Regiment received bad news—his colleague in Le Régiment de la Chaudière, Father Jean Dalcourt of Rimouski, had been killed by a mine. Father Dalcourt had asked for volunteers to recover bodies from some of the tanks that littered the battlefield. The bodies were placed in a carrier which started off to the rear. However, the carrier struck a powerful mine which blew the vehicle several feet into the air, killing or wounded all occupants.[9]

> A few hours later we stood around a hastily dug grave in the Bedburg cemetery as Father McCarney read the burial prayers over the lifeless body of Father Dalcourt, who, only a few hours before, stood on the same spot and read the same prayers over others. Yes, that is how uncertain death was in action! "He was a good priest."[10]

In the early phase of operations in the North West Theatre of operations, Honourary Major Jean Robert Amedée Josaphat Dalcourt was senior chaplain at the Canadian Base Reinforcement Group. He requested several times a posting to a more active post in the forward areas but, due to his state of health, was refused. Finally, however, he was granted permission, relinquishing his appointment as senior chaplain to come to the 8th Canadian Infantry Brigade and was attached to Le Régiment de la Chaudière.

From the very first day, he set a very high standard of devotion to duty. Daily, he made it a point to visit as many outposts as he could, this despite danger from enemy fire. On these daily trips, his permanently good humour and encouragement gave a boost to the morale of the soldiers.

It was the lot of the regiment to be in the line on Christmas Day. H/Major Dalcourt saw to it that every man had a good cause to remember that Holy Night of 1944. He personally visited every forward position of the regiment during the night, a trip of more than eight hours under enemy observation and fire. He brought with him good cheer, talking a few minutes with each soldier and exchanging greetings with all. All those who desired the consolations of the Church, that night, could obtain them without leaving their posts.

Throughout the campaign in the Netherlands, south of the Rhine, this chaplain was always handy, whatever the danger. During attacks, he always placed himself at the start line to hearten and encourage the men. He invariably followed behind the leading wave to be the first to provide relief and comfort to wounded and, on more than one occasion, distinguished himself by meritorious service.

It was during a particularly fierce engagement at Hollen near Keppeln in Germany, on February 28, that H/Major Dalcourt met his death while trying to bring back the bodies of two soldiers and some wounded from another unit supporting the regiment.

The high standard of devotion to duty of this officer, which ultimately resulted in his death, his personal bravery and entire disregard for danger, were a shining example for all ranks, and an incentive to further efforts to speed the end of the war.

For his actions, H/Major Jean Robert Amedée Josaphat Dalcourt was awarded the U.S. Bronze Star.

Some time later, on September 4, 1945 when peace had finally arrived, the officers and men of Le Régiment de la Chaudière held a requiem mass for Father Dalcourt in a little church in the Dutch town of Drieberben. Padre Laramée paid tribute to Father Dalcourt:

> Sa vie fut une prèdication,
> sa mort en est une aussi.
> Il avait le culte de devoir d'état,
> et c'est son zèle du devoir qui le
> menait aux avant-postes porter les
> consolations divines à nos héros . . .[11]

NOTES

1.   National Archives of Canada Record Group (RG) 24, Vol 15181, War Diary of Le Régiment de la Chaudière, September 1945, from the regimental newapaper, Fleur de Lys, dated 1 September, 1945:

> And the attack continues foot by foot, from one shell hole to another. The sky turns dark, clouds of dust fill the air, explosions thunder and leave behind pillars of black smoke . . . the wounded ask for help in an awful murmur . . . others lie partly burnt in a hole that is too small. Others cannot speak and in a desperate effort, they raise a bloody hand towards a stretcher bearer . . . and the advance continues.

2.   RG 24, Vol. 15170, Queen's Own Rifles War Diary, Feburary 1945, "Operation BLOCKBUSTER - Lessons Learned, " by Headquarters 8th Canadian Infantry Brigade dated 13 March 1945; RG 24, Vol 15181, Chaudière W.D., February 1945; Jacques Castonguay and Armand Ross, *Le Régiment de la Chaudière* (Le Régiment de la Chaudiére, 1983), p. 342; Col C. P. Stacey, *The Victory Campaign* (Ottawa: The Queen's Printer, 1966), p.499.

3.   Rev. R. Myles Hickey, *The Scarlet Dawn* (Fredericton: Unipress, 1980), p. 211.

4.   Hickey, pp. 210 - 211.

5.   RG 24, Vol. 15170, "Operation BLOCKBUSTER;" RG 24, Vol. 10572, Honours and Awards, 2 Canadian Corps, Deposition by Lt-Col. F. E. White.

6.   Will Bird, *North Shore (New Brunswick) Regiment* (Brunswick Press, 1963), pp. 509 - 510.

7.   W. Denis Whitaker and Shelagh Whitaker, *Rhineland* (Toronto: Stoddart Publishing Co., 1989), p. 203.

8.   RG 24, Vol 15181, Chaudière W.D., February 1945.

9.   Communication with Sergeant Leo Major, 11 October 1994.

10.   Hickey, p. 212.

11.   As reported in the regimental newspaper, *Fleur de Lys*, dated 15 September 1945, By Lieutenant P. A. Boutin:

> His life was a sermon,
> His death was one as well.
> He had the worship of duty,
> And it is his dedication to duty
> That led him to the outposts bringing
> divine consolation to our heroes . . .

-6-
BREAKING THE SCHLIEFFEN POSITION

MESSAGE OF THE GERMAN SECRETARY OF STATE
ON THE 25TH ANNIVERSARY OF THE NAZI PARTY,
FEBRUARY 1945

The Führer's devotion to duty did not permit him to leave his Headquarters on the day of the proclamation of the 25th anniversary of the National Socialist Programme was celebrated. In 1920 Germany had to face the same coalition of Bolshevism and Capitalism as today . . . If the soldiers at the front follow the example of the homeland and do their utmost, a whole world will be shattered by our unity. If the German people go on to deny the right of existence to cowards and saboteurs, our enemies will be hindered in their destruction of this nation. Then at the end of this conflict, there will be a German victory and we shall experience a proud happiness . . . Today, full of belief in success, I prophesy eventual Victory for the German Reich.[1]

The First Canadian Army now came up against the last of the German prepared defence lines–called the "Schlieffen Position" by the Germans and the "Hochwald Layback" by the Canadians. This was a continuous line of trench systems, protected by anti-tank ditches, minefields and belts of barbed wire, running from the Rhine River south to the area of Geldern. The German artillery support was powerful–over 700 mortars and 1,000 guns.[2]

In II Canadian Corps' sector, these defences ran along the western edge of the German state forests–the Hochwald, Tuschen Wald and Balberger Wald–heavily forested ridges which presented difficult obstacles for both infantry and tanks. The 2nd Canadian Infantry, 4th Canadian Armoured and 11th British Armoured Divisions struck these lines first on the last two days of February but, after heavy losses, could make no progress. On March 1, the 3rd Canadian Infantry Division moved into action to assist the armoured forces by clearing the Balberger Wald, the most southerly of the forests.

Major John Gerald Stevens was brigade major of the 7th Canadian Infantry Brigade from 3 August 1944 to 11 April 1945 and, during the period from 1 February 1945 was involved in a number of major engagements. This officer was responsible for all the detailed planning of the part played by the brigade in Operations VERITABLE. The care and forethought displayed by him was most certainly partially responsible for the success of the operation.

On many occasions, Major Stevens was subjected to enemy small arms and mortar fire whilst obtaining information from the battalions when normal communications were extended. One such occasion occurred on 28 February 1945 when the 7th Canadian Infantry Brigade was ordered to take over ground from the 11th British Armoured Division near Sonsbeck Germany. The brigade had no means of communication with this Division and only very scanty information was available. Reconnaissance and contact patrols had been sent out to liaise with the Monmouthshire Regiment but they could not be located. Major Stevens, realizing the necessity for obtaining this information in order that the brigadier could make his plans, volunteered to contact the 11th Armoured Division.

The speed of the advance of the brigade had left many isolated pockets of resistance and, in the darkness of the night, the journey was extremely hazardous. On at least five occasions, the car in which this officer was riding was fired on by riflemen and machine-gunners but, except for a few holes in the body of the vehicle, the occupants escaped injury. After about an hour's drive, Major Stevens encountered a company of one of the battalions the brigade was to relieve and, after being passed on to the brigade headquarters of that battalion, he obtained the full dispositions of the three battalions, thereby enabling the 7th Canadian Infantry Brigade to complete the relief by first light the following morning.

The services rendered by Major Stevens during the entire time he was brigade major were outstanding and the assistance which he gave to the battalion was invaluable. His energy, loyalty and cheerfulness was at all times worthy of the highest praise.

For his actions, Major John Gerald Stevens received the Military Cross.

Clearing the Tuschen Wald.

The 8th Brigade's plan was first to clear the smaller Tuschen Wald by launching an attack by one battalion through the area already seized by the 2nd Canadian Infantry Division. From this base, the other two battalions would attack south to clear their objective. Late on March 1, Le Régiment de la Chaudière received their orders to launch the opening attack on the Tuschen Wald. In continuing rain, the Chaudières were delayed in their move forward and the attack did not get going until almost 1900 hours. In the late winter day, with overcast skies, complete darkness fell on the regiment within half an hour of their entering the thick forest. The Germans ambushed the two leading companies, which had to withdraw in a series of delaying actions to avoid being cut off in the confused fighting. However, with a reorganized attack the next day, supported by tanks of the 6th Canadian Armoured Regiment, the woods were successfully cleared by midday.

On 1 March 1945, at 1815 hours, Le Régiment de la Chaudière attacked the Tuschen Wald and Maserhof features. It was imperative that these features be captured and the northern line of the Staatforst Xanten held to provide a firm base and a start line for the two following battalions to clear the lower Hochwald Forest.

The initial attack made good progress for some eight hundred yards when Le Régiment de la Chaudière was heavily counter-attacked. Lieutenant-Colonel Gustave Olivier Taschereau, appreciating the situation, immediately regrouped and reorganized the attack. The regiment was constantly under heavy mortar fire and extremely heavy shell fire, and by this time casualties were numerous.

At first light on 2 March 1945, Le Régiment de la Chaudière moved forward once again to attack the same objective. Lieutenant-Colonel Taschereau led the attack under heavy enemy shell, mortar and machine-gun fire and, with cool disregard for his personal safety and great determination, led his battalion to their objective.

The morale effect of this officer's fine example against an enemy determined to hold his positions at all costs was decisive in the battalion's success. It provided the remaining two battalions of the brigade with a firm base for attacking and overcoming their objective.

For his actions, Lieutenant-Colonel Gustave Olivier Taschereau was awarded the Distinguished Service Order.

Officers of Le Régiment de la Chaudière talking to General Crerar, Commander-in-Chief of the First Canadian Army (in the centre). Lt-Col Gustave Olivier Taschereau, Commanding Officer of the Chaudières, who was awarded the Distinguished Service Order for his actions in the Tuschen Wald, is on the left.
NAC, PA-192266

On 5 March 1945, Le Régiment de la Chaudière put in an attack to capture buildings immediately south of the Balberger Wald on the road to Sonsbeck Germany.

"B" Company advanced along the road and succeeded in clearing the buildings but then came under heavy enemy fire from a ridge east of the road. The ridge was supposed to have been cleared of enemy, but the other company had been pinned down by enemy fire, with the result that "B" Company was cut off in the hamlet. Ammunition was running low and none could be brought forward.

Casualties caused by heavy enemy shelling were numerous and it was impossible to evacuate the wounded. Private Florian Victor Veilleux, a stretcher bearer with "B" Company, entirely on his own initiative, went forward of our lines to tend the wounded. The hamlet was continually under heavy enemy machine-gun, artillery and mortar fire. Nevertheless, Private Veilleux kept on helping the wounded, cheering them up, going from farm to farm to visit them all. As soon as darkness came, he immediately started evacuating the casualties and worked through most of the night. His entire disregard for his personal safety and his cheerfulness was a great boost for the morale of the wounded and was a great inspiration to all of his comrades.

For his actions, Private Florian Victor Veilleux was awarded the Military Medal.

The Queen's Own Rifles and the North Shore Regiment now moved through to carry out the main clearance of the Balberger Wald. The task was difficult and exhausting; determined enemy resistance continued in the dense woods where wireless communications often broke down. Continuing wet weather caused the supporting tanks to bog down in the soft ground and made it difficult even to get food up to the forward platoons. Col Stacey wrote that:

> Every advance was counter-attacked, and more than once companies found their positions infiltrated in the darkness. Thickly-sown Schu-mines beset the path of the infantry . . . By the time the brigade reached the east edge of the woods on the afternoon of March 4, it had suffered more than 100 casualties.[3]

Lieutenant Owen Kevan Hugh Kierans was commanding a platoon of the North Shore (New Brunswick) Regiment, on 2 March 1945, when two companies were halted by heavy enemy machine-gun and small arms fire.

While the fierce fire fight which ensued was going on, Lieutenant Kierans, with great skill and dash, worked his way forward and located the enemy positions which he began to knock out one by one until the enemy resistance was broken, thus allowing the advance to continue.

Lieutenant Kierans, though wounded, continued to lead his inspired platoon with speed through to the objective, organized it in a defensive position and established contact so that a united front could be maintained before permitting himself to be evacuated.

Lieutenant Kierans, by his skill and courage, was an inspiration to all ranks; his initiative, endurance and devotion to duty was an example to all. His action contributed in great part to the success of this difficult operation.

For this action, Lieutenant Owen Kevan Hugh Kierans was awarded the Military Cross.

During the clearing of the Balberger Wald on 2 March 1945, Sergeant Austin Bennett was in command of a platoon of "D" Company of the North Shore (New Brunswick) Regiment. On the second day of the operation, all the of-

ficers and the company sergeant major of the Company became casualties. As the leading platoon commanded by Sergeant Bennett approached the company objective, they were held up by six snipers. The attack bogged down and Sergeant Bennett worked around to a flank from where he killed three snipers and took the remainder prisoner.

Sergeant Bennett then took over the company and disposed them on the objective. As this was going on, the company came under extremely heavy fire from a fortified house which was well beyond their objective. This non-commissioned officer, on his own initiative, then took a party of men and personally led the attack on the house. The brilliant attack, supported by the only available fire power, a group of PIATs, allowed Sergeant Bennett to seize thirty-four prisoners and was the deciding factor in the battalion attack.

The initiative, courage and quick action on the part of Sergeant Bennett permitted the following brigade to push through and continue the attack.

For his action, Sergeant Austin Bennett received the Distinguished Conduct Medal.

Wounded men of The North Shore Regiment being placed in a jeep ambulance during Operation BLOCKBUSTER
Donald I. Grant. NAC, PA-177595

Company Sergeant Major Maxwell Aiken Martin was temporarily commanding Number 7 Platoon, 1st Battalion, the Cameron Highlanders of Ottawa (MG) which was supporting the North Shore (NB) Regiment during the fierce fighting in the Hochwald Forest.

At 1630 hours on 2 March 1945, CSM Martin was ordered to take up a position on the forward edge of the Hochwald. CSM Martin immediately proceeded on his reconnaissance and, though he was considerably hampered by enemy snipers, one of which wounded him in the back, he completed his reconnaissance. Before darkness fell, he had his platoon in position on the forward edge of the forest where they remained during the night.

Soon after his platoon's arrival, CSM Martin observed an enemy mortar in action against a platoon of the North Shore (NB) Regiment on his right flank. Showing a cool disregard for his own safety, he personally directed the fire of his medium machine-guns against the enemy mortar and effectively silenced it.

During the night, despite intensive enemy shelling, CSM Martin personally directed numerous harassing shoots against known enemy positions. At first light, the enemy were observed in the vicinity of a dug-out some 200 yards distant. CSM Martin personally accounted with rifle fire for three of the enemy. Soon afterwards an enemy self-propelled gun was observed some 300 yards to the left front of his platoon position. CSM Martin sent back for one of our own self-propelled anti-tank guns and, on its arrival, moved forward to better observe the enemy. He personally directed the fire of our self-propelled gun with such accuracy that the first shell disabled the enemy gun and the second shot set it on fire. On moving forward as the battle progressed, 7 Platoon found in their target areas more than thirty enemy dead.

CSM Martin allowed himself to temporarily leave the battle to have his wound dressed only after fourty-eight hours of continuous action during which the counter-attacks of the enemy had been thwarted.

By his fine leadership and total disregard for his own safety, CSM Martin was an inspiration to his platoon on several occasions, enabling them to provide the infantry with the unfailing and very effective support. The success of this platoon's assistance to the infantry can be directly attributed to the courage, leadership, and devotion to duty of CSM Martin.

For his actions, Company Sergeant Major Maxwell Aiken Martin was awarded the Military Medal.

Sergeant Walter Arthur Cochrane served with the 3rd Canadian Anti-Tank Regiment from the landing on the Normandy beaches to the final cessation of hostilities in Germany. In every action in which his battery was involved, he acquitted himself in an exemplary fashion and was a constant source of inspiration, courage and resourcefulness to his men. On innumerable occasions, this non-commissioned officer has exhibited a degree of courage and coolness of a calibre which proved outstanding even when these attributes were considered commonplace.

On the evening of 3 March 1945, on the outskirts of Xanten Germany, it was evident that the enemy were preparing a counter-attack against the high ground held by our troops. This ridge was vital to the enemy's further defence of the area, and upon it were deployed anti-tank guns of the troop of which Sergeant Cochrane was troop sergeant. Enemy tanks were reported advancing against the position, and our infantry were somewhat uneasy at facing a tank attack since they had but little opportunity to consolidate the ground.

An outpost suddenly sighted an enemy tank at a range of 300 yards and reported its position to this non-commissioned officer. Since it was impossible to immediately engage this tank due to its hull-down position, Sergeant Cochrane mounted one of his self-propelled anti-tank vehicles and courageously manoeuvred it into a suitable location. At a range of less than 200 yards, he engaged the enemy tank and, by fearlessly exposing himself to obtain better vision, passed orders to the gun crew enabling them to knock out the enemy tank in spite of the closing darkness.

Not only did this feat eliminate the immediate threat of an enemy counter-attack, but it encouraged our infantry to a marked extent and so lowered the morale of the opposing forces that they evacuated the vicinity immediately.

For this action, Sergeant Walter Arthur Cochrane was awarded the Military Medal.

The Queen's Own Rifles were on the right flank of the advance and struggled to make headway in the closely wooded, heavily mined terrain. In the wet and cold weather, having been through many days of heavy fighting, the men were becoming exhausted. Major Ben Dunkelman wrote of "D" Company:

> We were in a sorry state after Mooshof. I was the only officer and I had almost no NCOs. We'd taken terrible punishment, the men were in urgent need of rest, and the company urgently needed to be reinforced and reorganized. It seemed unthinkable that we'd be sent into action in our present state.[4]

On the night of March 3, The Queen's Own found itself unable to advance and isolated from contact to the rear. The companies each entrenched in all-around defensive positions, harassed all night by enemy fire. They resumed the attack the next day, but found resistance had suddenly disappeared—the Germans had received orders to begin their withdrawal towards the Rhine. By last light on March 4, all objectives had been taken and the Balberger Wald had been cleared.[5]

Major Benjamin Dunkelman was Company Commander of "D" Company, 1st Battalion The Queen's Own Rifles of Canada on 4 March 1945. On that date, this battalion was given the task of clearing the Balberger Wald, east of the north-south road. "D" Company had the task of clearing the southern edges of the woods. Upon crossing the road which was the start line, the forward two platoons of "D" Company were immediately pinned down by intense machine-gun and Panzerfaust fire from the area of the edge of a clearing. The casualties suffered by these platoons were heavy and, due to the nature of the ground and the intense fire of the enemy, our troops were unable to press forward. Major Dunkelman picked up a PIAT, whose crew had been killed, and successfully silenced two of the enemy machine-guns. Then, rushing forward, led the remaining platoon into the attack upon the enemy positions.

Major Dunkelman personally killed ten of the enemy with his pistol and with his bare hands, all the time shouting to his men to press forward and to the enemy to "come out and fight." As a result of this gallant action and display of fearlessness, in the face of enemy fire, the platoon pressed home its attack and drove the enemy out of this area of the wood. "D" Company was then able to proceed and fight on to their final objective. The display of leadership, the coolness under fire, and the fighting qualities shown by Major Dunkelman struck fear into the heart of the enemy, and those that could fled from the scene of the action.

This gallant action on the part of Major Dunkelman was directly responsible for "D" Company successfully taking their objective and the battalion clearing the final objective.

For his actions, Major Benjamin Dunkelman was awarded the Distinguished Service Order.

On the morning of 4 March 1945, "A" Company, 1st Battalion The Queen's Own Rifles of Canada, took part in the attack on Balberger Wald at the southern end of the Hochwald. Number 8 Platoon was the right forward platoon in the assault. During the attack, Number 8 Platoon came under intense fire and suffered considerable casualties. One of these casualties was Rifleman John Joseph Robertson who received a wound in the stomach. He was advancing to the right flank of his platoon with the Number One of his section's Bren gun unit.

Notwithstanding his severe pain and with absolute disregard for his personal safety, Rifleman Robertson continued to keep the Bren gunner supplied with full magazines. To do so, it was necessary for him to crawl

Captain Benjamin Dunkelman, The Queen's Own Rifles of Canada, was awarded the Distinguished Service Order for his actions in the Balberger Wald, Germany.
NAC, PA-192249

over bullet–swept ground, in full view of the enemy, and secure additional magazines from casualties. During one of these trips to secure magazines, Rifleman

Robertson received another severe wound, this time in the leg. With supreme devotion to duty and outstanding courage, he continued to keep the Bren gun supplied.

The magnificent part played by Rifleman Robertson was in a large measure
responsible for Number 8 Platoon's success in taking its objective which resulted
in fifteen German dead and fourty prisoners.

For his action, Rifleman John Joseph Robertson was awarded the
Military Medal.

On the morning of 4 March 1945, "A" Company, 1st Battalion The
Queen's Own Rifles of Canada, was committed to an attack on Balberger Wald
at the southern end of the Hochwald Forest. In the initial stage of the attack, and
unbeknown to the platoon commanders ahead, the company commander of "A"
Company was severely wounded. The fighting at this particular time was confused and, due to the denseness of the woods, control was difficult to maintain.

Company Sergeant Major Charles Cromwell Martin described how, after the
two forward platoons of his company had been pinned down on a forward slope
by heavy machine-gun fire, the men were being picked off by snipers. Realizing
that something had to be done, he began working his way forward when he suddenly
came across a nest of snipers. Making a quick decision, he decided there was only one
thing to do.

I turned to Wilson, the Bren-gunner and said, "follow me and
keep that Bren on automatic" . . . [They fixed bayonets], the
thirty or forty of us who were left in A Company, and made
ready for a head-on straight-ahead charge . . . We were screaming like Apaches. It really was a do-or-die affair. We couldn't
stay and we couldn't go back so we went forward.[6]

Company Sergeant Major Charles Cromwell Martin of "A" Company picked
up a Bren gun and made his way under intense fire to the right flank of the company. Upon reaching the right flank, CSM Martin personally led the attack of
his men in a daring charge at the enemy. Firing the Bren gun from the hip and
constantly urging the men on, he inspired the men to great heights. The enemy
were completely routed and left behind twenty-six dead and fourty-seven prisoners. CSM Martin personally accounted for eleven enemy dead.

This magnificent example of courage, coolness in action, ability to inspire
men, and devotion to duty on the part of CSM Martin was mainly responsible
for the success of "A" Company, 1st Battalion The Queen's Own Rifles of Canada, in this attack.

For his action, Company Sergeant Major Charles Cromwell Martin was
awarded the Military Medal. CSM Martin was badly wounded in action on
April 16 at Sneek Holland during the advance to close the causeway across
the Ijssel Meer.

CSM Martin later wrote that:

All of us who survived must have been in the protection of God. Every man in that attack deserved the highest award a country can give, and the award they gave me belongs to everyone.[7]

NOTES

1.   National Archives of Canada Record Group (RG) 24, Vol. 15041, 1 Bn, The Canadian Scottish Regiment War Diary, March 1945.

2.   W. Boss, *The Stormont, Dundas and Glengarry Highlanders: 1783 - 1951* (Ottawa: The Runge Press, 1952), p. 247.

3.   Col C. P. Stacey, *The Victory Campaign* (Ottawa: The Queen's Printer, 1966), p. 513.

4.   Ben Dunkelman, *Dual Allegiance* (Toronto: MacMillan of Canada, 1976), p. 136.

5.   RG 24, Vol. 15170, Queen's Own Rifles War Diary, 3 and 4 March 1945.

6.   Charles Cromwell Martin, *Battle Diary* (Toronto: Dundurn Press, 1994), p. 127.

7.   Martin, p. 129.

-7-
VICTORY IN THE RHINELAND

FROM: Headquarters, 7th Parachute Division
5 March 1945

The Commander of Army Group H has ordered that:

In this tremendous battle which is critical now for Germany
and every German, the brave steadfast soldier is doing his hard
duty. There are only a few individuals who betray their own
people in this grave hour by shirking their duty. They trail
around behind the front line and make out that they are stragglers . . . The excuse of a straggler looking for his unit will NO
longer be accepted.

As from mid-day March 10, all soldiers in all branches of the
Wehrmacht who may be encountered away from their units . .
. and who announce that they are stragglers looking for their
units will be summarily tried and shot. To this end, Headquarters, Parachute Army, is creating as many mobile courts mar-
tial as possible which will be stationed at bridges and ferry
sites in particular.[1]

By the first days of March, the US Ninth Army was racing towards
the Rhine River from the south and, on March 3, American and British
tanks met on the outskirts of Geldern. The German First Parachute
Army was now caught in a pocket with its only means of escape being
the bridges over the Rhine at Wesel. Their losses had been terrible but
Hitler ordered General Schlemm to hold this bridgehead at all costs.

Late on the night of March 3/4, the Germans began to pull out of the
last positions they held in the Hochwald Layback defences. They anchored the southwest corner of their new line east of the Balberger
Wald on high ground, called the Hammerbruck Spur, dominating the
crossroad town of Sonsbeck. The 3rd Division was given the task of clearing this spur and then capturing the area of Sonsbeck, to allow the 4th
Canadian Armoured Division to pass south of the Balberger Wald. The
9th Brigade launched this attack initially with the Highland Light Infantry of Canada and the Stormont, Dundas and Glengarry Highlanders.

The Glen's attack began late on March 4 with "A," "C," and "D"
Companies leading, southwards out of the Balberger Wald. Despite

stubborn resistance, including several counter-attacks, all objectives were taken.[2]

On the night of 4/5 March 1945, at the southern edge of the Hochwald Forest, Germany, Lieutenant Alexander Harry Lawson Stephen of the Stormont, Dundas and Glengarry Highlanders, by his bravery, leadership, and determination, captured a difficult objective and assured the advance of the 9th Canadian Infantry Brigade.

The enemy had been forced to withdraw from the southern edge of the Hochwald Forest and had taken up previously dug defensive positions. These were mutually supporting and held in strength by troops of the German 7th Paratroop Division. The troops were directly supported by mortars, rockets, 88-mm guns and heavy artillery.

"A" Company of the Stormont, Dundas and Glengarry Highlanders were ordered to attack south from the perimeter of the Hochwald Forest. Lieutenant Stephen, a platoon commander, was ordered to attack the high feature across seven hundred yards of open rising ground, where the enemy had strong dug-in positions.

Shortly after crossing the start line, the left-hand platoon was forced to ground and was pinned down by enemy fire. Lieutenant Stephen then struck forward with great determination to the right flank of the company's objective. The enemy immediately attempted to break up this attack with machine-gun fire from four dug-in emplacements. This officer refused to be swerved from his intention and pressed home his attack with determination and courage. His platoon suffered heavy casualties and eventually were forced to ground by the enemy's machine-gun fire. Lieutenant Stephen then crawled forward, at grave personal risk, to the enemy position and cleared out a machine-gun nest with Number 36 Grenades and Sten gun fire. The valorous act allowed him to once again lead his platoon forward. His fearless leadership inspired his men, who, fighting furiously, enabled the company to gain a foothold on a portion of its objective where it could reorganize and complete its assigned tasks.

When Lieutenant Stephen had consolidated on his final objective, the enemy counter-attacked with twenty men and overran his rear section, killing the Bren gun crew. The enemy then took up positions in an anti-tank ditch and continued to shell the platoon position with artillery and rockets. Lieutenant Stephen, securing a Bren gun, and with complete disregard for his own safety, courageously fought his way to his overrun section, killing five and wounding eight Germans and forcing the remainder to withdraw.

The magnificent leadership shown during this action was an inspiration to all about him and resulted in opening the route for the advance of the reserve battalion of the brigade.

For his actions, Lieutenant Alexander Harry Lawson Stephen received the Military Cross.

On the night of 4/5 March 1945, at the southern edge of the Hochwald Forest, Germany, Corporal Melvin Louis Coulas of the Stormont, Dundas and Glen-

garry Highlanders, took command of Number 8 Platoon after the officer was killed. He continued the attack with such effect that he ensured the line of advance of the 9th Canadian Infantry Brigade.

The enemy had been driven from the southern fringe of the Hochwald Forest and had manned a ridge across seven hundred yards of open rising ground. This determined enemy, reinforced with extra MG 42s* and Panzerfausts, took up prepared positions, with direct mortar and artillery support.

Corporal Coulas was in command of Number 5 Section of Number 8 Platoon, "A" Company, which led the attack against this formidable enemy position. In the initial attack on the ridge, his platoon suffered severe casualties, one of which was his platoon commander. In the midst of withering cross-fire from four enemy machine-guns and through intense mortar bombardment, without hesitation and with complete disregard for his own personal safety, he assumed command of his platoon, quickly reorganized it and, with inspired leadership, killed or routed the enemy on the ridge and reached his platoon's objective. Immediately Corporal Coulas organized consolidation but, while engaged in this, the fanatical enemy attacked in force, driving one section from its position. Once again, Corporal Coulas, under direct fire from the counter-attacking force, led one of his remaining sections into the enemy positions. He killed eight and wounded fifteen of the enemy, causing such confusion that the enemy became completely disorganized and was forced to withdraw, leaving the ridge in our possession.

The initiative, courage, and determination shown by Corporal Coulas was an inspiration to all and in the highest tradition of the Canadian soldier.

For this action, Corporal Melvin Louis Coulas was awarded the Military Medal. Corporal Coulas was later wounded in action on April 10 near Deventer Holland.

Sergeant Charles Abbott Post, commanding Number 1 Section of the Carrier Platoon of the Stormont, Dundas and Glengarry Highlanders, during the battle of the Hochwald Forest on 6 March 1945, showed such gallantry, exceptional leadership and promptness of action that he was largely responsible for the success of the battalion's attack on the wood.

Sergeant Post was supporting "B" Company, the right flank company, on to its objective, with Bren gun and .50 calibre Browning machine-gun fire when he noted that the company was pinned down and unable to advance. Sergeant Post manoeuvred his carriers further to the flank to discover that "B" Company was being held up by fire from an enemy self-propelled gun. Completely disregarding the safety of himself and his section, Sergeant Post rallied his carriers and, with

---

*   The standard German light machine-gun which operated at a very high rate of fire.

Brownings blazing, he rushed the self-propelled gun and set it on fire, allowing "B" Company to advance on to their objective.

During the night, when the battalion was counter-attacked on the right flank, Sergeant Post held the fire of his guns until the enemy was within three hundred yards of the battalion's forward defended localities. Then, although under severe mortar fire, he opened up. The enemy was driven off, leaving forty dead and as many wounded. Few escaped his withering Browning machine-gun fire.

Through the gallant and determined actions of Sergeant Post, The Stormont, Dundas and Glengarry Highlanders were able to quickly gain and hold their objective against a most determined enemy in the battle of the Hochwald Forest.

For his actions, Sergeant Charles Abbott Post was awarded the Military Medal. Sergeant Post was later wounded in action on March 25 in the Rhine bridgehead.

Meanwhile, The Highland Light Infantry of Canada, 9th Brigade's other attacking battalion, also fought forward on March 5. On the left, "C" Company quickly captured its objective, which was three wooded knolls; but, on the right, the Company was stopped by a group of farm buildings that had been converted into a strongpoint. "C" Company renewed its attack later in the day with supporting fire from "A" Company and most objectives were taken just after dark. Fighting went on through the night and all objectives were secured by morning, allowing 7th Brigade to pass through in the next phase.

On the morning of 5 March 1945, Major Erwin Frank Klugman commanded the left forward company when the Highland Light Infantry of Canada attacked the Hammerbruch feature east of Hochwald Forest in Germany and displayed great courage and personal bravery. By his distinguished leadership, cool and skilful handling, his company successfully captured and consolidated ground vital to the brigade battle with a minimum of casualties to his own troops.

"A" Company, under a heavy artillery barrage, attacked and captured four small heavily defended wooded knolls on the battalion left flank. The company, inspired by the personal example of this officer, pressed closely behind the artillery barrage, accepting the obvious risk of casualties from their own artillery. The bulk of the enemy surrendered, stunned and amazed by the rapidity with which they were overrun.

The company now occupied a very exposed position which invited heavy enemy mortar and artillery fire and was also subjected to direct machine-gun fire from an adjacent high feature still in enemy hands. This feature was to have been attacked simultaneously by two other companies. Major Klugman realized that his rapid success could contribute much to the battalion battle. With utter disregard for the enemy about the area, he ensured proper consolidation and organized direct fire support to assist in the battle raging for the adjacent feature.

This officer also, at great personal risk, sought out strategic observation posts from which he could direct counter-fire measures against active enemy guns that he had spotted.

For his actions here and near Calcar, Major Erwin Frank Klugman was awarded the Distinguished Service Order. Major Klugman was later wounded in action in Holland on April 5.

On 5 March 1945, Sergeant Thomas Alexander Hopkins was in command of the leading platoon of "A" Company of The Highland Light Infantry of Canada during the initial attack on the strongly held Hammerbruch feature south east of the Hochwald Forest, Germany. The attack was launched just before first light behind a heavy artillery barrage and the infantry were instructed to follow the artillery as closely as possible. During the advance across open ground, subjected to spasmodic raking enemy machine-gun fire, several artillery rounds fell short among and dangerously close to Sergeant Hopkins' platoon, causing several casualties and creating serious confusion.

Realizing that to hesitate to reorganize his platoon would be suicidal and that the momentum of the attack must be maintained, Sergeant Hopkins, with utter disregard for his own safety, rallied those men nearest him and personally led an audacious charge straight at the enemy position. The assault was led with such dash and determination that the enemy were overwhelmed on the knoll which was the platoon's objective, numbers of them killed in their trenches, and approximately fifteen prisoners taken.

Three officers of The Highland Light Infantry of Canada after receiving their decorations from the King at Buckingham Palace. From left to right: Major Allan Kerr McTaggart awarded the Distinguished Service Order for his actions on the Hammerbruck feature; Major Joseph Charles King awarded the Distinguished Service Order for his actions at Bienen, Germany; Major Erwin Frank Klugman awarded the Distinguished Service Order for his actions near Calcar.

This non-commissioned officer, by his cool courageous action, established his platoon on ground vital to the continued success of the battalion and the ultimate consolidation of this whole commanding feature.

At all times during the ten months that Sergeant Hopkins served in active operations with The Highland Light Infantry of Canada, he displayed personal courage, leadership and initiative of an exemplary and meritorious nature.

For his actions on the Hammerbruch feature, as well as at Udem and at Sasput in the Scheldt, Sergeant Thomas Alexander Hopkins was awarded the Military Medal.

On 5 March 1945, Major Allan Kerr McTaggart, commanding "D" Company, The Highland Light Infantry of Canada, displayed outstanding courage and initiative.

The Highland Light Infantry of Canada had been ordered to capture the north half of the Hammerbruck feature, south of Xanten Germany. "C" Company was to precede "D" Company along a common axis, and the two companies were to fan out with "C" Company on the right and "D" Company on the left on the battalion objective. "C" Company came under intense machine-gun fire from a high feature on the axis, about half-way to the objective. Tanks were sent to aid "C" Company, but enemy mines and self-propelled guns knocked out eight of the nine tanks supporting the battalion.

Major McTaggart appreciated that, if he could bypass the high feature, he would cut off the enemy strongpoint. He therefore led his company down a narrow valley to the left of the feature without waiting for "C" Company. The enemy immediately brought heavy artillery and mortar fire to bear on the valley, inflicting heavy casualties on "D" Company.

Major McTaggart ordered his company to dig in and, ignoring the enemy fire, crawled forward onto the open sloping ground to the left of the high feature where he was under enemy observation and subject to mortar, small arms and self-propelled gun fire. He determined that there were no covered approaches to or around the high feature. Major McTaggart observed the enemy positions, returned to his company, and called for artillery and 3-inch mortar smoke on the enemy positions. Ordering his men to fix bayonets, he then led his company and rushed across the open ground and up the hill to the enemy position on the top. This action captured the dominating feature and allowed the battalion advance to continue.

The leading platoon of "D" Company, advancing across a forward slope to a wooded feature which was "D" Company's final objective, came under heavy machine-gun fire and was pinned to the ground, suffering eight casualties. Again exposing himself to the enemy fire, Major McTaggart immediately went forward across the open ground, reorganized the platoon, and observed the enemy fire until he had pin-pointed the location of eight enemy machine-gun posts. Returning to company headquarters, he called for artillery on the enemy positions, which silenced the enemy guns. He then led his company to its objective.

On consolidating his position, Major McTaggart was informed that a group of Germans had withdrawn to some nearby buildings. Having no reserve available to attack them, Major McTaggart personally contacted civilians in the nearest building and ordered them to tell the Germans to surrender or be wiped out by artillery fire. Twelve paratroops surrendered.

By his outstanding courage, initiative and leadership, Major McTaggart was directly responsible for the success of the battalion battle and the destruction of the German defence force.

For his actions, Major Allan Kerr McTaggart was awarded the Distinguished Service Order.

On 5 March 1945, Corporal Frank Reginald Jull was a section leader in Number 14 Platoon of "C" Company, The Highland Light Infantry of Canada. "C" Company was given the task of capturing a group of buildings and an orchard near Sonsbeck Germany, the approach to which was over three hundred yards of open ground.

Corporal Jull commanded the leading section of Number 14 Platoon, which was the left-hand platoon. While crossing the open ground, this section came under enemy rifle and machine-gun fire from the buildings and Corporal Jull was hit in the thigh by a rifle bullet. He continued to lead his section until it had cleared its objective, the first group of houses. He then had his wounds dressed by a stretcher bearer.

Enemy fire was still coming from an orchard just to the right of his section position. Refusing to be evacuated, Corporal Jull led his section in an assault on the enemy in the orchard. At this time, an enemy rifle bullet struck Corporal Jull's webbing pouches, igniting two phosphorus grenades he was carrying. These burned through his battle dress, scorching his body. In spite of severe burns, Corporal Jull continued to lead the assault until the orchard was cleared and then organized his section to defend the orchard. He remained there until Number 14 Platoon's position was consolidated.

Corporal Jull's outstanding courage and leadership materially affected the success of the company battle and he was personally responsible for the destruction of an enemy position.

For his actions, Corporal Frank Reginald Jull was awarded the Military Medal.

On 5 March 1945, H/Captain John MacMorran Anderson, Canadian Chaplain Service, was padre attached to The Highland Light Infantry of Canada. The regiment launched an attack from Balberger Wald over a mile of open ground, along a forward slope. "C" and "D" Companies were pinned down by heavy enemy machine-gun and small arms fire, and suffered over thirty casualties who had to be evacuated across the open ground under enemy fire.

*Tanks were sent across the start line to go to the assistance of the two compa-
nies but these were knocked out by enemy tanks and self-propelled guns on the forward slope before reaching "C and "D" Companies.*

*H/Captain Anderson, hearing of the casualties, proceeded forward on foot
across the bullet-swept ground to "C" and "D" Companies. Finding many casualties who required immediate attention, he returned to the battalion headquarters area near the start line and organized two available jeeps and a party of
volunteer stretcher bearers to return to the scene of the battle. Though warned
that tanks had been knocked out a few minutes before on the route, H/Captain
Anderson led the jeep party back and forth across the open ground until all casualties were evacuated.*

*During the day, a carrier and a tank had been knocked out by mines on the
route to the Regimental Aid Post. The enemy positioned a self-propelled gun and
machine-guns to cover the defile thus caused and successfully prevented the use of
the route by vehicles and marching personnel during the battle. H/Captain Anderson, knowing this, ignored the enemy fire and led his jeeps along the route. Although the enemy fired on the jeeps and destroyed one of them, H/Captain
Anderson continued to drive back and forth along the route throughout the battle.*

*By his complete disregard for his own safety, and by his outstanding courage
and initiative under heavy enemy fire, H/Captain Anderson successfully evacuated over thirty stretcher cases and thus saved the lives of many soldiers.*

For his actions, H/Captain John MacMorran Anderson was awarded a
Bar to his Military Cross.

The third battalion of the 9th Brigade, The North Nova Scotia Highlanders, also went into action on the right of the Highland Light Infantry of Canada as soon as the 8th Brigade had cleared the southern edge
of the Balberger Wald. As the battalion made their approach march on
a dark and rainy night, the command post carrier was blown up on a
mine. Fortunately, the battalion commander was only shaken up and he
managed to re-establish communications before the attack. Over the
next several days, the North Novas pushed ahead, often under severe
German artillery fire and with the ever present threat of German mines
underfoot. Losses were heavy, with one platoon of "D" Company reduced to only seven men. Under these circumstances, the close artillery
support by the 14th Field Regiment was especially valuable.[3]

*On the morning of 6 March 1945, Captain William Hopkins Quirk
Cameron of the 14th Field Regiment RCA, attached to the North Nova Scotia
Highlanders as a forward observation officer, attacked with "B" Company the
small wooded feature called Dursberg, immediately east of the southern limit of
the Balberger Wald. From this feature's eighty-metre eminence, the enemy commanded all approaches. The attack was made across ground sewn with anti-tank
and Schu-mines, a consideration which forced Captain Cameron to leave his carrier and go on foot with the infantry, using a Number 38 wireless set to send
message back to his main wireless set in the carrier.*

From the start, the company met machine-gun fire and about half-way to the objective, Captain Cameron was hit through the neck. His wound bled profusely, both internally as well as externally, cutting off his speech and seriously interfering with breathing. Although badly wounded, he recovered himself instantly and, showing a degree of resolution and courage as high as his sense of duty, pressed on undeterred in the face of continued fire. He continued to advance, controlling the fire of his supporting guns by writing his fire orders for his accompanying operator, being himself unable to speak, until after gaining another two hundred yards, he collapsed near the foot of the objective.

This officer's example of courage and devotion to duty was an inspiration to the soldiers with him and was undoubtedly a contributing factor to the success of the attack.

For his action, Captain William Hopkins Quirk Cameron was awarded the Military Cross.

On the morning of 6 March 1945, The North Nova Scotia Highlanders attacked the high ground east of the Balberger Wald. Battalion Tactical Headquarters, comprising the battalion commander's wireless carrier and the artillery representative's wireless carrier, was moving up from the Assembly Area to the Forming Up Position when, about five hundred yards from its destination, it ran into a minefield and the commander's carrier was knocked out. The battalion command post, to which the battalion commander and battery commander then proceeded on foot, was now without communications to brigade headquarters other than by the Artillery Number 19 Wireless Set. This set, however, required a five-hundred-yard remote connection across the fire-swept minefield. In addition, there was no mine-sweeping apparatus available to assist anyone in crossing this area.

Since the infantry wireless personnel were all casualties or temporarily unfit, the spare artillery operator took over the Number 18 Set control to maintain communications with the rifle companies. This left only Gunner Benjamin Satten of the 14th Field Regiment RCA to lay and maintain this long remote entirely on his own.

With all possible speed, Gunner Satten laid cable through the minefield under almost continuous mortar, machine-gun and sniper fire. The line was cut three times by mortar fire and each time Gunner Satten repaired it. He was then ordered to abandon the cable and try to recover one of the Infantry Number 22 Wireless Sets if he could find one not too badly damaged. To do this, he made two more trips across the fire-swept minefield and salvaged one set and enough undamaged components to get it working as a ground station in the battalion command post, thus establishing the only secure communication with brigade headquarters.

Gunner Satten's complete disregard for his own safety, resolution, skill and initiative in setting up and maintaining vital communications before the battalion launched its attack contributed beyond doubt to its success.

For his actions, Gunner Benjamin Satten was awarded the Military Medal.

By the early morning of March 6, the main objectives on the Hammerbruch spur had been taken and 7th Brigade launched the next phase, attacking the area of Sonsbeck itself.

On the morning of 6 March 1945, The Royal Winnipeg Rifles were ordered to attack and secure the high ground in the area north of Sonsbeck. "A" Company attacked on the left and "D" Company on the right. Sergeant Norman Joseph Lowe accompanied "A" Company as mobile fire controller for the mortar platoon. During the advance, Sergeant Lowe was subjected to very heavy shelling. The company was held up by this shelling and Sergeant Lowe was required to bring down mortar fire.

To obtain a suitable observation post, it was necessary for Sergeant Lowe to cross a heavily mined area and endure further heavy shelling. With outstanding courage and without thought of his own personal safety, this non-commissioned officer made his way through the minefield and, although wounded by shell fragments, reached the observation post from which he directed mortar fire on the enemy.

Due to the determination and bravery of Sergeant Lowe, the enemy were routed and "A" Company was able to advance to its objective.

For his action, Sergeant Norman Joseph Lowe was awarded the Military Medal.

"C" Company, The Royal Winnipeg Rifles, was ordered to attack and clear the high ground northeast of Sonsbeck Germany on 6 March 1945. After crossing the Start Line, the company sustained heavy casualties from shelling and from Schu-mines which were sown thickly over the area.

Rifleman Bernard Cyr, a stretcher bearer in "C" Company, with magnificent personal courage and showing great devotion to duty, took prompt action to evacuate the casualties. He moved about the area fearlessly and without thought of the great danger involved, rendering succour to all the wounded and supervising their evacuation.

His outstanding courage was a fine example to all ranks in the company and contributed strikingly to the high morale which enabled the company to attain its objective quickly.

For his action, Rifleman Bernard Cyr was awarded the Military Medal. Rifleman Cyr was later wounded in action on April 7 near Deventer Holland.

On 6 March 1945, The Royal Winnipeg Rifles, under command of 9th Canadian Infantry Brigade, were ordered to clear a high wooded feature two miles southeast of Xanten Germany. "D" Company, in which Rifleman Mervyn Frank Milson MM was a stretcher bearer, led the attack and almost immediately came under terrific shelling. The ground over which the attack was made was also heavily mined and booby-trapped.

Many casualties were caused to the members of "D" Company. Rifleman Milson MM, with great courage and bravery and without thought of self, went out into this mined and booby-trapped area during the heavy shelling, dressed the wounds of his comrades, and brought in the casualties. His coolness under fire, complete disregard for his own safety and prompt action saved the lives of many men.

The courage displayed by this soldier was an inspiration to all ranks and contributed greatly to the maintenance of the high degree of morale. His gallant action undoubtedly saved the lives of the wounded men and his courage was an inspiration to all ranks of the battalion, and was worthy of the highest traditions of this Regiment and the Canadian Army.

For his actions, Sergeant Mervyn Frank Milson MM was awarded a Bar to his Military Medal.

At 1400 hours, 5 March 1945, in Balberger Wald, an enemy mortar concentration blew up a Kangaroo armoured vehicle and a 6-pounder anti-tank gun. Two carriers and two jeeps were adjacent to these two vehicles. Although mortar fire was continuous, an armoured vehicle was burning, and ammunition was exploded in all directions, Gunner William John Maynes of the 13th Field Artillery RCA was able to drive the two carriers and one jeep a safe distance away. The second jeep was burning when he tried to drive it away. He was unable to start it and just left it momentarily before it blew up.

Heavy vehicle casualties on carriers had recently been suffered in the forest fighting. Saving these two carriers was of immediate assistance to the operation, one of them containing the forward observation officer's communications equipment for artillery support. By his disregard for his own safety and by his skilful driving, Gunner Maynes saved vehicles which contributed successfully to the operation south of the Balberger Wald.

For his action, Gunner William John Maynes received the Military Medal.

At approximately 1000 hours on 9 March 1945, in the forward area, a party of Canadian infantry were laying wire about fifty yards in front of the anti-tank gun position of Sergeant Edward Joseph Corbett, 3rd Anti-Tank Regiment. One or more of the infantry personnel stepped on a Schu-mine and four of the party were wounded. Sergeant Corbett, who had been trained in first-aid skills, immediately organized a carrying party to remove the wounded and, without the slightest hesitation, proceeded to the scene of the accident, although he knew that the area was thick with mines. Having tended the wounded, Sergeant Corbett was evacuating one man from the mine area when he stepped on a mine and was wounded to the extent of losing his leg.

The coolness, courage and organizing ability displayed by Sergeant Corbett in tending and evacuating the wounded through what he knew to be an extremely dangerous area was of the highest calibre. It served as a magnificent example and steadying influence on all ranks.

For his action, Sergeant Edward Joseph Corbett received the Military Medal.

While the 3rd Division was fighting to clear the southwest corner of the German bridgehead, other units of II Canadian Corps closed in on the western anchor of the German line at Xanten, and British and American forces pushed in from the south and east. The Germans contested every defendable position even though, late on March 6, the German High Command finally gave permission to evacuate the bridgehead. Canadian forces occupied Sonsbeck with practically no opposition although the Germans left plenty of mines and booby traps.

The German withdrawal from the west bank was carried out very efficiently with most of the German equipment getting across the Rhine before the last bridge at Wesel was blown up. On March 11, the Germans were gone from the west bank.

Thus ended more than a month of continuous bitter fighting by the First Canadian Army in which weather and ground had seemed almost invariably to side with the enemy. Day after day, clouded skies had robbed the Army of its air support; flood and mud had too frequently immobilized its armour. The enemy had concentrated an unusual amount of firepower, which in General Crerar's phrase "had been more heavily and effectively applied than at any other time in the army's fighting during the present campaign." The German opposition had been formidable in both quantity and quality . . .

In these circumstances, the victory, inevitably, was costly . . . [The Canadian, British and American forces had sustained about 23,000 casualties for the period February 8 to March 10.] Canadian casualties totalled 243 officers and 3395 other ranks . . .

The loss inflicted on the enemy had been much heavier. During the whole period from the beginning of "Veritable" until the German withdrawal east of the Rhine . . . Thus the two armies' [i.e. First Canadian and Ninth US Armies] converging operations had cost the Germans, according to our best figures, approximately 90,000 men.[4]

HQ 3 CID
Memorandum No 10
13 Mar 45

At the conclusion of Operations "VERITABLE" & "BLOCK-BUSTER" I wish to send you my most sincere congratulations on your magnificent fighting achievement against a tough enemy and under appalling conditions of ground & weather.

There will be no one in "The Water Rats" who will forget the amphibious battles to clear the flooded Rhine polders. 7 CIB will long remember the clearing of the wooded area overlooking MOYLAND and the fierce German counter attacks which they beat off. 8 CIB will not easily forget KEPPELN or the SPORTSPLATZ or the BALBERGER WALD. 9 CIB (The Highland Bde) will often recall the capture of UDEM & the HAMMERBRUCK feature . . .

We now have an opportunity to rest, refit and train for the tasks ahead. There will be hard fighting in the future battles. The German is fighting on home ground amongst his own supporters. It will require for each one of us the highest standard of physical fitness, mental alertness & above all an eager determination to see this thing thru to an early finish.

At this great moment before the crossing of the Rhine, I recall to your attention Drake's Prayer.

"Oh Lord God, when Thou givest Thy servants to endeavour any great matters, grant us also to know that it is not the beginning, but the continuing of the same, until it is thoroughly finished, which yieldeth the true glory; through Him that for the finishing of Thy work laid down His life, our Redeemer, Jesus Christ."

(D C Spry) Maj-Gen
GOC 3 Cdn Inf Div

NOTES

1.   National Archives of Canada Record Group (RG) 24, Vol; 15077, The Highland Light Infantry of Canada War Diary, March 1945, "3 CID Intelligence Summary No 81 " dated 9 March 1945.

2.   W. Boss, *The Stormont, Dundas and Glengarry Highlanders: 1783 - 1951* (Ottawa: The Runge Press, 1952), p. 247.

3.   Will R. Bird, *No Retreating Footsteps* (Kentville: Kentville Publishing Co.), p. 325.

4.   Col C. P. Stacey, *The Victory Campaign* (Ottawa: The Queen's Printer, 1966), p. 522.

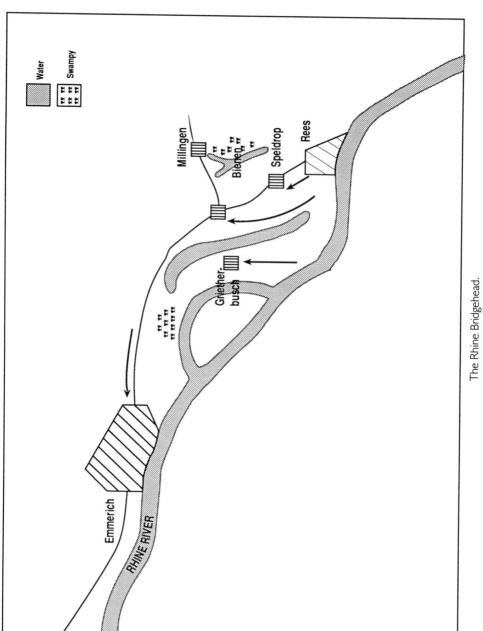

The Rhine Bridgehead.

-8-
RHINE BRIDGEHEAD

21 ARMY GROUP
PERSONAL MESSAGE
FROM THE COMMANDER-IN-CHIEF

On the 7th of February I told you we were going into the ring for the final and last round; there would be no time limit: we would continue fighting until our opponent was knocked out. The last round is going very well on both sides of the ring . . .

21 ARMY GROUP WILL NOW CROSS THE RHINE

The enemy possibly thinks he is safe behind this great river obstacle. We all agree that it is a great obstacle; but we will show the enemy that he is far from safe behind it. This great Allied fighting machine, composed of integrated land and air force, will deal with the problem in no uncertain manner.

And having crossed the Rhine, we will crack about in the plains of Northern Germany, chasing the enemy from pillar to post. The swifter and the more energetic our action, the sooner the war will be over, and that is what we all desire: to get on with the job and finish off the German war as soon as possible.

Over the RHINE then, let us go. And good hunting to you all on the other side.

May "the Lord mighty in battle" give us victory in this our latest undertaking as He has done in all our battles since we landed in Normandy on D-day.

Signed (B. L. Montgomery)
Field-Marshal,
C-in-C
21 Army Group[1]

At the end of March 1945, the Allied forces were in position to launch the final offensive to end the war in Europe. The strategy had been agreed upon early in the year—the main strike would take place in the area of Field-Marshal Bernard Montgomery's 21st Army Group.

The Rhine marked the last major obstacle to releasing the Allied forces into the heart of Germany. At the same time, it was known that the German forces would now fight with whatever strength they could muster to defend their homes.

With the withdrawal of German forces to the east bank of the Rhine, the German First Parachute Army was assigned the defence of the sector designated for the British assault. The Germans had suffered heavy losses in men in the Rhineland but, among any reinforcements that could be scraped up, the paratroops would no doubt remain the most fanatic in their resistance. In addition, General Schlemm had managed to save a good part of his equipment, with about 150 artillery pieces including a large number of medium and heavy guns. Many of these were concentrated on the Hoch Elten heights seven miles west of Emmerich, where they could dominate this stretch of the river. Even more ominous, the Army Group Reserve, the still dangerous 15th Panzer Grenadier and 116th Panzer Divisions under 47th Panzer Corps, were located only a few miles northeast of Emmerich.[2]

Montgomery's plan for the crossing, Operation PLUNDER, called for a combined amphibious-airborne assault with massive strength on the stretch of the Rhine between Emmerich in the west and Wesel in the east. The British Second Army would cross on the left in the area of Rees with the US Ninth Army crossing on their right in the area of Wesel. Once a firm bridgehead was established, both armies would break out eastward: the British thrusting towards Munster while the Americans swept around the northern edge of the vital Ruhr industrial area to link up with the 12th US Army Group, coming up from the south.

The First Canadian Army would not have a role in the crossing itself. However, the 3rd Canadian Infantry Division was placed temporarily under command of the left flank British Division, the 51st Highland. When the 51st Highland Division had taken their initial objectives, the 9th Canadian Infantry Brigade would attack westward along the bank of the Rhine, securing the flank of the bridgehead by capturing Emmerich. In particular, they were to eliminate the artillery threat from the Hoch Elten feature so that a major supply bridge could then be built at Emmerich.[3]

Shortly after sunset on March 23, on a warm spring evening, over 2,000 guns of the 21st Army Group opened fire on the German bank of the Rhine. After a massive three-hour bombardment, the assault troops crossed over with surprisingly little difficulty. In most areas, the German forward lines were quickly overrun from Wesel to Rees. On the left flank, however, as the 154th Brigade of the 51st Highland Division tried to push inland early on March 24, their advance was violently stopped by a battlegroup of the 6th Parachute Division in the village of Speldrop.[4]

Movement of XXX British Corps came to standstill until this flank could be cleared. Here, however, the unique nature of the Rhine River floodplain made an ideal defensive situation. The main Rees-Emmerich highway passed through an isthmus formed on the left by an old river bed of the Rhine and, on the right, by stretches of stagnant water left from winter meanders of the river. Both areas were boggy and not passable. Within this narrow passage, the land was broken up by dykes, the largest of which was the main flood dyke, ten to sixteen feet high. There was only one way out of the bridgehead in the area, and that was along this highway which passed first through Speldrop and then Bienen. Inside the dykes, the land was flat and devoid of cover. There was no alternative but to attack Bienen frontally, despite the casualties that could be expected.[5]

Speldrop

The Highland Light Infantry of Canada crossed the Rhine at 0400 hours, March 24, as the first unit of the 9th Canadian Infantry Brigade to move up in support of the 51st Highland Division. They found that the Black Watch (154th Brigade of the 51st Division) had been thrown back from Speldrop by fierce German counter-attacks supported by tanks and self-propelled guns. The British troops were exhausted and had left two companies cut off in the village. The HLI of Canada were now called on to attack as soon as possible to capture the village and relieve the British troops.

The attack was launched with "B" Company leading at 1630 hours, March 24, with powerful artillery support from six field and two medium regiments, as well as two heavy artillery batteries. The leading company successfully crossed the open ground but met stubborn resistance in the western edge of the village. "A" Company attempted to pass through to clear the rest of the village but could make no progress. At dusk, however, supporting weapons in carriers managed to cross the open ground under fire from self-propelled guns, to break the resistance and "A" Company finally secured its objectives. The German paratroops still hung on to a number of entrenched positions requiring the remaining companies of the regiment to continue the fight through the night to overcome these.[6]

The HLI War Diary described that:

> the battle continued well on into the morning. Houses had to be cleared at the point of the bayonet and single Germans made suicidal attempts to break up our attacks. Wasp flame-throwers were used to good effect. It was necessary to push right through the town and drive the enemy out into the fields where they could be dealt with.[7]

On 24 and 25 March 1945, Major Joseph Charles King, commanding "B" Company, The Highland Light Infantry of Canada, displayed a great coolness, courage and leadership in battle.

On 24 March 1945, The Highland Light Infantry of Canada had been ordered to captured Speldrop, a strongly held German town which was preventing
the development of the 51st Highland Division bridgehead north of the Rhine.
"B" Company, the leading company of the battalion, was given the task of securing a firm base in the north end of the town, through which other companies
would pass.

Major King led his company across one thousand yards of open ground and
seized the first group of buildings. Here, two of his platoon commanders were
killed and the third wounded, leaving only corporals to command platoons. Major
King personally supervised the each platoon in taking its objective, and he moved
freely throughout the company area, though it was swept by German machine-
gun fire and subjected to direct fire from three German tanks sited to cover the
approaches.

A group of fortified buildings beyond Major King's objectives proved to be a
strongpoint and the Germans there subjected "B" Company's area to withering
machine-gun and Panzerfaust fire. Major King, even though he had not been told
to clear these buildings, seized the initiative. He appreciated the necessity for close
support and called for Wasps and anti-tank support. When these arrived, Major
King organized an attack with one platoon on the strongpoint and captured it.
This action disorganized the German defences and enabled the following companies to pass through to their objectives.

On the following day, March 25, Major King's company was ordered to clear
a group of buildings in Bienen, a nodal point which was blocking further advance
by the bridgehead forces. Major King again fearlessly led his platoons to their objectives, personally supervising the clearing of each building.

By his initiative, leadership and courage, Major King contributed materially
to the success of the battalion's battles, which broke the German Rhine defence
line and enabled rapid expansion of the bridgehead.

For his actions, Major Joseph Charles King was awarded the Distinguished Service Order. Major King was later wounded on April 4 during the
advance into Holland, but was able to remain on duty.

On 24 March 1945, Lance Sergeant Cornelius Jerome Reidel was a section
leader in Number 12 Platoon, "B" Company, The Highland Light Infantry of
Canada. The Highland Light Infantry of Canada had been ordered to capture
Speldrop Germany, a strongly defended nodal point which was preventing the development of the 51st Highland Division's bridgehead north of the Rhine. "B"
Company, the leading company, was ordered to attack across one thousand yards
of open ground and to secure a foothold in the west half of the town.

Number 12 Platoon, the leading platoon, came under intense fire from enemy
20-mm and machine-guns located in an orchard and a group of fortified buildings, beyond which was the objective of the platoon. The platoon commander was
killed and the platoon scattered to cover.

Lance Sergeant Reidel, realizing that this initial bite into the town was vital to the success of the battalion battle, immediately took command of the platoon, ordered the men to fix bayonets and, taking a Bren gun, led the platoon into the orchard in the face of heavy small arms fire. The platoon captured the orchard and cleared the buildings beyond, killing ten Germans and capturing fifteen prisoners, along with three 7.5-cm infantry guns.

Lance Sergeant Reidel's initiative and great courage so inspired his men that they were able to destroy a force of German paratroops superior in number to themselves. The success of the platoon action enabled the battalion to gain a foothold in the town and eventually to capture the nodal point.

For his action, Lance Sergeant Cornelius Jerome Reidel was awarded the Military Medal.

On 24 March 1945, Lieutenant George Oxley Macdonald was platoon commander in Number 8 Platoon, "A" Company, The Highland Light Infantry of Canada. The Highland Light Infantry of Canada was ordered to capture Speldrop Germany, a strongly held nodal point blocking the expansion of the 51st Highland Division's bridgehead north of the Rhine. "A" Company was attacking the eastern half of the village which was strongly held by the enemy who had machine-gun posts sited in at least three buildings. Lieutenant Macdonald's platoon was ordered to attack in daylight, under covering fire of a carrier section.

Lieutenant Macdonald led his platoon across two hundred yards of open ground and successfully assaulted the first enemy positions although two more enemy machine-gun posts beyond the objective and to the flank subjected the platoon to a withering fire. All non-commissioned officers in the platoon became casualties but Lieutenant Macdonald personally organized the consolidation of the objective and encouraged his men to hold the building, though it was discovered that at least two enemy tanks were active in the immediate area.

As a result of his courage and determination, the platoon held the buildings and successfully contained the enemy machine-gun posts, enabling another platoon to get into a position to clear them. This courageous and brilliant action largely contributed to the success of the Highland Light Infantry of Canada's attack.

For his action, Lieutenant George Oxley Macdonald was awarded the Military Cross. Two days later, Lieutenant Macdonald died of wounds received in the battle for the Rhine bridgehead.

On 24 March 1945, Captain Donald Albert Pearce, carrier platoon commander of The Highland Light Infantry of Canada, displayed courage and initiative beyond the call of duty. The Highland Light Infantry of Canada had been ordered to capture Speldrop, a German nodal point which was preventing the expansion of the 51st Highland Division's bridgehead north of the Rhine.

Captain Pearce was ordered to place his guns to protect the left flank of the battalion's approach to the town. During the approach, a group of German guns opened fire from the left, at a point not covered by the carrier platoon guns. Captain Pearce ignored the enemy fire and moved about the open ground to his gun positions, directing their fire onto specific enemy machine-guns, forcing them to cease fire.

Officers of The Highland Light Infantry of Canada soon after crossing the Rhine: Major John Alexander Ferguson, commanding Support Company, on the left, and Captain Donald Albert Pearce of the Carrier platoon on the right. Both won the Military Cross for their actions at Bienen and Speldrop.
Donald I. Grant, NAC, PA-192264

After the capture of the first company objective, it became evident that it was necessary to get supporting weapons across the open ground into the town to assist the rifle companies to their objective. Captain Pearce organized two Wasps, two sections of carriers, and four 6-pounder anti-tank guns to be ready to dash across the open ground into the town. An artillery smoke screen was called for to obscure the line of sight of three German tanks sited to cover the approach. The artillery smoke screen was delayed due to the employment of the artillery elsewhere.

Appreciating the necessity for speed, Captain Pearce in his own carrier, without waiting for the smoke screen, led the convoy into the town. Then, using his own carrier as a test, he moved about in view of the enemy to determine suitable firing positions for his weapons.

Though the area was swept by German fire, Captain Pearce then personally directed fire against enemy weapons and enabled the infantry to cross the open ground to gain access to the German-held buildings.

By his great initiative and courageous example, Captain Pearce enabled the battalion to take its objective and clear the way for expansion of the bridgehead.

For his actions, Captain Donald Albert Pearce was awarded the Military Cross.

On the night of 24 March 1945 at Speldrop Germany, the Highland Light Infantry of Canada had been given the task of capturing the village of Speldrop. Sergeant Wilfred Francis Bunda, in command of a section of anti-tank guns, was given the task of protecting the right flank of the battalion position. The area in which Sergeant Bunda had to site his guns was under constant enemy mortar and small arms fire.

Because the roads had not been checked for mines, it was necessary for Sergeant Bunda to go on foot ahead of his guns to lead them into position. With an enemy self-propelled gun in the area, it was of the utmost importance to get the guns into position to consolidate the battalion position. Sergeant Bunda personally directed the siting and digging in of his section of guns.

By his total disregard of enemy fire and his example and leadership, the men in his gun crews were inspired to a greater effort. If it had not been for Sergeant Bunda's example and direction, the consolidation of the anti-tank defences of the battalion area would not have been accomplished in such a short time. Even when some of his men were wounded during the consolidation phase, Sergeant Bunda kept right on with the direction and leadership of his section, removing his wounded only after his task had been completed.

For his actions at Speldrop and again at Bienen the next day, Sergeant Wilfred Francis Bunda was awarded the Military Medal.

A corner in the village of Speldrop after the battle has been won
NAC, PA-190843

Major John Alexander Ferguson of The Highland Light Infantry of Canada had consistently displayed great daring, courage, outstanding initiative and devotion far beyond the normal call of duty, and at great personal danger.

During the attack on Speldrop Germany, 24 March 1945, as Support Company commander of the Highland Light Infantry of Canada, Major Ferguson, riding in his jeep, personally led supporting arms over roads unchecked for mines and subjected to sweeping enemy machine-gun and deadly mortar fire to effect immediate tank-proof consolidation of the forward companies against an expected counter-attack by enemy self-propelled guns and infantry known to be in the vicinity.

For this action at Speldrop and for his action the next day at Bienen, Major John Alexander Ferguson was awarded the Military Cross.

Bienen

It had quickly become apparent that the original plan for the employment of the 9th Canadian Infantry Brigade was no longer realistic. Instead of taking over from the 154th Brigade at Bienen, the Canadians would now have to fight their way forward to capture the village themselves. Accordingly, as soon as the other two battalions of the brigade crossed the Rhine, they were ordered into battle.

Unfortunately, as the Canadians were moving across the Rhine, units of the 15th Panzer Grenadier Division was also moving towards Bienen. As soon as the German High Command had confirmed that Montgomery had launched his offensive, the German strategic reserve was ordered to execute what was apparently a pre-planned counter-attack converging on Rees, with one wing striking through Bienen. Held up by Allied night bombing and artillery, the 115th Panzer Grenadier Regiment did not arrive in the area until the afternoon of March 24.[8]

On the warm and sunny morning of March 25, the North Nova Scotia Highlanders launched their attack on Bienen which would become one of their most difficult battles. The main flood dyke followed a north-south line to the west of the village, providing good cover to get closer to the village, although 800 yards of flat open country would still have to be crossed. "A" and "B" Companies began their move along the dyke, with the intention of crossing over this obstacle when they were opposite the village and making a dash under the cover of an artillery smoke screen.

The attack began to go wrong very quickly. Because the Glens had not yet taken their objective to the west, the North Nova companies came under machine-gun, mortar and sniper fire before they reached their Start Line. They were then hit by a continuous hail of machine-gun fire as they crossed the top of the dyke. Heavy casualties disrupted the platoons and these were pinned down, isolated from one another.

The reserve companies, "C" and "D" were ordered to go forward at 1430 hours accompanied by tanks and Wasps, with a renewed effort by the artillery to cover them with smoke. These companies managed to reach the edge of Bienen, but only after losing many men which forced "C" Company to reorganize on a two-platoon basis. The North Novas in the village began to fight their way from house to house, supported by tanks. The War Diary reported that "in spite of heavy pounding given them by supporting weapons, [the enemy] were determined not to yield." German self-propelled guns entered the town at dusk and an armoured battle erupted between them and the supporting Sherman tanks.

With the North Novas stretched to their limits, Brigadier Rockingham decided to commit the Highland Light Infantry, which had just cleared Speldrop, to reinforce the attack in Bienen. "A" and "C" Companies of the Highland Light Infantry moved through the forward units of the North Novas at 2300 hours that night and they too met bitter resistance. However, they fought though the night and, at first light, the remaining two companies of the HLI were also committed. This added strength finally secured the final objectives ending the battle for Bienen.

As Will Bird later wrote:

> The fight for Bienen was one of the hardest the North Novas experienced. During the whole operation, the excellent support of the guns were never able entirely to dampen the enemy machine-gun fire. The Germans realized the importance of the position and held on with annoying tenacity . . .[9]

On 25 March 1945, when commanding "C" Company, North Nova Scotia Highlanders, Major Lloyd Christian Winhold showed leadership and bravery of a very high order which influenced the capture of Bienen Germany, a vital position in the Rees bridgehead of the River Rhine.

The village of Bienen, which had been attacked four times before "C" Company's attempt, constituted a key to the perimeter of the Rees bridgehead. It provided the only exit from the western part of the bridgehead and was very strongly held. The initial assault by "C" Company was made over about five hundred yards of open ground. A large number of casualties, including the platoon commander and sergeant of Number 14 Platoon, were sustained from machine-gun and mortar fire. Many times, while passing through this devastating fire, Major Winhold, with entire disregard for his personal safety, climbed on one of the tanks supporting the attack, in order to direct its fire.

After the first platoon had crossed the open ground, it assaulted a strongly held house by a main road, but did not have enough remaining strength to capture it. The commander and sergeant of Number 15 Platoon were also wounded. Major Win-

hold personally reorganized the platoon and led the assault successfully through withering fire coming from the front and both flanks. He immediately proceeded to reorganize his depleted company into two platoons and deployed them.

Major Winhold then directed a new attack into the main enemy defences in Bienen, from an exposed position. Each platoon started on a separate axis and he personally led one of them. After proceeding some distance, the area was counter-attacked by three enemy self-propelled guns and a strong body of infantry. It was getting dark so he moved around in the area of the enemy self-propelled guns, forming a firm line onto which he withdrew his leading section, and successfully repulsed the enemy attack. When the reorganization was progressing, he again climbed onto one of the tanks and directed its fire in the darkness during the whole of the armoured fire fight, in which one of his supporting tanks and one of the enemy self-propelled guns were knocked out. The remaining two enemy guns then withdrew.

The inspired leadership and great personal bravery exhibited by Major Win-hold were the means whereby this very strong enemy position was cleared for the further operations of XXX British Corps in the western part of the Rees bridge-head. His conduct during the whole six hours of the operation was beyond praise.

For his actions, Major Lloyd Christian Winhold was awarded the Distinguished Service Order.

Lieutenant William Myers, "C" Company, North Nova Scotia Highlanders, on 25 March 1945, led Number 15 Platoon at Bienen Germany with such un-flinching courage that it penetrated the strong outer defences of the village, ena-bling the follow-up force to get into the village and break through.

The village of Bienen Germany was located at the bottleneck of the western part of XXX British Corps bridgehead across the Rhine River. Several unsuc-cessful attempts had been made to capture Bienen. "C" Company, with Number 15 Platoon leading, launched its attack on the main crossroads at the south edge of the village. The approach was over open ground for about five hundred yards and, from the outset, the platoon came under extremely heavy machine-gun fire from the edge of the village and suffered heavy casualties. Lieutenant Myers led his platoon with such bravery that, although there were only eight men remaining in the platoon, they reached the edge of their objective.

At this point, the platoon was under fire from both flanks and from a strongly held house across the road. Under this fierce machine-gun fire, Lieutenant Myers organized an assault with his remaining men and led them across the road, at-tacking the house and neutralizing the fire from the flanks.

Although he was so seriously wounded himself as to be completely paralysed, his inspired leadership and example had been such that the objective was reached, assisting the following platoons to capture their objectives. This main crossroads was vital to the defence of Bienen. Its capture enabled following troops to seize the village and others to break out of the western part of the Rhine River bridgehead.

In this vital action, Lieutenant Myers' leadership and bravery were of the highest order. He inspired all about him with his fine example.

For his actions, Lieutenant William Myers was awarded the Military Cross.

Sergeant Joseph Prokopchuk came to The North Nova Scotia Highlanders as a private in August 1944. He was put in Number 14 Platoon, "C" Company, and fought with this platoon through all their actions until March 1945 when he was made platoon sergeant. In the attack on Beinen, March 25, Sergeant Prokopchuk led his platoon with great courage and with no regard for personal safety until evacuated with wounds in both legs.

"C" Company was ordered to attack Bienen Germany, a vital position in the Rees bridgehead of the River Rhine. One battalion had already failed in this and two previous company attacks by this battalion had also failed. It was very heavily held by paratroops, with numerous machine-guns, mortars and self-propelled guns and, as happened with previous attacks, the company came under very heavy fire and sustained many casualties. This included Sergeant Prokopchuk, who was wounded in both legs. Not being able to continue leading his platoon, this non-commissioned officer started to evacuate other wounded soldiers and, in spite of continued heavy fire and great pain, he evacuated twelve casualties personally until too weak to do any more. He was then evacuated himself.

This man's great personal bravery and unselfish devotion to duty were the means of saving the lives of several men and his conduct, all the way throughout the entire campaign, was of the highest order.

For his actions, Sergeant Joseph Prokopchuk was awarded the Military Medal.

Sergeant George Stewart, "C" Company, North Nova Scotia Highlanders, was a platoon sergeant of Number 13 Platoon during the company's attack on Bienen Germany, an enemy strongpoint holding up the advance on the left flank of XXX British Corps across the Rhine River on 25 March 1945.

In order to break into the southwest outer defences of Bienen Germany, "C" Company made an assault across five hundred yards of open flat ground, devoid of any cover. For the entire distance, the whole Company came under intense enemy machine-gun fire from the town itself which, although it did not stop the advance, caused many casualties. Sergeant Stewart spotted a number of enemy machine-gun positions on the left flank of the advance and, entirely on his own initiative, took one of his sections, leading it straight toward the enemy. He then placed it in a fire position from which its fire neutralised a number of these machine-gun posts. By doing so, he reduced the intensity of the enemy fire considerably, thus saving many lives and enabling the company to reach the outskirts of the town in sufficient strength to destroy the outer defences. Sergeant Stewart, having placed his fire section, moved forward along across the bullet-swept field and rejoined his platoon.

On arriving at the edge of the town, the company, owing to casualties, had to reorganize on a two-platoon basis. There was only one officer left and Sergeant Stewart was the only sergeant. He was placed in command of Number 13 Platoon. When the company proceeded with the clearing of the town, Sergeant Stewart showed great skill in handling his platoon. The job of house clearing was almost completed when an enemy counter-attack of infantry supported by armour made it necessary for "C" Company to move back slightly to a firm position. By means of Sergeant Stewart's inspiring coolness, sound tactics and excellent fighting spirit, his platoon held the counter-attack and forced the enemy to retire.

For his actions, Sergeant George Stewart was awarded the Military Medal.

Private Gordon Francis Scott, "C" Company, North Nova Scotia Highlanders, was a platoon stretcher bearer in the Company's attack on Bienen Germany, an enemy strongpoint on the left flank of XXX British Corps bridgehead across the Rhine River on 25 March 1945.

During the assault on the southwest outer defences of Bienen, the entire company had to move across five hundred yards of flat open cultivated ground, all of which was swept by devastating machine-gun fire from positions situated approximately three hundred and fifty yards on the left flank of the assault.

Over thirty men, including two other stretcher bearers, were hit during the first five minutes. Private Scott accompanied his platoon across the field and carried on giving first aid to the wounded even though he saw the other two stretcher bearers shot and killed while performing their duties.

Noticing that the company's ambulance jeep would not be able to evacuate all the stretcher cases in sufficient time to save their lives, he ran back to the Forming Up Place in search of another jeep. Finding one unattended, and being unable to locate the driver of the jeep, he drove it out to the middle of the bullet-swept field and, with complete disregard for his own safety, evacuated the wounded. He made the trip time and time again, and was instrumental in saving the lives of several seriously wounded men.

The initiative and courage shown by Private Scott in his devotion to duty are of the highest order.

For his actions, Private Gordon Francis Scott was awarded the Military Medal.

Company Sergeant Major Harry Jardine Bishop, "D" Company, North Nova Scotia Highlanders, exhibited a high degree of devotion to duty, personal bravery and inspired confidence during the company's attack on Bienen Germany, an enemy strongpoint on the left flank of XXX British Corps bridgehead across the Rhine River on 25 March 1945.

"D" Company attacked this strongly held position on the left flank of "C" Company and the company commander was seriously wounded in the first few minutes of action. Upon hearing that his company commander was wounded,

Company Sergeant Major Bishop immediately went forward across the open ground under intense enemy machine-gun fire. The forward platoons were out of communication with company headquarters and with each other. Company Sergeant Major Bishop contacted both platoons and coordinated the company's effort until it was firm on the first part of its objective. While doing this, he was hit in the shoulder by shrapnel but he refused to have his wounds attended until "D" Company came under command of "B" Company some six hours later.

As soon as the company was firm on the first part of its objective, Company Sergeant Major Bishop organized the evacuation of casualties, personally directing the removal of the more seriously wounded men. He stayed in the field directing these operations even though the machine-gun fire had not been stopped. Time and time again, he crossed the open ground, regrouping his men and keeping in communication with the command post.

By his daring conduct and inspiring actions during this operation, Company Sergeant Major Bishop was responsible to a very great extent for the successful company consolidation and holding of the first part of the objectives. His fine example of leadership and bravery was unsurpassed.

For his actions, Company Sergeant Major Harry Jardine Bishop was awarded the Military Medal.

On 25 March 1945, during the attack on Bienen Germany, Private Daniel Isaac Shanks, "D" Company, North Nova Scotia Highlanders, showed utter contempt for withering enemy fire, discharged his duties as senior stretcher bearer with such complete disregard for his own personal safety, that everyone was inspired by the bravery and self-sacrifice of this soldier.

"D" Company encountered extremely heavy fire at the opening phase of the attack. Severe machine-gun and small arms fire swept the high winter dyke which flanked the western part of Bienen. Private Shanks made a total of fourteen trips with his jeep along and over this dyke in direct view of the enemy. All but two of these trips were alone.

At the height of this fierce battle, Private Shanks realized that only one company stretcher bearer remained unwounded. He crossed the bullet-swept dyke on foot and organized volunteer stretcher parties from Support Company personnel. This brave soldier led them into the battle and set them to work with the greatest speed and efficiency. He continued to assist the regimental medical officer dressing the wounded long after his normal duties had ceased.

The complete disregard for his own personal safety and outstanding display of initiative and bravery shown by Private Shanks resulted in the evacuation of a large number of badly wounded soldiers to safety and medical aid. This soldier undoubtedly saved very many of his comrades' lives.

For his actions, Private Daniel Isaac Shanks was awarded the Military Medal. Private Shanks was later wounded in action on April 8 during the attack to cross the Schipbeek Canal in Holland.

When The Highland Light Infantry of Canada moved up to continue the attack at Bienen, they found the enemy's determination had not weakened at all.

> Progress was slow as the enemy fought like madmen. Isolated houses had to be cleared and proved most difficult. The enemy artillery and mortars poured shells into our troops continually. Again, single paratroopers made suicidal charges at our advancing troops. They were consistently chopped down but sometimes not before they had inflicted casualties on our sections.[10]

On 25 March 1945, Sergeant Frederick James Jarman, platoon sergeant in Number 13 Platoon, "C" Company, The Highland Light Infantry of Canada, displayed outstanding courage and devotion to duty.

The Highland Light Infantry of Canada had been ordered to capture Bienen Germany, a town and road centre which was blocking expansion of the 51st Highland Division bridgehead north of the Rhine. "C" Company was ordered to clear the east half of the town, and Number 13 Platoon to clear a strongly defended group of buildings. Sergeant Jarman as in command of Number 13 Platoon.

During the approach to the first buildings on its objective, 13 Platoon was subjected to heavy machine-gun and small arms fire from the buildings, and Sergeant Jarman was wounded in the head and arm. Completely ignoring his wounds, he continued to lead his men until the platoon was firmly established in the buildings. He then returned to company headquarters where his wounds were dressed, and he was told he would be evacuated immediately.

Sergeant Jarman, realizing that his platoon had no officer or sergeant, insisted upon returning to his platoon. He organized the platoon and once more led it in the attack on his final objective. The attack was successful, but the position was subjected to heavy small arms fire at close range. Sergeant Jarman refused to leave his platoon until his objective was completely consolidated and another platoon had passed through.

Sergeant Jarman's courage and great devotion to duty were an inspiration to his men, and were responsible for the success of the platoon and company battle.

For his actions, Sergeant Frederick James Jarman was awarded the Military Medal.

At Bienen Germany, during the night of 25/26 March 1945, when anti-tank guns moving up on consolidation were obstructed by a road-block, Major John Alexander Ferguson, commander of Support Company, The Highland Light Infantry of Canada, personally supervised the laborious manhandling of these weapons around the road-block while under heavy mortar fire. Though wounded, he remained on duty throughout, successfully navigating the road-block and delivering the guns to the companies.

This same night, Major Ferguson, with utter disregard for his own personal safety, moved on foot ahead of supporting self-propelled anti-tank guns and guided them to company areas through the constant crump of enemy shells and the debris of the town as yet only partially cleared of enemy. This action enabled the guns to be in position by first light when they knocked out an enemy self-propelled gun which was denying the use of the main road and preventing the further advance along this axis of the lead battalion of another brigade awaiting to pass through.

This officer's superb courage and devotion to duty have been an inspiration to all, and his unceasing efforts to ensure that supporting arms are moved forward on the heels of the attacking infantry greatly assisted the forward troops to consolidate their positions against enemy counter-attacks.

For his actions at Bienen and earlier at Speldrop, Major John Alexander Ferguson received the Military Cross. Major Ferguson was wounded on March 26 but remained on duty.

On 26 March 1945, The Highland Light Infantry of Canada had just completed the capture of Bienen Germany, and an entrenchment and anti-tank ditch about one thousand yards north of the town. Enemy self-propelled guns and tanks had been encountered during the battle, and Sergeant Wilfred Francis Bunda, in command of a section of anti-tank guns, was ordered to site his section to cover the entrenchment and anti-tank ditch areas. The route up to the position was under enemy observation and small arms fire from the right flank. The section of guns led by Sergeant Bunda proceeded up a route which was known to be mined and encountered a road-block. Here they came under heavy enemy mortar and machine-gun fire. The block was at a defile, and the guns had to be uncoupled and manhandled to turn them around.

Sergeant Bunda, knowing that his guns must be sited immediately, ignored the heavy enemy fire, dismounted from his carrier, and coolly directed the extrication of his guns by manhandling. An alternative route was found and Sergeant Bunda led his section to their destination. Here they were once more under observation and were immediately subjected to mortar and machine-gun fire.

Sergeant Bunda, again completely ignoring his own personal safety, moved freely about in the open ground, direction the siting and digging in of his guns, and reorganizing one gun crew which had been decimated by enemy fire. He was to be seen everywhere, inspiring confidence and encouraging his men.

By his superb example and his great devotion to duty, Sergeant Bunda successfully completed the consolidation of the battalion's anti-tank defences. This consolidation was necessary to complete the brigade task of protecting the Rhine bridgehead against imminent enemy armoured counter-attack.

During the continuous fighting from D-Day onwards, Sergeant Bunda displayed personal courage and leadership in all active operations, thereby assisting the battalion to consolidate its objectives early and strongly.

For his actions both at Bienen and at Speldrop, as well as continually since D-Day, Sergeant Wilfred Francis Bunda was awarded the Military Medal.

Grietherbusch

Early on March 24, The Stormont, Dundas and Glengarry Highlanders crossed the Rhine and, that evening, relieved the front-line Scottish troops to be "in the unique position of being on the left of the whole Allied advance." The next day, while the initial attacks by the North Novas were launched on Bienen, the Glens advanced to clear that flank of the isthmus, where the German defences centred on Grietherbusch. The battalion was held up initially in its attack by fortified houses and entrenchments. However, by nightfall, it had taken all objectives.

At Grietherbusch in the Rhine bridgehead on 25 March 1945, Captain John Alexander Dure, Acting "D" Company commander of The Stormont, Dundas and Glengarry Highlanders, did so brilliantly and daringly lead his Company as to overrun an enemy stronghold and thereby secure the left flank of the 9th Canadian Infantry Brigade.

After crossing the Rhine on 24 March 1945, the Stormont, Dundas and Glengarry Highlanders were assigned the task of securing and holding the left flank of the 9th Canadian Infantry Brigade. "D" Company was to assault and capture Grietherbusch, a vital link in the enemy defence line and a menace to the Allied bridgehead. Grietherbusch was strongly held by the enemy with infantry, well–positioned medium machine-guns and four mortars. Captain Dure launched his attack in the face of intense fire from the enemy dug-in positions. Due to the terrific firepower of the enemy, the leading platoon was pinned down. Captain Dure immediately, and with complete disregard for his own safety, worked his way forward, ordered the leading platoon to support him with fire, and personally led the remainder of the company in an assault on the enemy's left flank. Cover was inadequate and fire was brought to bear on Captain Dure from both Grietherbusch in front, and from Grietherorth, an enemy–defended locality one thousand yards to his left flank. Undaunted, Captain Dure continued the advance, his exceptional courage an example that was followed by his men, and the enemy position was captured. Severe casualties were inflicted on the enemy. Fourteen Germans were killed and twenty-two taken prisoner. All medium machine-guns and mortars were destroyed.

It was due to Captain Dure's magnificent leadership, personal bravery and steadiness under fire that "D" Company of The Stormont, Dundas and Glengarry Highlanders was able to capture Grietherbusch and thereby ensure the safety of the left flank of the 9th Canadian Infantry Brigade.

For his action, Captain John Alexander Dure was awarded the Military Cross.

On 25 March 1945 on the consolidation of the Rhine bridgehead at Tillhaus, Corporal Clifford John Handley, section commander of The Stormont, Dundas and Glengarry Highlanders, took over command of his platoon when his platoon commander and platoon sergeant became casualties. He continued the advance and captured the company objective, thereby securing the battalion's left flank.

The Stormont, Dundas and Glengarry Highlanders were assigned the task of securing the left flank of the 9th Canadian Infantry Brigade after crossing the Rhine River. Tillhaus was an enemy strongpoint menacing the left flank of the battalion. "B" Company attacked this strongpoint and the leading platoon, of which Corporal Handley was section commander, was subjected to intense and accurate machine-gun and mortar fire. The platoon commander and platoon sergeant were wounded and the leading section pinned down.

Corporal Handley, without hesitation and in the face of heavy observed fire, went forward alone to read the battle, and discovered that the leading section had all become casualties with the exception of one man. Corporal Handley then sent for a troop of tanks and a section of flame throwers, and personally led this battle group towards the objective. His well-planned attack was completely successful and it overran the heavily defended enemy stronghold, destroyed the defenders by flame and bullet. A colonel of the 6th Paratroop Division and his adjutant were taken prisoner. No enemy escaped.

Through Corporal Handley's quick appreciation, prompt action and personal bravery, Tillhaus, a vital link in the enemy defence line, was captured and the left flank of the 9th Canadian Infantry Brigade secured.

For his action, Corporal Clifford John Handley was awarded the Military Medal. Corporal Handley was wounded in action four days later, on March 29.

Lance Sergeant Alvin Clifford Dolan, commanding Number 2 Flame Section of the Carrier Platoon of The Stormont, Dundas and Glengarry Highlanders, during the battle for the Rhine bridgehead on 25 March 1945, showed such gallantry, exceptional leadership and promptness of action as to be largely responsible for the success of "B" Company's attack on the Tillhaus strongpoint north of Grietherbusch Germany.

Lance Sergeant Dolan was supporting "B" Company of The Stormont, Dundas and Glengarry Highlanders on to Tillhaus, the final battalion objective and the regimental headquarters of the enemy garrison. Five hundred yards from the strongpoint, the enemy opened fire with heavy and medium machine-guns. Several casualties were inflicted on "B" Company, including the company commander. "B" Company was forced to ground and unable to advance through this withering fire. Sensing the seriousness of the situation, and with complete disregard for the safety of himself or his section, Lance Sergeant Dolan signalled his flame crews forward. Without any covering fire, he led his carriers forward to the strongpoint, flushing the enemy fortifications and trench systems with flame and chasing the defences screaming from their hide-outs. This bold action allowed "B" Company of the Stormont, Dundas and Glengarry Highlanders, to advance and mop up Tillhaus. A score of enemy were killed and wounded. Among the prisoners taken were the lieutenant colonel and adjutant of the German garrison.

Through the gallant and determined action of Lance Sergeant Dolan, "B" Company of The Stormont, Dundas and Glengarry Highlanders was able to quickly capture and consolidate on the forward battalion objective which was on the extreme left flank of the Rhine bridgehead.

For his action, Lance Sergeant Alvin Clifford Dolan was awarded the Military Medal.

On the afternoon of 25 March 1945, during the consolidation of the bridge-head across the Rhine River at Rees, Private James Allan Whitacre of Number 10 Platoon, "B" Company, The Stormont, Dundas and Glengarry Highland-ers, by his outstanding bravery, extricated his platoon from a position of extreme danger and strongly influenced the capture of the command post of the German 6th Paratroop Battalion.

Private Whitacre's platoon had been assigned the task of taking a fortified house on the outskirts of Grietherbusch. Surrounding the house were trenches and machine-gun emplacements, and the windows of the house were loopholed. The en-emy manning the defences resisted stubbornly.

As Private Whitacre's section advanced onto its objective, it came under in-tense machine-gun fire from concealed flanking positions, as well as from its objec-tive, and was pinned down. Another section of Number 10 Platoon was brought up and came under the same fire. It was forced to ground with heavy casualties. Private Whitacre courageously faced the machine-gun fire, exposed himself in or-der to return to his company for tanks to assist in overcoming the strongpoint. Reaching his headquarters, he immediately obtained the tanks and once again showed extreme bravery by guiding them to his platoon position under heavy ma-chine-gun fire. Despite this fire, he gathered two men from his pinned-down sec-tion and bravely assaulted the strongpoint. The fanatical enemy resistance was overcome by this determined attack and the strongpoint was captured. The pris-oners taken included the colonel of the battalion and the adjutant.

During the whole of this action, Private Whitacre displayed courage, devotion and initiative far beyond the call of duty. His efforts contributed largely to the capture of this most important strongpoint.

For his action, Private James Allan Whitacre was awarded the Military Medal. Private Whitacre was later wounded in action in April.

Brigadier John Meredith Rockingham, with his 9th Canadian Infantry Bri-gade, was under command of the 51st (Highland) Division for the assault cross-ing of the Rhine at Rees on 23 March 1945. The role of the brigade was to pass through a brigade of the 51st (Highland) Division which was to capture the vil-lages of Speldrop and Bienen, and to expand the bridgehead to the north-west.

Elite German paratroops, skilfully led, provided stiff opposition to the assault and follow-up, and only the outskirts of Speldrop and Bienen had been reached by 1730 hours on March 24 when Brigadier Rockingham was ordered to take over the battle with his brigade.

From the first, this officer demonstrated outstanding qualities of leadership, skill and personal courage under fire, which have characterized his command throughout the hard fighting in Normandy, Belgium and Holland.

He spurred on his battalions in valorous attacks on heavily fortified positions. Speldrop fell that night. Bienen was only taken on March 25 after Brigadier Rockingham, in view of the enemy and under heavy fire, made a fresh appreciation and realigned his attacking units. Then, with an additional infantry battalion placed under command, thirty-six hours of the heaviest type of close infantry fighting followed against a fanatic enemy.

Largely through the unceasing day and night personal direction of Brigadier Rockingham, by March 26, the 9th Canadian Infantry Brigade had captured the villages of Speldrop, Grietherbusch, Bienen, Millingen and Praest; effected a heavy toll of enemy dead and wounded; captured over five hundred prisoners; and expanded the bridgehead to the north-west.

For his actions, Brigadier John Meredith Rockingham was awarded a Bar to the Distinguished Service Order.

Brigadier J. M. Rockingham, who was awarded the Bar to the Distinguished Service Order for his actions in the Rhine bridgehead, conferring with officers of the 9th Canadian Infantry Brigade and the Royal Canadian Engineers.
Donald I. Grant, NAC, PA-130232.

On the night of March 25/26, despite the fierce fighting that continued, the Rhine bridgehead had been secured. W. Boss would recall the conclusion of that night because of the:

tremendous artillery activity. The whole horizon was lit by the continuous flashes of guns, and rockets, too, could be occasionally seen. Indicative of the superb artillery support given it may be said that units of the Royal Canadian Artillery fired until their guns were too hot for further action.[12]

NOTES

1. National Archives of Canada Record Group (RG) 24, Vol 15123, North Novas Scotia Highlanders War Diary, April 1945.

2. RG 24, Vol 15041, 1 Bn, The Canadian Scottish War Diary, March 1945, "3 CID Intelligence Summary No. 87," dated 12 March 1945.

3. Will R. Bird, *No Retreating Footsteps* (Kentville: Kentville Publishing), p. 338.

4. Col C. P. Stacey, *The Victory Campaign* (Ottawa: The Queen's Printer, 1966), p. 534; Jack Bartlett, 1st Battalion, The Highland Light Infantry of Canada: 1940 - 1945 (Galt: The Highland Light Infantry Association, 1951), p. 97.

5. RG 24, Vol. 15123, North NS Hghlrs W.D., March 1945, "51st Highland Division Planning Intelligence Note No. 1," dated 18 March 1945; Bird, p. 338.

6. Bartlett, p. 98.

7. RG 24, Vol 15077 HLI W.D., March 25, 1945.

8. RG 24, Vol 15041, 1 C Scot W.D., March 1945, "3 CID Intelligence Summary No. 90,"dated 26 March, 1945.

9. Bird, p. 351.

10. RG 24, Vol 15077, HLI W.D., March 26, 1945.

11. Lt Col W. Boss, *The Stormont, Dundas and Glengarry Highlanders: 1783 - 1951* (Ottawa: Runge Press, 1952), p. 251.

12. Boss, p. 253.

-9-
RHINE BREAK–OUT

By the morning of March 26, the Rhine bridgehead had been firmly established. However, the 9th Canadian Infantry Brigade had run head on into units of the 15th Panzer Grenadier and 6th Paratroop Divisions which, despite their reduced strength, were the best German units on the Western Front. It would take the heaviest hand-to-hand fighting to expand the left flank of the bridgehead and, ultimately, break out.

The first task of the First Canadian Army was to extend the Rhine bridgehead westward by capturing the town of Emmerich where a major supply bridge could be built. Rather than attack the town frontally, across the river, the 7th Brigade of the 3rd Division would advance through the 9th Brigade, along the east river bank to attack Emmerich from the rear.

The North Nova Scotia Highlanders and Highland Light Infantry of Canada had finally broken the resistance in the village of Bienen itself. However, the violent resistance had thrown the original plan off schedule and it was necessary to bring up the North Shore Regiment from the 8th Brigade to reinforce the advance north of Bienen, to clear the way to Emmerich.

The North Shore Regiment began their advance at noon on March 26 with "A" and "B" Companies leading, crossing 1500 yards of level ground without any cover. Their objective was Millingen, a village on the main railway line between Emmerich and Wesel. Its capture would open up the neck of the narrow isthmus which was hindering the expansion of the left flank of the bridgehead. The defenders consisted of 600 paratroops supported by self-propelled guns and tanks. Despite continuous mortar and artillery fire directed against them, the North Shores managed to advance and clear the village, house-by-house.

On 26 March 1945, The North Shore (New Brunswick) Regiment was ordered to take the town of Millingen where the enemy made a determined stand to prevent the enlargement of the bridgehead across the Rhine. The main axis of advance of the unit was along the main road from Bienen to Millingen. Three companies advanced along the road with support of tanks and an artillery barrage, while one company advanced on the left flank.

Captain Harry Lorne Hamley commanded "B" Company which advanced along the left flank. As they advanced, they came under direct machine-gun fire which originated from some buildings off to the left flank. The clearing of these buildings on the extreme left of the area was not included in the original plan of the attack, but the enemy fire from these positions was so devastating that Captain Hamley quickly appreciated that the main advance of the battalion would be held up. He immediately regrouped his company. The flexibility of his plan and the skill of his manoeuvres resulted in the destruction of the enemy in these positions.

On one occasion, the leading elements of the company came under particularly intense machine-gun and mortar fire. Captain Hamley personally led his men in on the attack and, as they approached the defended group of houses, they encountered numerous shots from enemy Panzerfausts which caused the company to hesitate. However, this officer, through his courageous leadership and cool thinking, rallied his men in time to continue the attack which destroyed or captured the enemy within the buildings.

By this time, the company had moved considerably off its original axis and were in danger of being cut off. Captain Hamley, with great skill, fought his way back to the original axis of advance and, at the same time, destroyed the enemy positions which were holding up the advance of the battalion.

This officer, by his personal leadership and cool decisive actions, inspired his officers, non-commissioned officers and men to overcome the fanatical enemy resistance. His efforts contributed greatly to the success of the battalion which permitted the continued advance of a division.

For his actions, Captain Harry Lorne Hamley was awarded the Military Cross. Captain Hamley was later wounded in action on April 5 at Zutphen Holland.

On 26 March 1945, The North Shore (New Brunswick) Regiment was ordered to take the town of Millingen which was held by the enemy in considerable force and which prevented the enlargement of the bridgehead across the Rhine. "B" Company was ordered to clear the left flank of the main axis of advance. The enemy had set up a strongly defended locality in some buildings from which they were able to sweep the main axis with accurate and direct machine-gun fire.

Corporal Reginald Alastar Shepherd, section leader of Number 4 Platoon of "B" Company, was advancing with his section when his company was pinned down by severe machine-gun fire. Corporal Shepherd quickly appreciated the situation and pin-pointed the enemy fire as coming from a house on his flank. He manoeuvred his section of six men, under direct fire, across open and difficult ground with great skill and daring. Once in position, he led his section in an assault against the strongly defended house. After a fierce fight, he and his section captured four enemy machine-guns and twenty-three prisoners. Corporal Shepherd, by quick thinking and determination, took out the last machine-gun position single-handedly. Once the house had been cleared, "B" Company was able to continue to advance and to clear out the rest of the enemy positions, which were delaying the main advance of the battalion.

The initiative, skill and courage of this non-commissioned officer provided inspired leadership to his men. His undaunted efforts destroyed the enemy stronghold, thus permitting the advance of his company and, in turn, allowing the battalion to advance on its objective.

For his action, Corporal Reginald Alastar Shepherd was awarded the Military Medal. Corporal Shepherd was later killed in action on April 5 at Zutphen Holland.

During the attack on Millingen on the 26th of March 1945, Sergeant Joseph Lawrence Hennigar was platoon sergeant of the leading platoon in "C" Company. His platoon was heavily shelled on the Start Line and suffered casualties, but this non-commissioned officer very coolly went among the sections, showing complete disregard for his own safety.

The platoon objective having been taken, the company came under murderous machine-gun fire from houses to the front and had to take cover in trenches which had just been cleared. Sergeant Hennigar, to obtain a field of fire, had to move into the open and, in this exposed position, by his daring action and accurate fire, caused the enemy fire to become greatly reduced. At this moment, an enemy tank appeared from around the corner of one of the houses and opened fire on the platoon position. Sergeant Hennigar immediately secured a PIAT and, with a well-directed bomb, forced the enemy tank to retire.

During the action, this non-commissioned officer also used the PIAT on a fortified house which the enemy were defending with determination, and forced the remaining ten German soldiers to surrender after two direct hits on the house.

The cool determination and bravery of this non-commissioned officer, in the face of heavy odds, allowed the rest of the company to get on to their objective, which was a vital point in the enemy's defences and was holding up the advance of the rest of the company. Sergeant Hennigar was a tower of strength to his platoon and company, and contributed greatly to the success of the operation.

For his actions, Sergeant Joseph Lawrence Hennigar was awarded the Military Medal. Sergeant Hennigar was later wounded in action on April 23.

Even though the North Shores won their battle that day, tragedy struck. Just prior to the start of the attack, a German artillery barrage came down, killing their commanding officer, Lieutenant-Colonel John Rowley who had been awarded the Distinguished Service Order at Keppeln. Padre Hickey later wrote:

> Unable to contact the Highland Light Infantry by wireless . . .
> he started off over open country to contact them himself. He
> leaped up on one of our tanks that was passing and, as he did,
> a German shell picked him off. In that moment, the regiment
> lost one of the greatest men it ever had.[1]

On the morning of the March 26, The Stormont, Dundas and Glengarry Highlanders also attacked, passing through the forward positions of the HLI and pushing northward. "A" Company managed to advance as far as one thousand yards in front of the battalion.[2]

On the night of 26 March 1945, during the battle of the Rhine bridgehead in the Rees sector northwest of Bienen Germany, Major James Wallace Braden, "A" Company of the Stormont, Dundas and Glengarry Highlanders, by his cool efficiency and resourcefulness, disrupted and finally defeated a powerful armoured and infantry counter-attack which threatened the entire left sector of the Rhine bridgehead.

Major Braden's company had attacked northwest out of Bienen and secured positions in the battalion forward area, with his company some one thousand yards in front of the battalion. Having successfully completed his attack, Major Braden was checking the consolidation of his forward platoon when the enemy launched a counter-attack in strength supported by five Tiger tanks. Heavy artillery fire was required urgently and the forward artillery officer had been killed. Major Braden then personally directed the artillery fire against the enemy force which was now within the perimeter of his company defences with steady coolness and great skill. A the same time, he organized his company and controlled their movement to repel the infantry counter-attack.

Major Braden then concentrated his efforts on the tanks. Round after round fell among them, causing great confusion. The fire which Major Braden directed was so intense and so accurate, his control of his company so secure and complete, that the entire German force was compelled to retreat, badly damaged and depleted, too weak to launch another attack.

Major Braden's resourcefulness, his sure and steady anticipation and appreciation of the enemy's intention and action, and his inspiring example of coolness and determination were the principal factors which defeated the enemy in this vital action. It allowed the assembling of break-out forces to continue east of the Rhine without interruption or impediment.

For his actions, Major James Wallace Braden was awarded the Distinguished Service Order.

The German forces defending the line of the Rhine River were now so weak that they could no longer hold a coherent line. The 15th Panzer Grenadier Division was pulled out of the area to try to plug holes opening up further south. The German defence now pulled back to concentrate at Emmerich, where fresh units of the 346th Infantry Division from Holland had arrived. This division was considered one of the last first-grade divisions left in the West.[3]

The Canadian Scottish Regiment of the 7th Canadian Infantry Brigade began moving into the outskirts of Emmerich on the night of March 28. As described by Col C. P. Stacey:

> Emmerich, which had a normal population of about 16,000, had been heavily bombed and was "completely devastated except for one street along which a few buildings were more or less intact." (When the 1st Canadian Division passed through

Emmerich nine days later it recorded that "only Cassino in Italy looks worse.")[4]

Infantry of The Canadian Scottish Regiment advancing at Emmerich, Germany
Donald I. Grant, NAC, PA-137323

The Germans had made good use of the piles of rubble, sprinkling them with mines and booby-traps, and turning the cellars into strongpoints, many of these connected by holes through which small groups of defenders could move. The defenders were well supported by mortars and guns located north and northwest of the town. On March 29, The Regina Rifles joined the battle.

The heavily bombed town with road-blocks and rubble presented difficulty in keeping direction and in denying the use of close supporting arms, tanks, Crocodiles* and Wasps, so vital in an attack of this type. It was in a sense guerilla fighting. Each house had to be cleared as the infantry advanced, no telling which could hold snipers. The number of automatic weapons was out of proportion to what would normally be encountered. Mines proved a bug-bear, particularly the demoralizing AP** Schu-mines. . . . The enemy did have self-pro-

*   Flame-throwing tanks.

**   Anti-personnel.

pelled guns in the area that were very difficult to pinpoint and through the denial of the roads to us made our anti-tank defences quite weak till road blocks were removed and anti-tank guns brought up.[5]

On the 28th of March 1945, at Emmerich Germany, Lance Corporal Albin James Kellerman, a regimental signaller attached to "A" Company, 1st Battalion, The Canadian Scottish Regiment, displayed great personal courage and a devotion to duty which was inspiring to all ranks.

The 1st Battalion, The Canadian Scottish Regiment, was given the task of breaking through the enemy defences on the outskirts of the town in order that the town could be cleared of enemy troops. "A" Company was assigned the forward position in the initial stages of the attack. Immediately the attack had commenced, "A" Company was subjected to heavy fire from cunningly concealed mortars. Lance Corporal Kellerman, carrying his wireless set, worked his way into a position from which he could see the enemy mortars. Whilst the company commander was engaged reorganizing his men, this aggressive soldier, amidst the storm of mortar fire, and despite the efforts of German snipers to knock him out, personally directed through the medium of his wireless set the counter-mortar fire onto the enemy positions. His complete disregard for his own safety and his resourceful initiative were undoubtedly instrumental in disrupting the enemy's defensive plan, thus making possible the company's advance to the final objective.

Lance Corporal Kellerman's bravery and offensive zeal were an inspiration to all ranks of his company and contributed in no small measure to the successful conclusion of the battalion's attack on this day.

For his action, Lance Corporal Albin James Kellerman was awarded the Military Medal.

Lieutenant Robert Alfred Warriner was in command of Number 2 Troop, "C" Squadron, 27th Canadian Armoured Regiment (Sherbrooke Fusilier Regiment). This troop was supporting the Canadian Scottish Regiment in their attack on Emmerich, 29 March 1945.

As he was crossing the Start Line, his own tank was put out of action by a direct hit from enemy shell fire. Without delay, he took over another tank in his Troop and carried right on with the attack. Before they had progressed very far, his sergeant's tank received a hit from an enemy self-propelled gun and brewed up.* With complete disregard for the very heavy enemy mortar fire and fire from a German machine-gun sited only thirty yards away, he immediately jumped out and pushed to rescue the crew of the burning tank. He managed to get three men out, the other two having been killed. During the rescue, he was hit twice by enemy fire. Despite his wounds in the shoulder and arm, he returned to his tank and continued the advance.

---

*   Commonly used termed meaning that a tank burst into flames.

A third tank of his troop broke down within a short time, leaving only one to support the infantry. With his one tank, he led the infantry, shooting up strongpoints on the way, until they had reached their objective. Once the objective was reached, he remained there supporting the infantry. This was done despite repeated attempts of enemy Panzerfaust teams to destroy him and in spite of the fact that he was nearly out of ammunition. The enemy counter-attacked time and time again but, with supreme courage, he held his ground until relieved by another troop of tanks from his squadron.

This display of courage and daring was a wonderful inspiration to the attacking force. Lieutenant Warriner, by grim determination and great devotion to duty, made possible the successful conclusion of this operation at Emmerich.

For his actions, Lieutenant Robert Alfred Warriner was awarded the Military Cross.

Tanks of the Sherbrooke Fusiliers moving up to assist the infantry in clearing Emmerich
Lieutenant DeGuire, NAC, PA-192258

On the 28/29th of March 1945, the Regina Rifle Regiment was responsible for clearing the outskirts of Emmerich Germany in preparation for taking the town itself. "B" Company was moving into position among a group of buildings when they came under heavy concentrations of enemy mortar and machine-gun fire from the town itself. The company had lost one of its platoon stretcher bearers and Rifleman James Donald Innes volunteered to take over the job.

As his platoon came under fire, the leading section had two very serious casualties. Without hesitation, Rifleman Innes ran forward to them in the open and attended their wounds. To reach the furthest man, it was necessary to run across an open stretch of about seventy-five yards which was "alive" with enemy mortar and small arms fire. While attending the wounded, a bomb landed, killing two of the men in the section who were trying to help him. At this time, one of our own tanks was hit and Rifleman Innes ran to the burning tank and safely rescued one of the crew who had been wounded.

Rifleman Innes, volunteering for this dangerous job at the last minute, showed superb courage in carrying out his duties and saving the lives of the wounded members of his company.

For his actions, Rifleman James Donald Innes was awarded the Military Medal.

At Emmerich Germany on the morning of the 29th of March 1945, at 1000 hours, two companies of the Regina Rifle Regiment were advancing into the town with the task of clearing and holding the eastern half of this important stronghold. "B" Company, commanded by Major Leonard Vincent McGurran was on the right, with one troop of Crocodile tanks in support.

On the advance to the town, the companies were subjected to very heavy shelling and mortaring and it required the highest standard of leadership to keep the companies advancing. Immediately on reaching the town, "B" Company came under intense small arms fire and the fighting became very confused. Although the right flank of the company was entirely open and the town was fanatically defended from prepared positions, Major McGurran maintained the impetus of the attack by his courageous and skilful leadership and daring personal liaison with all his platoons.

In the latter stages of the battle, Major McGurran was painfully wounded in several places but he refused to be evacuated until his company had gained all their objectives and completed their consolidation.

It was undoubtedly due to the courage, resourcefulness and the utter disregard of personal safety by Major McGurran that this position was taken and held.

For his actions, Major Leonard Vincent McGurran was awarded the Distinguished Service Order

At Emmerich Germany at 1000 hours on the 29th of March 1945, the Regina Rifle Regiment was ordered to clear and hold this important stronghold so that bridging operations could commence across the Rhine. On the initial attack, "D" Company, under command of Captain Herbert Sinclair Roberts, was the right reserve company, moving up behind "B" Company.

Once "B" Company gained their objective, "D" Company passed through at 1330 hours to an objective some six hundred yards further into the town. For two hours, Captain Roberts' company fought hand-to-hand in the rubble against fiercely determined enemy, killing many and taking twenty-five prisoners. In this phase of the battle, the supporting Crocodiles could not advance because of road-

blocks, but with the courageous and determined leadership of Captain Roberts, they gained and held their objective.

This position was held, despite the absence of all supporting weapons and while under constant mortaring and shelling. At 2330 hours, Captain Roberts' company was ordered to advance in conjunction with two other companies. By 0500 hours, 30th of March, the objective had been gained by continuous and bitter combat. Many times, the fearless example of Captain Roberts inspired his weary men to continue. When the objective was taken, an enemy self-propelled gun penetrated the company position and Captain Roberts personally supervised the coordination of his infantry and the anti-tank guns, which had by this time arrived, and succeeded in routing the gun which was subsequently destroyed by a flanking unit. By this time, Captain Roberts had been without sleep for forty-eight hours but, when ordered to exploit forward of the town, he skilfully planned and executed a platoon attack which suffered heavy casualties but materially aided those troops who were to follow.

The magnificent leadership, cheerfulness in the face of fatigue and constant danger, and the utter disregard of personal safety displayed by Captain Roberts was the factor which enabled his men to successfully carry out this operation which was instrumental to the attainment of the battalion's objective.

For his actions, Captain Herbert Sinclair Roberts was awarded the Military Cross.

In the operations involved in crossing the River Rhine, the 7th Canadian Infantry Brigade was to break out of the initial bridgehead and seize the town of Emmerich to enable bridges to be built for the II Canadian Corps. The task of clearing out the central portion of Emmerich was allotted to The Regina Rifle Regiment. The enemy, realizing the importance of the position, offered stubborn resistance and had built numerous road-blocks and fortified houses throughout the town.

The plan as evolved by Lieutenant Colonel Allan Stuart Gregory, and the manner in which this officer directed his battalion, resulted in at least half of the central part of the town being cleared by last light on the 29th of March 1945, the day on which the clearing had commenced. This was done despite determined opposition from infantry in prepared positions in houses supported by self-propelled guns. Lieutenant-Colonel Gregory, disregarding his own safety during the day, had positioned himself in the town despite consistent enemy shelling and sniping. During the evening, Lieutenant-Colonel Gregory quickly regrouped his battalion which was becoming fatigued at this stage after having continuously been advancing against or fighting the enemy for over forty-eight hours. The actions and energy of this officer proved to be an inspiration to the troops under his command, and the task allotted to his battalion was completed when the town was cleared by the following day. This operation, accomplished with only light casualties by our troops, contributed to the early commencement by II Canadian Corps of bridging operations across the River Rhine.

The success which The Regina Rifle Regiment achieved and the aggressive eagerness displayed by this unit may be attributed to a great extent to Lieuten-

ant-Colonel Gregory. *This officer, by his leadership, persistence, energy and cool-ness in action against the enemy, was an example to all ranks.*

For his actions, Lieutenant-Colonel Allan Stuart Gregory was awarded the Distinguished Service Order.

Lieutenant-Colonel Allan Stuart Gregory, commanding officer of The Regina Rifles, addresses his men. Lt-Col Gregory was awarded the Distinguished Service Order for his actions at Emmerich, Germany.
Ken Bell, NAC, PA-116304

Throughout the battle, German forces continued to resist stubbornly, even launching local counter-attacks.

On the morning of the 30th of March 1945 at Emmerich, Sergeant Darrow Gomez, of the 3rd Canadian Anti-Tank Regiment RCA, was the non-commis-sioned officer in charge of a 17-pounder self-propelled Valentine gun which was a part of a troop of the 105th Canadian Anti-Tank Battery in support of The Royal Winnipeg Rifles. The enemy had determinedly counter-attacked the posi-tion during the previous night and, with daylight, came the knowledge that self-propelled guns had been brought up to support these attacks. These enemy guns had assumed a most aggressive role and were rapidly rendering untenable the area occupied by a company of The Royal Winnipeg Rifles. Since they were de-ployed on the high ground and at short range, any movement on the part of our infantry was extremely hazardous.

At approximately 1100 hours, Sergeant Gomez pin-pointed the location of one enemy gun after performing a reconnaissance under intense rifle and ma-chine-gun fire. Sergeant Gomez then manoeuvred his 17-pounder Valentine gun into a favourable position and succeeded in knocking out the enemy self-propelled vehicle. Not content with this one success, he immediately commenced another reconnaissance with the commander of "D" Company of the Royal Winnipeg Rifles. After considerable time, they located the position of another enemy self-propelled gun which was pinning down an entire company of our infantry. Notwithstanding the fact that the infantry company commander was killed at his side and the driver of his own vehicle had become severely wounded, Sergeant Gomez fearlessly commenced to advance his gun to a suitable position. Although his own gun was twice hit by enemy shell fire, this non-commissioned officer attained his objective and, laying the gun himself, destroyed the enemy self-propelled gun with one round.

Shortly after this incident, a strong enemy fighting patrol attacked the position occupied by Sergeant Gomez. Although his gun was clearly exposed to this part of enemy and, at very short range, he unhesitatingly manned the machine-gun mounted on his vehicle and brought fire to bear on the infantry. One of the enemy patrol was consequently killed, seven taken prisoner and the remainder forced to retire.

Throughout these actions, Sergeant Gomez displayed magnificent leadership and absolute disregard for his own personal safety. There is no doubt that the example he set enabled our infantry, despite heavy casualties, to hold this vital area in the face of spirited enemy counter-attacks.

For his actions, Sergeant Darrow Gomez was awarded the Distinguished Conduct Medal.

On the morning of March 30, the last German strongpoint was finally taken by "A" Company of the Reginas after three Wasps flamed the buildings from end to end. Then, as the regimental historian wrote, "on good Friday, 1945, Emmerich was declared 'kaput'."

Meanwhile, on the 28th of March, II Canadian Corps Headquarters crossed the Rhine River and began operating at Bienen. By the 30th of March, both 2nd Canadian Infantry and 4th Canadian Armoured Divisions were in the bridgehead, ready for the break-out. By this time:

> the bridgehead was 35 miles wide and extended to an average depth of 20 miles. All opposition had virtually collapsed . . . Poised ready to advance into the North German plain, Montgomery had 20 divisions and 1,000 tanks, all up to strength and eager to go . . . The Battle of the Rhine was over and the way open to the Elbe and beyond.[6]

NOTES

1.   Rev. R. Myles Hickey, *The Scarlet Dawn* (Fredricton: Unipress, 1980), p. 214.

2.   Lt-Col W. Boss, *The Stormont, Dundas and Glengarry Highlanders: 1783 - 1951* (Ottawa: The Runge Press, 1952), p. 253.

3.   National Archives of Canada Record Group (RG) 24, Vol 15041, 1 Battalion, The Canadian Scottish War Diary, March 1945, "3 CID Intelligence Summary No. 91," dated 28 March, 1945.

4.   Col C. P. Stacey, *The Victory Campaign* (Ottawa: The Queen's Printer, 1966), p. 542.

5.   RG 24, Vol 15042, "The Battle for Emmerich: Battle Narrative–Regina Rifles," by Lt-Col A. Gregory.

6.   H. Essame, *The Battle for Germany* (New York: Charles Scriber's Sons), p. 185.

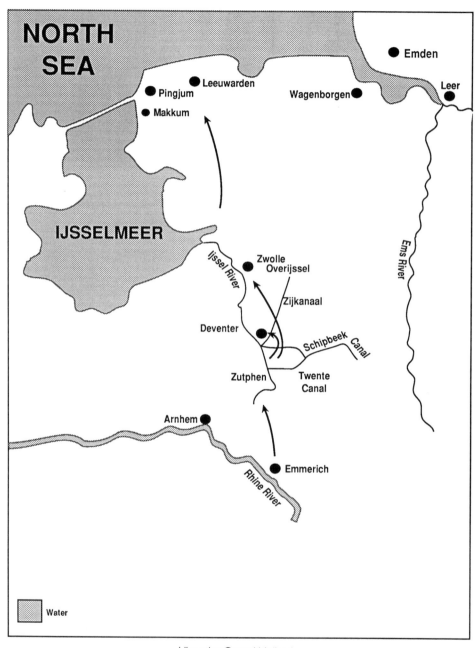

Liberating Central Holland.

-IO-
LIBERATING CENTRAL HOLLAND

Wherever we have met determined resistance during the past
few days, the enemy's fighting qualities have belied any sugges-
tion that recent disasters have diminished the German Army's
will to fight. Although the terms "hodge podge," "odds and
sods," "scrapings" etc. are accepted epithets for such an order
of battle as he now discloses on our front, the skill and fighting
spirit of individual units has been to the standard of elite
troops. Even though the soldiers are often youths from Training Centres, they are fanatical and brave.[1]

> 3 Canadian Infantry Division
> Intelligence Summary No. 95,
> 7 April 1945

On 28 March 1945, Field Marshal Montgomery declared the Battle of
the Rhine had been won and issued his orders for the next phase. While
the Second British Army advanced westwards, the First Canadian Army
would use II Canadian Corps to attack north, driving along the east bank
of the Ijssel River to cut off the remaining German forces in western Holland. After achieving this task, II Canadian Corps would clear northeast
Holland and then the German North Sea coast. In the meantime, I Canadian Corps, now having arrived from Italy, would liberate western Holland.

Allied intelligence had been watching the German forces in Holland
to see whether they would abandon that country as their forces west of
the Rhine were forced back. Looting of the Netherlands became increas-
ingly evident with a steady stream of equipment and personnel crossing
into Germany; however, the line of the Rhine River to the sea continued
to be held in strength. Furthermore, a north-south line of defence had
been constructed along the Ijssel River to hold any Allied forces which
might cross into western Holland. Civilian forced labour was employed
to construct pillboxes, especially in the area of the city of Zutphen
where the headquarters of Army Group H was located.[2]

The II Canadian Corps would break out of the Rhine bridgehead
with the 3rd Division on the left, 2nd Division in the centre, and 4th
Canadian Armoured Division on the right flank. The task of the 3rd Division was to clear the east bank of the Ijssel River with particular attention to the area between Zutphen and Deventer, which 1st Canadian

Division would then use as a base for its drive westward across the river.

The Canadian line of advance would thus outflank the German Ijssel River line, but would likely encounter resistance on the natural lines of resistance running in an east-west direction—the Twente Canal originating at Zutphen and the Schipbeek Canal starting at Deventer. The Canadians' old opponent, the German 6th Parachute Division, held this area and now pulled back to the Twente Canal, reinforced by numerous rear area units such as the 31st Reserve Parachute Regiment.[3]

The advance northwards was launched by the 9th Canadian Infantry Brigade on March 31. They met little resistance and, on April 1, the Highland Light Infantry of Canada passed through to clear the first Dutch town to be liberated, s'Heerenberg, situated only a little more than a kilometre north of Emmerich. Here, "C" Company of the HLI met resistance at an anti-tank ditch in front of the town. The ditch was bridged under fire and the advance continued against a number of strongpoints based on a large castle and a monastery.

Sergeant Peter Joseph Steinman, while serving with The Highland Light Infantry of Canada in the campaign for the liberation of Holland, displayed great courage, leadership and selfless devotion to duty. On the afternoon of 31 March, 1945, "C" Company of the Highland Light Infantry of Canada was assigned the task of crossing a blown bridge south of s'Heerenberg and clearing the enemy from the dominating trench system beyond, to enable the construction of a new bridge. The enemy were firmly entrenched on the north of the bridge itself and surrounding area was in plain view of the enemy. Enemy snipers were located in high buildings on the outskirts of s'Heerenberg, overlooking the bridge.

Under covering fire of a troop of tanks and supporting artillery fire, Number 15 Platoon, in which Sergeant Steinman commanded a section, was to force the bridge. The remainder of the company would then follow when an initial success had been gained. Sergeant Steinman's section was the leading section.

The importance of his task was pointed out to him by his company commander and the fact that, if there was any hesitation in the initial assault and success was not immediately attained, the whole attack would bog down. This intrepid non-commissioned officer, with calculating coolness, unshakable determination and practised skill, manoeuvred his section into position for the assault over the ruins of the bridge. Enemy fire inflicted several casualties but, at the appointed hour, this dauntless section leader led his section with great dash and utter disregard for his own personal safety and successfully secured a foothold in the enemy trench system, thus beating down the enemy fire and enabling the remainder of the platoon and company to come forward and clear up the remaining enemy.

This action made possible the immediate construction of a bridge, subsequent move forward of the brigade group and speedy development of this important main axis.

For his action, Sergeant Peter Joseph Steinman was awarded the Nether-lands' Bronze Cross.

When the 3rd Division surged through s'Heerenberg as their advance got under way on April 1, they found it difficult to pass through this town, despite the fact that German resistance had been overcome. The North Nova Scotia Highlanders noted:

> Progress was slow through the town because of the cheering and waving crowds of Dutch lining the street. The First Cana-dian Army was liberating again and it certainly was a change from the sullen mass of Germans we continually bumped into on the other side of the Rhine and up to Emmerich . . . After five years of oppression, the Dutch people were expressing their joy and thanks at being liberated.[4]

General Keefler decided that the 7th Reconnaissance Regiment and the 9th Canadian Infantry Brigade would spearhead the drive north, ad-vancing as fast as possible, while 7th and 8th Brigades would peel off to deal with stubborn enemy strongpoints as required.

On the 2nd of April 1945, "C" Company of the 1st Battalion, The Queen's Own Rifles of Canada, advancing near Vogelhorst Germany, were held by en-emy fire coming from a farmhouse directly in their path.

Sergeant Ernest Crain was given the task of clearing the enemy from the house. Leading a patrol of five men, he boldly crossed one hundred and fifty yards of open ground, under intense fire, never wavering or faltering in his stride, to clear the house. The coolness and the courage displayed by Sergeant Crain and the audacity of the attack of this small patrol unnerved the enemy to such an ex-tent that they fled in confusion from the rear of the building. Sergeant Crain and his men killed four of the enemy and took four prisoners. It is estimated that there were forty enemy in there, and several of these were also wounded. Only the pa-trol's instructions not to proceed beyond the house prevented them from inflicting further casualties on the enemy and determining the number of wounded who had been carried away by their comrades.

The success of the patrol, due to the able leadership of this non-commissioned officer, eliminated a strong enemy threat to the continued advance of the battalion onto its objective.

For his action, Sergeant Ernest Crain was awarded the Military Medal.

On the morning of 3 April 1945, Lance Corporal Raymond Wickens of the 4th Canadian Provost Company was detailed to point duty at Baak Holland. The divi-sion axis swung east at this point and the enemy were holding positions to the north and west. Baak was under shell and mortar fire. "F" Echelons and ammunition sup-ply convoys were rolling through and it was essential to the success of the action that the Baak crossroads be continuously controlled. Enemy mortars were ranging on the crossroads, where a number of cheering civilians were waving to passing troops.

A mortar shell fell in the crowd, killing six and wounding several others. Transport drivers left their vehicles and took shelter, but Lance Corporal Wickens continued to stand on the point and, by his example and encouragement, persuaded the transport drivers to continue their journey and, at the same time, directed the removal of the dead and wounded although mortar and shell fire continued. Lance Corporal Wickens' fine example undoubtedly kept the divisional route open and must have contributed in no small measure to the success of that phase of the operation.

By his devotion to duty and courage, this non-commissioned officer has contributed to the success of operations on frequent occasions. The cool and capable manner in which he had carried on with his duties despite heavy enemy fire has been an inspiration and example to all men of the company.

For his action, Lance Corporal Raymond Wickens was awarded the Military Medal.

The 7th Reconnaissance Regiment, in leading the advance into enemy territory, was finally carrying out a role for which it had been specially trained. Its armoured cars fanned out in different directions, seeking the best roads for the infantry to follow. As the regimental history described, it was:

> as if someone had finally started unclogging the holes of the salt cellar they had been in for the last few months and all that was necessary was for someone to "tip it" and the fast Recce patrols, shaking the last few bits of mud from their wheels, would begin pouring all over the country . . . Maj-Gen Keefler tipped the salt cellar and out poured the Regiment.[5]

On 3 April 1945 at the railway station near Wehl, Sergeant Cedric Godfrey Whittall of the 7th Canadian Reconnaissance Regiment, in command of a patrol, was held up by heavy enemy 20-mm, machine-gun and small arms fire. He pulled the patrol back and worked the patrol forward where it again was held up by heavy 20-mm, mortar and Panzerfaust fire. Sergeant Whittall dismounted from his vehicle and, under heavy fire, worked his way forward to an observation point where he was able to pin-point the enemy position. Returning to his car, he then rushed this position with all weapons firing and eliminated all enemy resistance, killing five Germans and taking seven prisoners.

Later the same day, still searching for a crossing, Sergeant Whittall was fired at three times by anti-tank fire from a position near Hulthuizen and again rushed this position, killing seven of the enemy; the remainder fled to the north. This final action cleared all resistance south of the railroad. By his prompt, cool and decisive actions, with complete disregard for his own personal safety, Sergeant Whittall was responsible for clearing the way for the advance of the 7th Canadian Infantry Brigade to their objectives in that area.

For his actions, Sergeant Cedric Godfrey Whittall was awarded the Military Medal.

On 3 April 1945, the 1st Battalion, The Queen's Own Rifles of Canada was committed to an attack on the village of Laag Kappel, Holland, with "C" Company assigned the task of leading the assault. Shortly after crossing the start point, "C" Company came under intense small arms and mortar fire together with accurate sniping which inflicted heavy casualties. The deadly sniping wounded three of the company's stretcher bearers but in spite of this Rifleman John Wilfred Leonard Johnston, with complete disregard for his personal safety, went forward and evacuated nine of the wounded men. During this period he found time to render first aid to three men who were in need of immediate attention.

This extreme devotion to duty, carried out under withering fire from the enemy, was an outstanding example of bravery far beyond the normal call which undoubtedly saved the lives of some of the wounded men who were so efficiently evacuated by Rifleman Johnston's action.

For his action, Sergeant John Wilfred Leonard Johnston was awarded the Netherlands' Bronze Lion.

During the night of 5 April 1945, the 1st Battalion, The Queen's Own Rifles of Canada was forming an independent battle group on the east bank of the Ijssel River, holding the area from Doesburg to Emmer. Due to the area involved, communication was difficult and it was of the utmost importance that it be maintained. Enemy action constantly cut lines and the line parties working on the repairs carried on without a break. Lance Sergeant Nicholas John Perry, the signal platoon sergeant, was directing this work going from point to point, helping and encouraging the men to greater speed. Lance Sergeant Perry went forward under the fire of enemy machine-guns from across the river and repaired the line, thus inspiring the men under his command.

The Support Company was burned out at their headquarters and they were forced to move back to a new position east of the road, along which the line ran, and this non-commissioned officer, heedless of the fire which the enemy laid down on the road and the possibility of patrols, kept checking this stretch of line. Due to his efforts, contact was maintained with the forward company which was attacking at that time.

This is only one example of the fine work done by Lance Sergeant Perry from D-Day to V-E Day. He has always been an outstanding example to the men of the platoons, with his cool quick thinking and calm courage in the face of any emergency.

For his actions, Lance Sergeant Nicholas John Perry was awarded the Netherlands' Bronze Cross.

Zutphen

Zutphen. That queer sounding name will mean little to many. To Dutchmen, it pictures a pretty town on the Dutch-German border. To many a veteran it awakens a nightmare, something akin to Keppeln and Carpiquet, for here we slugged out our last big fight with fanatical Nazis, now fighting with the desperation of cornered rats.[6]

Padre R. Myles Hickey,
North Shore (New Brunswick) Regiment

In order to defend the line of the Ijssel with the minimum troops, the Germans pulled back their forces to concentrate in the towns of Zutphen, Deventer, and Zwolle which they turned into strongholds. The Zutphen garrison was built around III Battalion, 3rd Parachute Training and Reinforcement Regiment, a well-equipped unit made up of fanatical teenagers led by experienced instructors, and therefore particularly determined. The town of about 25,000 people made a naturally strong defensive position, with the Ijssel River on the west side, half-circled to the east and south by the River Berkel. The need to mount a well-prepared assault soon became clear as armoured cars of the 7th Reconnaissance Regiment were met by a hail of fire on all access routes leading into town. As the 9th Brigade slowly pressed in on the outlying villages, they found that:

> heavy machine-guns and 88-mm fire made progress slow. In some cases, the Germans had erected machine-guns in the trees; others were located in village cemeteries where heavy tombstones could be used for protection. The brigade fought for each yard of ground . . .[7]

On 4 April 1945, at Loeston Holland, Sergeant Alexander Lawton, "B" Company of the Stormont, Dundas and Glengarry Highlanders, by his initiative and courage, enabled his platoon to carry out its task, thereby assuring the start line for the battalion at a time when it was gravely menaced by fanatical enemy resistance.

Early in the afternoon of 4 April, "B" Company was leading the battalion into Loeston when it came under heavy machine-gun fire from well-concealed snipers on their flank across open ground. His platoon leader was killed when the enemy opened fire. Sergeant Lawton, despite the open ground where they were pinned down, succeeded in reorganizing the scattered platoon and soon was able to return the fire though they could not clear the situation.

When Sergeant Lawton's runner was killed, he personally contacted the following platoon to inform them of the position, returning immediately to his own men. "B" Company had by this time lost half their effectives to the fanatical enemy but, despite the heavy fire, Sergeant Lawton continued to rally his remaining men and, at the same time, completely disregarding his own safety, acted as company runner, keeping the battalion informed of the progress of the battle.

This situation continued for two hours, during which time Sergeant Lawton was exposed to vicious enemy sniping and machine-gun fire until sufficient support in the form of flame–throwers enabled the battalion to relieve his platoon of their task.

For his action, Sergeant Alexander Lawton was awarded the Netherlands' Bronze Cross.

The North Nova Scotia Highlanders were given the task of securing the village of Warnsveld, just east of the outskirts of Zutphen. "A" and "B" Companies led the advance, but both ran into trouble from young paratroops who would not surrender even when their resistance was hopeless. "A" Company's attack did not start until late in the day and was held by a road–block and machine-gun posts in a wood and cemetery. Under heavy mortar fire, these were cleared after dark with the help of flame-throwing Wasps.

Sergeant William Lemuel MacKay landed with The North Nova Scotia Highlanders on D-Day and carried out many commendable acts, including escaping after being captured in Normandy.

In the battalion's attack on Warnsveld Holland in early April 1945, "A" Company was leading and Sergeant MacKay, without an officer, was commanding Number 9 Platoon. It was nearly dusk and the company was advancing, with Number 9 Platoon leading. They came under fire from a road–block position. Sergeant MacKay took a section and personally led the assault on this position, killing or wounding all the defenders. He reorganized his platoon and proceeded forward. He had just started when they again came under fire, resulting in casualties. This time it was from a house and, again, Sergeant MacKay, with no regard for his own personal safety, rushed the place and took twelve prisoners. By this time, it was nearly dark and the whole company came under fire from the main position, a woods just behind the house. A company attack was put in and again Sergeant MacKay distinguished himself by clearing his part of the objective and then assisting the rest of the company in their sectors. During this action, Sergeant MacKay was the mainstay of his platoon. He was always in the fore, personally taking several prisoners, and acting with great bravery throughout.

The services rendered by this sergeant since coming back to the unit in October 1944, during which time he never missed an action, cannot be too highly praised. He was always a splendid example to his men and his personal disregard for danger, and his devotion to duty, were of the highest order.

For his actions, Sergeant William Lemuel MacKay was awarded the Netherlands' Bronze Lion.

On the 4th and 5th days of April 1945, during the approaches to and the battle on the eastern edge of Zutphen, an enemy strong point on the east bank of the Ijssel River, Private Waldo James Cousins, driver of the stretcher bearer jeep in "D" Company, North Nova Scotia Highlanders, showed bravery, courage and complete disregard for his personal safety when he faced devastating machine-gun fire from the enemy to bring in casualties that could not be removed otherwise.

On the 4th of April, "D" Company was ordered to protect the left flank of the battalion. In order to do this, the company had to control the ground on the east side of the Ferry Crossing at Bronkhurst. An attack was ordered for this purpose and, while crossing open ground, ten casualties were suffered from enemy machine-gun fire. Private Cousins, with complete disregard for his personal safety, time and time again, drove his jeep through this fire and picked up the casualties.

On his last trip, machine-gun bullets hit his radiator and he had to get out and repair it in order to continue the evacuation of the remaining casualties.

Again, on the following day, "D" Company was engaged in clearing a street on the eastern outskirts of Zutphen when word reached the company commander that a man was seriously wounded in a house some one hundred and fifty yards further up the street. At this time, the street was covered by very heavy enemy Spandau fire from a distance of four hundred yards. Without hesitating, Private Cousins jumped in the stretcher bearer jeep and drove up the street, parked the jeep beside the house, dashed inside, picked up the wounded man, carried him out to the jeep and then drove back down the street to safety through another devastating hail of bullets. The jeep was so full of bullet holes that it had to be sent to the rear area for repairs.

There is no doubt that this soldier's fine display of courage and initiative under fire has been the means of saving the lives of many wounded men. During the whole of operations, Private Cousins' example of bravery and actions beyond the call of duty has been of the highest order.

For his actions, Private Waldo James Cousins was awarded the Military Medal. Private Cousins was wounded in action several days later on April 8 during the attack to cross the Schipbeek Canal.

General Keefler did not want 9th Brigade diverted too long from pressing the advance northwards. Therefore, he ordered 8th Canadian Infantry Brigade to finish the capture of Zutphen while 9th Brigade disengaged and moved on. The 8th Brigade attacked Zutphen from the east before dawn on April 6 with Le Régiment de la Chaudière on the left, North Shore Regiment on the right. "B" Company of the North Shore Regiment under Major Hamley was held at a blown bridge and became engaged in heavy hand-to-hand fighting. Major Hamley, who had been awarded the Military Cross for his actions at Millingen, was wounded when the Germans attempted to overrun the company headquarters. The situation became critical as "B" Company's platoons became pinned down by fire from both flanks. At this point:

> "D" Company under Major Carroll made a desperate effort to get in to help "B" Company, but enemy fire was so intense that little could be done. Seeing the situation, Colonel Gordon ordered the two companies to withdraw, which they were able to do under the screen of covering fire laid down by Captain Harvey's mortar platoon. All night long the enemy kept shelling, and the clatter of machine-gun fire kept patrols on the alert . . .[8]

Meanwhile, the Chaudières were also held up on the edge of town by Germans firing from windows of the cellars, main floors and upper floors of buildings converted into strongpoints. When the Chaudières managed to gain a foothold in the town, Acting Brigadier Lett formed a plan whereby two companies of the North Shores passed through the Chaudières' flank position to enter the town.

However, on April 7, fierce resistance continued and two-thirds of the town was still held by the Germans that evening. After dark, Major Armand Ross of the Chaudières and six men made a silent reconnaissance further into the town and found a route by which "B" and "D" Companies of the Chaudières could infiltrate to reach the edge of the Ijssel. They found such a route and Major Ross then led a platoon through to surprise the defenders from the rear. The objective was occupied at 0400 hours on April 8 and, five hours later, the remainder of the regiment was able to take control of all their sector of Zutphen.[9] At the same time, the North Shore Regiment renewed their advance with support from tanks and Crocodiles and had consolidated their final objectives by mid-afternoon.

Personnel of "C" Company, The North Shore Regiment, crossing a canal in Zutphen, Netherlands, 7 April 1945
Donald I. Grant, NAC, PA-130059

On 6 April 1945, the North Shore (New Brunswick) Regiment attacked the city of Zutphen. "B" Company led the assault along the railway which passes through the city. The company reached a point near its final objective when it encountered heavy opposition and was subjected to very heavy machine-gun, sniper and mortar fire.

Private Ernest Fowlie Watling, the operator of the "B" Company wireless set, accompanied the company commander with the leading platoon which became pinned down and cut off. A brisk hand-to-hand engagement ensued, resulting in bitter and confused fighting. The company commander and the platoon commander became casualties.

In spite of the continuous and direct fire brought to bear upon him, Private Watling with exceeding coolness continued to send vital messages. As the fighting became more fierce, he used his Sten gun with great effect against the enemy and, at the same time, kept the battalion headquarters informed as to what was happening.

When it became necessary to withdraw the leading platoon to a place of contact with the rest of the company, Private Watling remained with the wounded officers to provide covering fire until the platoon had withdrawn. Then, with great presence of mind and courage, he helped both the platoon officer and company commander to cross over an open and bullet-swept piece of ground to safety, thereby permitting the company commander to get in a position to regain control of his company in time to save a critical situation from becoming disastrous.

The courageous action in operating his set, the skilful and effective fighting which this soldier displayed over and above his normal duties, permitted his wounded company commander to retain control of the company. This was instrumental in allowing the company to hold its newly won positions, thus enabling the battalion to continue in its operation against the city of Zutphen.

The utter disregard for personal safety and the cheerfulness on the part of Private Watling was an inspiration and steadying influence on the whole company.

For his action, Private Ernest Fowlie Watling was awarded the Military Medal.

On 6 April 1945, The North Shore (New Brunswick) Regiment attacked the city of Zutphen. Private Norman Edward Fisher was a signaller in "A" Company during this attack. It was necessary to pass "A" Company through another battalion to gain entrance to the city. Immediately on passing through, the company came under heavy Panzerfaust, machine-gun and sniper fire. Private Fisher accompanying the company commander was cut off and pinned down. Although wounded, Private Fisher refused to be evacuated and remained by his set, operating it under great difficulty. In spite of continuous and direct fire, he continued to send vital messages, keeping battalion headquarters informed.

The courageous action in operating his set assisted the company to gain its objective and enabled the rest of the battalion to be committed properly. The utter disregard for personal safety and the cheerfulness on the part of Private Fisher was an inspiration and a steadying influence on the whole company.

For his action, Private Norman Edward Fisher was awarded the Netherlands' Bronze Cross.

On 6 April 1945, Le Régiment de la Chaudière was engaged in very bitter action against stubborn enemy troops of the Hitler's Youth defending Zutphen. During this fierce battle, Private Maurice Lacasse displayed a very high standard of devotion to duty and personal bravery in his duties as stretcher bearer.

The outskirts of Zutphen were heavily defended by machine-gun fire, and artillery fire was sweeping some three hundred yards of very open ground. Many casualties were incurred. This gallant soldier, constantly exposed for some twelve hours, went from wounded to wounded man, providing comfort and preparing them for evacuation. His utter contempt for danger was a high source of inspira-

tion to all ranks. He was also one of the first to enter Zutphen and devoted many hours to the treatment of civilian casualties

The high standard of devotion to duty, personal bravery and utter disregard for his personal safety assisted materially in saving many lives of our soldiers and those of Dutch civilians.

For his actions, Private Maurice Lacasse was awarded the Netherlands' Bronze Lion.

On the 6th of April 1945, during an attack by le Régiment de la Chaudière on the town of Zutphen in Holland, Lieutenant Gerard Jean, pioneer officer of the unit, displayed unusual bravery and leadership.

It was necessary that there should exist a very close cooperation between infantry, tanks and flame–throwers in order to subdue and eliminate the garrison of young German fanatics. Early in the attack, an anti-tank ditch was encountered and sappers with bulldozers were called for. Lieutenant Jean led his men forward and started the preliminary work of sweeping for mines and demolition charges; he thus cleared the axis allowing the bulldozers to come forward. All this had been accomplished under intense enemy fire from machine-guns, mortars and artillery.

Later on, two companies reached the bridge which the enemy blew up before they could get across. The infantry went forward but tanks could not negotiate the obstacle. This officer, still under intense fire, made a reconnaissance of the area and found a shallow spot in the stream suitable for a tank crossing. To do the necessary work to permit tanks to cross was out of the question due to an enemy position close by. Since no infantry was in the immediate vicinity, Lieutenant Jean gathered a few of his men, attacked and succeeded in overcoming the enemy positions, killing one enemy, wounding another and scattering two others; one light machine-gun was abandoned by the enemy.

This done, he proceeded to have the necessary trees cut, to reinforce the crossing. The enemy, appreciating the purpose of this work, intensified their fire. Lieutenant Jean remained cool, refused to take cover, and urged his men on. As a result, in a short while, it was possible for the tanks to cross. This officer stayed at this fire-swept spot for four hours, reinforcing with timber this crossing which deteriorated with each tank crossing effected.

It is certain that the personal bravery of this officer, his display of superb leadership and initiative, and his entire disregard of danger was the decisive factor that permitted the battalion to get forward onto its objective.

For his actions, Lieutenant Gerard Jean received the Military Cross.

On the 6th of April 1945, Le Régiment de la Chaudière was given the task of attacking Zutphen from the northeast. The regiment was supported by tanks and it was imperative that the tanks and the Wasp flame–throwers get forward to clear strongly held houses. The advance of these tanks was held up by an anti-tank ditch and a bridge which was destroyed. Both of these obstacles were covered by observed enemy machine-gun and mortar fire.

Major Hardy Lawrence Main of the 16th Canadian Field Company RCE, in support of Le Régiment de la Chaudière's attack, was called forward by the commanding officer. It was extremely hazardous to move in the vicinity of these obstacles as both were on high ground and all movement drew additional enemy fire. Notwithstanding the intensity of the enemy fire, Major Main personally made a reconnaissance of the sites for bridging and, remaining in an exposed position, ignoring his personal safety, directed the bridging operation, an example and inspiration to the men working under him.

On completion of the bridging at the anti-tank ditch and, as the tanks pushed forward to give fire support to the second bridging operation, the enemy became fully aware of the plan to bridge this second obstacle. Notwithstanding the savagely increased enemy fire now directed on the locality, Major Main once again remained in an exposed position and directed the bridging operation. For fourteen hours, this officer remained in the foremost position of our troops, under intense fire and with complete disregard of the enemy, ensuring the completion of the task in order that the infantry might forge ahead and reach their objective.

His calmness under fire and his cool example influenced his men, giving them heart to carry out their tasks under the most trying conditions, and permitted le Régiment de la Chaudière to carry through to their final objective.

For his actions, Major Hardy Lawrence Main was awarded the Distinguished Service Order.

During a battalion attack on the town of Zutphen Holland, on the 6th of April 1945, Major Joseph Armand Ross, commanding "C" Company of le Régiment de la Chaudière, displayed unusual leadership and gallantry in the face of stubborn and fierce enemy resistance.

The garrison of Zutphen consisted of young fanatics of the Hitler Youth, who preferred death to surrender. The company commanded by this gallant officer had the task of penetrating the western outskirts of the town. For many hours, his company moved inch by inch forward in the face of a most intense concentration of enemy fire from all types of weapons. The company was finally forced to ground and unable to move forward again. A battalion attacking on the right flank was also in the same predicament.

Without waiting for orders, Major Ross gathered six soldiers of his company and, despite the intensity of the fire directed at anything that moved, he personally led this small patrol to find a way into the town. In doing so, this small patrol suffered three casualties but he was successful in finding an unguarded entrance. He came back, bringing the wounded with him, still under intense enemy fire.

Without pausing, he led the first platoon in and sent guides for the other. He personally led the first platoon in mopping up the enemy from the rear. This action had the result of forcing the enemy to give up this key position and retire into another part of the town, which relieved a critical situation, thus allowing the balance of the battalion and the flanking battalion to proceed according to plan.

The brilliant leadership on the part of this officer, his initiative, personal bravery, utmost gallantry and entire disregard for his personal safety in the face of enemy fire have been a high source of inspiration to his men and a most important contribution to the success of operations throughout the campaign.

For his actions, Major Joseph Armand Ross was awarded the Distinguished Service Order.

Officers of Le Régiment de la Chaudière talking to General Crerar, Commander-in-Chief of the First Canadian Army (on the left). Major J. Armand Ross, who was awarded the Distinguished Service Order for his actions at Zutphen, Netherlands, is on the right.

On the afternoon of 7 April 1945, during the second day of the attack by Le Regiment de la Chaudière on the town of Zutphen in Holland, Sergeant Israel Maurice Deslippe of "A" Company displayed unusual bravery and initiative.

His platoon was to capture the only undamaged bridge in the town, vital to our future plans. The enemy had the bridge and its approaches under heavy and accurate machine-gun fire. The platoon was soon forced to take cover and the attack seemed to be bogging down. It was then that Sergeant Deslippe, without waiting for an order, took a Bren gun and several magazines, and made a dash to a flank. From a vantage point in open ground, he engaged enemy positions, one after another, causing casualties to the enemy, with the result that soon the bulk of the enemy fire was directed at him. However, he still went on firing, allowing the rest of the platoon to dash forward and secure its vital objective.

The superb display of initiative of this non-commissioned officer, his entire disregard for personal safety, his personal courage and utter coolness under fire, was an inspiration to all his men, being the decisive factor in securing this most important objective. This magnificent action was instrumental in capturing the whole town the next day. During his entire service, Sergeant Deslippe, by his bravery, skill and devotion to duty, has set an inspiring example to his men, enabling them to carry their objective in the face of heavy enemy resistance.

For his actions, Sergeant Israel Maurice Deslippe was awarded the Military Medal.

At the end of this battle, Padre Hickey of the North Shore Regiment reported that:

> the next morning, I said Mass for the men in the remains of a schoolhouse in Zutphen. I gave a general absolution and, as the men came up to Holy Communion, in each war-weary face I could read my own fondest hope—the hope that the end was near.[10]

Deventer

While the battle for Zutphen was still going on, General Keefler became aware that Deventer, about ten kilometres to the north, was also strongly held and would take several days of fighting to clear. He therefore ordered the 9th Canadian Infantry Brigade to swing around and bypass it to the west, while the 8th Brigade was given the task of capturing Deventer.

The approaches to Deventer, as with Zutphen, were covered by a series of waterways. The Schipbeek Canal was the first major obstacle, beginning just south of Deventer and running westward. Just behind it, the second major canal, the Zijkanaal, ran northeast forming a kind of natural moat for "Fortress" Deventer. The garrison consisted of two battlegroups made up of remnants of the 16th and 17th Parachute Regiments, the Fleiger Horst Battalion along with elements of a number of miscellaneous units such as a penal servitude battalion.

On the evening of April 6, The Royal Winnipeg Rifles established a bridgehead over the Schipbeek Canal just south of the city. The Germans reacted quickly with heavy artillery support, concentrating all the forces that they could. The Regina Rifles crossed the next day to reinforce the bridgehead, and the entire 7th Brigade was across by April 8.

On 7 April 1945 during the advance on Deventer, The Royal Winnipeg Rifles arrived at the Schipbeek Canal to find the enemy holding the far bank in strength. There was a blown bridge immediately opposite "D" Company on the left and, to approach closer than within five hundred yards of this bridge, it was necessary to cross open fields under enemy fire. Realizing that a reconnaissance would be necessary to prepare an operation for crossing the canal, Captain Arthur Thomas Edwin Fairweather, acting as company commander, set out with one non-commissioned officer. They crawled forward through short grass until they found a German-dug trench which enabled them to advance under cover to the approaches of the bridge. Captain Fairweather made a detailed reconnaissance, although under heavy small arms and Panzerfaust fire. Returning to his

company, Captain Fairweather reported his findings to the battalion commander
and asked permission to undertake the crossing that day. This was granted and Captain Fairweather launched one platoon, supported by flame-throwers and covered by
smoke, to seize the far end of the bridge. When this attack had been completed, he
personally directed the crossing of the remainder of the company. This was a very
hazardous undertaking as planks had been used to bridge breaches in the damaged bridge, and it was under heavy and accurate fire from a distance of a few
hundred yards along each flank. However, with the assistance of fire from a section of carriers, this was accomplished sufficiently to allow the passage of the remaining two platoons. Several hours of daylight remained and, during this time,
Captain Fairweather fought a hard battle to hold his limited bridgehead in the
face of determined efforts to wipe it out. Although the casualties in the company
were heavy, and they were under constant enemy fire, they were successful, largely
due to the fact that Captain Fairweather went from position to position directing
the men as the other officers of the company became casualties. With the arrival
of darkness, the rest of the battalion passed through "D" Company and, after
bitter fighting, enlarged the bridgehead, taking almost two hundred prisoners, and
thus making it possible for the rest of the brigade to cross.

For his actions, Captain Arthur Thomas Edwin Fairweather was awarded
the Military Cross.

On 7 April 1945, The Royal Winnipeg Rifles were ordered to cross the
Schipbeek Canal and establish a bridgehead in the preparation for an assault on
the city of Deventer Holland by the 7th Canadian Infantry Brigade. The crossing of the Schipbeek Canal was of vital importance for the success of the brigade
operation. It was very strongly held and it was due only to the determination and
boundless courage of Lieutenant Donald Charles MacKenzie that a quick crossing was made possible without heavy casualties. The enemy had a battlegroup
dispersed around the bridge approaches on the far bank and had blown the
bridge, making it impassable.

Lieutenant MacKenzie, in command of the unit pioneers attached to "D"
Company, had the responsibility of bridging the canal so that a bridgehead could
be rapidly built up, ready for a break–out. The enemy fire was intense, but with
covering fire from "B" Company, Lieutenant Mackenzie succeeded in crawling
out onto the bridge, dragging a couple of planks. He was working well within grenade range of the enemy and at least six grenades exploded close by, wounding
him by shrapnel and blast. With complete disregard for his own safety, he continued working until he had four planks in position, allowing the company to
cross quickly and secure a solid bridgehead.

His dauntless spirit and untiring efforts inspired the men around him and resulted in the momentum of the advance being maintained.

For his action, Lieutenant Donald Charles MacKenzie was awarded the
Military Cross. Lieutenant MacKenzie was later killed in action, on April
22, during the attack on Appingdam.

On 7 April 1945 at Schipbeek, southeast of Deventer, "D" Company of The Royal Winnipeg Rifles established a bridgehead over the canal. Corporal Frank Hole, a section commander of Number 16 Platoon, was ordered to take his men to a spot on the canal bank where he could bring down enfilade fire to protect the party building the bridge. To reach the position, it was necessary to move over a stretch of open ground, one hundred and fifty yards in length, covered by heavy enemy machine-gun fire. This corporal did twice, first to make his reconnaissance to see if it was actually suitable and secondly to lead his men in.

When the bridge was completed, Corporal Hole's section was one of the first to cross and after was ordered to advance a further two hundred yards to clear several enemy–occupied buildings. While doing this, the section came under mortar fire and the corporal was wounded. However, he refused to permit himself to be evacuated until his task was done which, under his brilliant leadership, was soon accomplished.

This non-commissioned officer's determination, leadership and personal bravery, and the example he set, were the inspiration that made possible the successful completion of his platoon's tasks.

For his action, Corporal Frank Hole was awarded the Military Medal.

On 7 April 1945, "A" Company of The Royal Winnipeg Rifles was leading company of a battalion attack in the area around Kolmschate, near Deventer Holland. The first objective was some very strongly held mutually supporting farm buildings and an adjacent wood near this small town. Sergeant Alfred Francis Richardson, who was acting as platoon commander, led Number 9 Platoon in the spearhead of the attack. An artillery preparation of six minutes was laid down on the target in an effort to cut down the intense enemy machine-gun fire which poured continuously from the area of the farmhouses. Sergeant Richardson formed the platoon up as the artillery began firing and, while there was still one minute left of the barrage, he led his platoon onto the objective in the face of heavy enemy machine-gun fire from the flanks. He kept shouting encouragement to the men as they moved in and their objective was taken with very few casualties. Five machine-guns and thirty of the enemy were captured in the area of the farm buildings. As soon as the farm had been secured, Sergeant Richardson, using a captured enemy machine-gun, raked the nearby woods with fire, thereby enabling the remainder of the company's objective to be quickly taken. By doing this, an additional fifteen of the enemy, some of them wounded, were flushed out.

In all these brilliant actions, Sergeant Richardson showed absolute disregard for his own safety and was a contributing factor in his company's quick successes.

For his actions, Sergeant Alfred Francis Richardson was awarded the Military Medal. Sergeant Richardson was wounded in action the next day, April 8.

"D" Company of The Royal Winnipeg Rifles, on the night of the 7th of April 1945, succeeded in obtaining a bridgehead over the canal at Schipbeek, southeast of Deventer Holland. Rifleman George Henry Webster, a driver on strength of the company headquarters, was detailed to evacuate casualties in his vehicle.

All roads leading to the bridgehead were being heavily shelled and mortared by the enemy and, during the action, the company had suffered many casualties. Time and time again, Rifleman Webster drove that hazardous route, carrying the wounded to the Regimental Aid Post though every trip meant a few more shrapnel holes in the body of his vehicle. This self-sacrificing soldier refused to rest until the battle was successfully completed and all wounded had been brought back to the care of the unit medical officer.

His personal courage and cheerful manner with his wounded comrades kept their morale high throughout the whole of that hazardous journey, and his devotion to duty was undoubtedly instrumental in saving several lives.

For his actions, Rifleman George Henry Webster was awarded the Military Medal.

On 7 April 1945, Lieutenant Neville Whitney Mann, of the 6th Canadian Field Company RCE, was detailed to be in charge of an engineer party in support of the 7th Canadian Infantry Brigade in their crossing of the Schipbeek River approximately two miles southeast of Deventer Holland. He was with the forward infantry battalion, the Royal Winnipeg Rifles, and it was imperative that an improvised crossing be constructed. Lieutenant Mann, in full view of the enemy who were about twenty-five yards away, proceeded to construct this improvised bridge. With only small arms fire to cover him, this officer braved the enemy fire which consisted of machine-gun, rifle and grenade fire and succeeded in erecting a bridge of planks so that the infantry could cross and proceed with the advance of the brigade. It is without doubt that, but for Lieutenant Mann's courageous and daring act, the attack could not have gone through and any delay would have been costly. The infantry, thus inspired by Lieutenant Mann's disregard for his own personal safety and his bravery, crossed over the bridge and succeeded in their attack. Their admiration for this engineer officer will long be remembered by The Royal Winnipeg Rifles.

For his action, Lieutenant Neville Whitney Mann was awarded the Military Cross.

On the night of April 8/9, the 7th Canadian Infantry Brigade opened its attack to cross the last barrier, the Zijkanaal. In the main attack from the south, The Regina Rifles managed to gain a bridgehead over the canal although the important bridge over the canal was blown up in their face. It was then decided to swing the Canadian Scottish around this barrier to cross from the east. This attack was successful just after midnight of April 9/10 and the regiment occupied Schalkhaar, a village about two miles west of the canal.

The Germans reacted in the early morning by trying to launch a counter-attack from the northern flank, but ran into a carrier section and mortar detachment which successfully foiled the attempt. As the morning mist cleared, the enemy became apparent to Sergeant Minnis, the commander of the carrier section, and:

the three Bren guns opened fire immediately. Those of the enemy who were both lucky and quick enough leaped into a
ditch and tried to crawl away but the Bren gunners pinned
them down and the nearby mortar detachment, happy for the
opportunity, lobbed some bombs into their midst.[11]

*On 10 April 1945, at Schalkhaar Holland, the carrier platoon of the 1st
Battalion, The Canadian Scottish Regiment, was detailed to protect the right
flank of the battalion on the advance to the objective. Sergeant Alfred Robertson
Minnis, with his section, was placed on the extreme right flank. This post was
taken up just before dawn in a thick mist and, owing to the rapid advance of the
battalion, was soon isolated. As the sun rose, the mist evaporated and visibility
became better. At about 0800 hours, movement was seen to the section's right
front and, on closer examination, the movement proved to be the enemy in some
force supported by tanks.*

*Sergeant Minnis, realizing that his position had been discovered, opened fire
and was successful in killing ten of the enemy and wounding an undetermined
number. The enemy then opened fire with its tanks and succeeded in getting a direct hit on the building the sergeant was in, wounding three and killing the second
in command of the section.*

*Undeterred by this fire, the section continued to put down a heavy curtain of
small arms fire from its automatic weapons, thus enabling the rest of the platoon
to be deployed to assist them. Through his wireless set, Sergeant Minnis was able
to get support from the 3-inch mortars and so effectively controlled the fire that
twenty enemy were killed. Sergeant Minnis, noticing that twenty-three of the enemy were trapped in a communication trench by our fire, personally led his section forward and succeeded in taking them prisoner.*

*This non-commissioned officer displayed great personal courage and excep-
tional leadership throughout the whole of this action, and his cool demeanour inspired his men to fight off a determined attack by the enemy which, had it been
successful, would have jeopardized the whole battalion.*

For his actions, Sergeant Alfred Robertson Minnis was awarded the Military Medal.

*On the night of 9 April 1945, the 1st Battalion, The Canadian Scottish
Regiment took up positions on the outskirts of Deventer Holland. The 3-inch
mortar platoon moved up behind the infantry in support the following morning at
0630 hours. This particular morning was very foggy and, when it cleared, the
platoon found themselves completely cut off by the enemy.*

*Corporal Frederick James Nicol was in charge of one mortar which was ex-
posed to enemy fire from all sides. As the fog lifted, the enemy attacked with infantry and tanks. Corporal Nicol, ignoring enemy fire, remained at his post,
firing the mortar at one hundred yards range. This not only had very great effect
on the enemy but also endangered his own life, as the shrapnel effect from a mortar bomb extends two hundred yards. He successfully broke up the attack, ena-*

bling his platoon to take thirty prisoners as well as killing and wounding many others. He saved the battalion from a grave situation and assisted greatly in clearing the way into Deventer.

Throughout his service, Corporal Nicol has inspired confidence in his abilities and has been an inspiration to the men he commanded. The way he showed utter disregard for his personal safety and his able leadership in action were a credit to the regiment. This non-commissioned officer played a part which assisted materially in the liberation of Holland.

For his action, Corporal Frederick James Nicol was awarded the Netherlands' Bronze Lion.

At noon on April 10, The Canadian Scottish and Royal Winnipeg Rifles launched the final attack, meeting strong resistance at an anti-tank ditch on the edge of the city. The leading companies suffered heavy casualties and it seemed that they would not have the strength to break through. However, supporting tanks were brought up to eliminate the German strongpoints. This force broke the German resistance and then opened the way to Deventer.[12]

On 10 April 1945 at about 1100 hours, "B" Squadron, 27th Canadian Armoured Regiment was in support of the 9th Canadian Infantry Brigade, attacking north from Deventer with the 1st Battalion, The Canadian Scottish as point battalion. This battalion was held up and pinned down by two self-propelled 75-mm guns and a line of small arms fire. The troop of tanks in support of this battalion had not as yet been employed owing to the extremely open nature of the ground and the lack of good cover. The situation rapidly deteriorated with the infantry suffering many casualties from self-propelled, high explosive and small arms fire. Since only a few yards separated them from the enemy and the situation was quite confused, our artillery did not dare to engage the enemy positions.

Sergeant Arthur Rigby, a crew commander with the 27th Canadian Armoured Regiment, after making as detailed a reconnaissance as was possible, felt that he could help. Therefore, making use of every patch of cover, he guided his tank into a position to the left flank of our infantry and carefully searched the ground ahead for the enemy.

At this moment, the self-propelled gun fired again and Sergeant Rigby saw its flash. He had approached so well, with such skilful use of cover and ground that he found himself within five hundred yards of the enemy gun. Information had been received that there were two of these guns, but he could not detect the position of the second one. He decided, although it probably meant his own demise, to risk giving his position away in order at least to knock out the one self-propelled gun which was causing such severe casualties amongst the infantry. Therefore, although he knew his blast would most certainly be observed by the still–concealed gun, he carefully laid his gunner on the target and fired. He scored a direct hit the first round and the self-propelled gun exploded.

At almost the same moment, he detected further movement and saw the second self-propelled gun moving into position to engage him. He fired, scoring a direct hit which damaged the enemy armoured fighting vehicle and put it out of action. Enemy infantry who had been dug into well-prepared positions in the area of the self-propelled guns dropped their weapons and began to run. Sergeant Rigby did great execution among them with high explosive shells and .30-calibre machine-gun fire. About forty surrendered and, as our infantry reorganized and again advanced, they met little or no opposition for several miles.

Obviously, the enemy had intended to hold strongly and Sergeant Rigby's skill, coolness and courage were a major factor in restoring a critical situation. This kept up the impetus of the advance which was vital to the success of the attack against Deventer.

For his actions, Sergeant Arthur Rigby was awarded the Military Medal.

Corporal Edwin Garfield Harvey, 27th Canadian Armoured Regiment, distinguished himself in many actions but particularly in his contribution to the successful attack on Deventer Holland.

"C" Squadron, with two flame-throwers, was in support of the Regina Rifles Regiment. Corporal Harvey, commanding the point tank of the leading troop, was well forward with the infantry when the advance was halted by heavy machine-gun, mortar and anti-tank fire from a group of buildings on the outskirts of town. The flame–throwers could not advance within range since it was necessary to cross open ground. Corporal Harvey immediately assessed the situation and, without hesitation, worked his tank to an intermediary position, but was halted by a Panzerfaust team around the corner of a building.

Taking two grenades, he dismounted from the tank, crawled through the cellar of the house and destroyed the Panzerfaust team from the rear. He then crawled back to his tank and continued on to a favourable position from which he knocked out the enemy anti-tank gun. Through his initiative and fortitude, the flame-throwers were allowed to advance and deal with the remaining enemy.

Corporal Harvey, through his cool and decisive actions, has proven himself a praiseworthy crew commander. His initiative and disregard for personal safety have won him a high place in the annals of his regiment.

For his action, Corporal Edwin Garfield Harvey was awarded the Netherlands' Bronze Lion.

As the Canadians advanced into the town, they were met by the Dutch resistance, wearing orange armbands, who pointed out enemy positions and guided the Canadians through the streets. The citizens of Deventer thronged the streets, celebrating their liberation even as the fighting continued. Captain S. L. Chambers reported taking two platoons and going:

> down the main streets while the Dutch soldiers scoured the
> back alleys catching the Germans as they popped out of back

doors. At one point my platoon was mobbed by fifty delirious happy girls from a nursing school who flung themselves about the necks of my men amidst the odd burst of machine-gun fire and stray shells . . .[13]

By late in the day, April 10, Deventer was effectively cleared, the remaining Germans escaping across the Ijssel River. The German's Ijssel line had now been essentially eliminated and only Zwolle blocked the way to northern Holland.

NOTES

1.   National Archives of Canada Record Group (RG) 24, Vol 15042, 1 Battalion, The Canadian Scottish Regiment War Diary, April 1945.

2.   RG 24, Vol 15042, 3 CID Intelligence Reports No. 89 and 94, dated 25 March and 4 April 1945 respectively.

3.   Col C. P. Stacey, *The Victory Campaign* (Ottawa: The Queen's Printer, 1966), p. 546.

4.   RG 24, Vol 15123, North Nova Scotia Highlanders War Diary, April 1945.

5.   Capt Walter G. Pavey, *An Historical Account of the 7th Canadian Reconnaissance Regiment in the World War 1939 - 1945* (Montreal: privately printed, 1948), p. 107.

6.   Rev. R. Myles Hickey, *The Scarlet Dawn* (Fredricton: Unipress, 1980), p. 216.

7.   Lt Col W. Boss, *The Stormont, Dundas and Glengarry Highlanders: 1783 - 1951* (Ottawa: The Runge Press, 1952), p. 255.

8.   Hickey, p. 217.

9.   Jacques Castonguay and Armand Ross, *Le Régiment de la Chaudière* (Levis: Le Régiment de la Chadière, 1983), p. 352.

10.   Ibid.

11.   R. H. Roy, *Ready for the Fray* (Vancouver: The Canadian Scottish Regiment, 1958), p. 409.

12.   Ibid, p. 411.

13.   Quoted in Roy, p. 412.

-II-
THE DRIVE TO THE ZUIDER ZEE

The enemy was returning from northern Holland [to Germany] in headlong flight and 9 CIB [Canadian Infantry Brigade] was rolling through. The Dutch people were nearly going crazy, lining the route and cheering and waving. There was orange bunting everywhere . . .

War Diary
North Nova Scotia Highlanders[1]

The task of the 3rd Canadian Infantry Division, as part of II Canadian Corps' advance into Holland, was to push along the east bank of the Ijssel River and cut off the escape routes of the German forces in western Holland, by reaching the North Sea coast near Leeuwarden. With organized German resistance in eastern Holland crumbling by the end of the first week of April, the division's commander, General Keefler, was determined to keep up the momentum of his advance. Therefore, while Deventer was being cleared by the 7th Canadian Infantry Brigade, he ordered the 9th Brigade to swing to the right and bypass the city to continue the advance north.

"C" Squadron of the 7th Reconnaissance Regiment led the way and "for a day and a half . . . probed, pushed and fought their way to the objective." At one point, enemy observers spotted the armoured cars and brought down a mortar barrage, wounding the squadron commander and his second in command.[2]

On April 8, about ten kilometres west of Deventer, the North Nova Scotia Highlanders attacked across the Schipbeek Canal with the task of establishing a bridgehead at the village of Bathmen, at which point a Bailey bridge would be built quickly as the main route for the drive into northern Holland. The attack, with "C" Company on the left and "D" Company on the right, found the enemy holding the canal line in strength and "D" Company became pinned down.

On the first attempt to cross, both companies were stopped by machine-gun and mortar fire . . . "C" Company called for tanks to neutralize the machine-guns in farms in the left front, and for 3-inch mortar smoke across their front . . . 14 Platoon then crossed on debris of a demolished bridge, entered the houses on the opposite side and brought their small arms fire

on the enemy position on the opposite bank. 14 Platoon suffered 8 casualties in the assault. The remainder of the company crossed immediately and the clearing of the town began.[3]

Corporal Joseph William Campbell was a section commander in "C" Com-
pany, North Nova Scotia Highlanders, from the Nijmegen break–out until the
8th of April 1945. On that date, during the advance of the 9th Canadian In-
fantry Brigade into the north of Holland to cut off the enemy forces in the west,
The North Nova Scotia Highlanders were ordered to secure a bridgehead over the
canal at Bathmen Holland. "C" Company was given the task of making the in-
itial assault crossing.

At the Forming Up Point, the company came under heavy machine-gun and
mortar fire and also found that the approaches to the demolished bridge were
heavily mined. Corporal Campbell, resolutely leading his men right to the edge of
the canal, with utter disregard for his personal safety, kept them steady by mov-
ing from one to the other with words of encouragement. When the signal was
given for the leading section to rush across, Corporal Campbell (with outstanding
coolness and courage) led his men across the wreckage of the blown bridge. A
smoke screen hid his movement from the enemy, positioned at a distance from the
canal, but Corporal Campbell soon found that there were two machine-gun posts
dug right into the opposite bank. In spite of the deadly cross-fire which suddenly
came at him from close range, hitting two of his men, Corporal Campbell led the
remainder of his section in a swift attack on the opposite dyke. Using his Sten
gun with great effectiveness, he personally dealt with one of the enemy machine-
gun posts. He then placed his Bren gun in position to cover him, and led his rifle-
men in a bayonet assault on the other Spandau. At point-blank range, the enemy
weapon opened up on him. Corporal Campbell was killed a few seconds before his
men, whom he had inspired by his leadership, jumped into the enemy trench and
finished his job.

The dyke was cleared and the remainder of his company immediately moved
across the canal and into the town of Bathmen. Corporal Campbell's outstanding
bravery in this action enabled his battalion to continue its swift advance into
northern Holland, without giving the Germans the delay they wanted. He gave
his life in a manner that was beyond praise.

For his action, Corporal Joseph William Campbell was awarded the
Netherlands' Militaire Willems-Ordre.

The 9th Brigade stayed in Bathmen only long enough to secure the
bridgehead and rebuild the bridge. Then, as described by Col Stacey:

> The 9th Infantry Brigade became the vanguard in a dash for
> Leeuwarden, nearly seventy miles in a direct line north of De-
> venter and only ten miles from the coast. The infantry rode in
> borrowed "Rams" (armoured gun tractors) of the 6th Anti-
> Tank Regiment RCA and miscellaneous vehicles of the 14th
> Field Regiment RCA and 27th Armoured Regiment. Delayed

only by demolitions, Brigadier Rockingham's men drove north
to the Overijsselsch Canal, southeast of Zwolle . . . [4]

*Lieutenant Colonel Charles Alexander Baerman has commanded the 7th Ca-
nadian Reconnaissance Regiment from October 1944, through the Scheldt, Operation VERITABLE, the break–out to the Rhine, the crossing of the Rhine, and
the present advance through Holland into northern Germany.*

*During the advance through Germany and Holland in April 1945, the re-
connaissance squadrons under his command were deployed between Emmerich
and the Hoch Elten in front of the leading infantry brigade. The German opposition—artillery, machine-gun and small arms fire—was heavy and every bridge
was blown along the axis of advance.*

*This officer personally set an example, to the three squadrons of his regiment,
of extreme aggressiveness, of coolness under fire, of initiative of getting around obstacles and of improvising bridges and by-passes. This resulted in the whole regiment accomplishing more than its directed objectives, enabling the infantry to
continue its fast advance.*

*On 10 April 1945, north of Bathmen Holland, "C" Squadron was held up
by heavy anti-tank and mortar fire. The squadron leader and the second in command were both wounded. Lieutenant Colonel Baerman, from his tactical headquarters forward of the brigade headquarters, took over the squadron, personally led
it in by-passing the enemy strongpoint, captured the position from the rear, wiped
out the enemy with heavy casualties, and then resumed his overall command.*

*The leadership and courage displayed by Lieutenant-Colonel Baerman
throughout this series of actions have been outstanding.*

For his actions, Lieutenant Colonel Charles Alexander Baerman was
awarded the Distinguished Service Order.

On April 10, the Stormont, Dundas and Glengarry Highlanders,
leading the Brigade forward, moved up the highway towards Raalte,
about half-way to Zwolle, where the road crossed the Zijkanaal.

*On 10 April 1945 on the line of the Zijkanaal near Raalte Holland, Corpo-
ral Hugh Charles Atchison, section leader in "A" Company, the Stormont, Dundas and Glengarry Highlanders, crossed the canal alone under heavy enemy
machine-gun fire. He procured a boat from the enemy side and made possible the
establishment of a bridgehead.*

*"A" Company of the Stormont, Dundas and Glengarry Highlanders, was the
leading company of the leading battalion of the 9th Canadian Infantry Brigade.
The advance was held up by a blown bridge across the Zijkanaal. Corporal
Atchison volunteered to cross the canal to try and get a boat which was noticed
moored to the enemy bank. By scouting under fire along his side of the canal, this
non-commissioned officer found a kayak in which he crossed the canal. The enemy
intensified their fire and swept the canal with small arms fire. Corporal
Atchison, with exceptional coolness and bravery, continued to paddle his unreli-*

able craft across the canal and reached the enemy boat. He then recrossed the canal with the serviceable craft and began ferrying riflemen across.

This brave action, far beyond the call of duty, made possible the formation of a firm bridgehead through which the entire battalion was able to pass. The resourcefulness and daring shown in the face of heavy enemy fire was an inspiration to his comrades.

For his action, Corporal Hugh Charles Atchison was awarded the Military Medal.

On April 12, The Stormont, Dundas and Glengarry Highlanders, continuing as the vanguard of the brigade, were ordered to seize a bridgehead over the Overijssels Canal as they advanced on Zwolle. After a wild early morning ride on tanks of the Sherbrooke Fusiliers, the battalion reached the canal and crossed it on a girder of a partially destroyed bridge. The small enemy defensive force was completely surprised and driven off. However, at 2045 hours, the Germans returned in force and counter-attacked under a concentrated artillery and mortar barrage, supported by armoured fighting vehicles. Three German armoured cars penetrated the defensive perimeter, and the Glens' commander quickly brought down defensive artillery fire to within fifty yards of the forward Canadian troops. Because of the blown bridge, the battalion had been unable to move their heavy anti-tank weapons across the canal. The situation hung in the balance, as the battalion's second in command collected a force of drivers and cooks to attempt to get the anti-tank weapons across the canal.

Captain Roger Nelson LeBaron, of 66 Battery, 14th Canadian Field Regiment RCA, was acting as forward observation officer supporting The Stormont, Dundas and Glengarry Highlanders during the advance of the 9th Canadian Infantry Brigade on the east side of the River Ijssel. By the afternoon of 12 April 1945, the battalion had crossed on foot the Overijssel Canal north of Heino. All bridges had been blown and it was not possible to bring across any vehicles or anti-tank guns.

The country was wooded, close and flat, with the only observation post being from a conspicuous narrow sand ridge behind the centre forward infantry company. This ridge was being subjected to fire from both flanks, including mortars, small arms and shelling, a high proportion of which was air bursts. In spite of this, Captain LeBaron proceeded to establish an observation post there, leaving his signaller a few yards away at the base of the ridge in a place of safety.

At about an hour before dark, an enemy counter-attack of armour supported by infantry developed against the bridgehead and seriously threatened the whole battalion position which was without anti-tank guns and not yet securely consolidated to meet the threat.

From his position, Captain LeBaron saw four tanks, each followed by infantry, moving from a concealed position behind trees and close in on "D" Company, the left company. He immediately reported this and brought down a concentration of artillery and mortar fire on the enemy. Enemy shelling of the sand dune increased and a direct hit was made on the adjacent slit trench within six feet of Captain LeBaron. Despite this fire, Captain LeBaron stayed at his post. While the enemy tanks were still being engaged on the left, Captain LeBaron observed three heavy armoured cars approaching, one of which moved to a position sixty yards to his flank. These cars opened direct fire with 20-mm cannon on Captain LeBaron's position and on "B" Company. In face of this fire, he crossed the ridge to reach his signaller and called down artillery fire on this new close target. He then returned to his observation post and remained there in order to control the fire and report on the situation.

The counter-attack was beaten off, principally by the artillery fire which was laid down for a period of one hour and twenty minutes. The battalion was thus able to hold its ground while a bridge was constructed and anti-tank guns brought up to consolidate the bridgehead through which the brigade was able to continue its advance the next morning.

For his action, Captain Roger Nelson LeBaron was awarded the Military Cross.

On the night of 12/13 April 1945 at the Overijsselsch Canal, Lance Corporal Hector John King Edwards, "A" Company of The Stormont, Dundas and Glengarry Highlanders, while in charge of his company's ammunition stores, displayed initiative and courage beyond the call of duty in order to ensure that the riflemen could carry out their tasks in holding the bridgehead over the canal.

"A" Company had crossed the canal over a single span on the blown bridge and immediately contacted the enemy who reacted vigorously with 20-mm Flak guns, two tanks and other small arms fire. For several hours, the situation was unsettled as no support could be brought over the canal until early in the morning. With ammunition running low, three enemy scout cars penetrated the battalion position and were engaged with PIATs. Lance Corporal Edwards, realizing that the ammunition supply was becoming serious, managed with great difficulty to manoeuvre his carrier across the broken bridge which was only partially repaired at the time and was constantly under heavy enemy mortar fire. Ignoring the mortars and the 20-mm fire as he advanced, he brought his carrier up to the company position, following the enemy scout cars so closely that he was almost engaged by his own company PIATs.

By his action, the company was enabled to repulse the enemy counter-attack and thus establish the bridgehead and assure the advance of the 9th Canadian Infantry Brigade.

For his action, Lance Corporal Hector John King Edwards was awarded the Netherlands' Bronze Cross.

During the advance northwards, "C" Squadron of the 7th Reconnaissance Regiment led the way, fanning out in front to find the best routes forward. The squadron's 11 Troop was assigned the probe to the west where they ran into a strongly defended enemy position. The leading armoured car was knocked out by a Panzerfaust and the crew, who had bailed out of the burning vehicle, were pinned down by machine-gun fire.

On 12 April 1945, 11 Troop of "C" Squadron of the 7th Canadian Reconnaissance Regiment was patrolling to examine the bridge over a canal near the town of Wijhe. The leading armoured car, which carried the troop officer, was hit and knocked out by a Panzerfaust. The crew, although wounded, had bailed out but were pinned down by machine-gun fire. The guns of the second armoured car had jammed and were unable to give covering fire.

Corporal Allan Sheppard, commanding the leading carrier, quickly sized up the situation and, without hesitation, moved across six hundred yards of open country under heavy machine-gun and Panzerfaust fire directed at him. He engaged the enemy with such hot and accurate fire that he succeeded in partially neutralizing their fire. He then got out of his carrier, exposing himself to further fire, and helped the wounded men into it.

After he removed the wounded men to a place of safety, he again went forward under heavy machine-gun and Panzerfaust fire to within eighty yards of the enemy's positions. He engaged them hotly until seriously wounded by a close burst from a Panzerfaust. This non-commissioned officer, by his coolness and exceptional courage, not only saved the lives of his comrades but, by repeatedly exposing himself and drawing the enemy fire, enabled the crew of the second armoured car to observe the enemy's dispositions. This armoured car was able to extricate itself from a difficult position without casualties. The information about the enemy's estimated strength and dispositions, given by the crews of the second armoured car and by the wounded who were saved by this non-commissioned officer's bravery, materially assisted the 9th Canadian Infantry Brigade to cross the canal that night and proceed on to the ultimate liberation of Zwolle.

For his action, Lance Corporal Allan Sheppard was awarded the Netherlands' Bronze Lion.

Following the capture of Deventer, The Canadian Scottish were assigned to screen the city on the north. Patrols soon identified that the village of Olst, about five miles north, was held in strength by the enemy. Orders were given for "B" Company of The Canadian Scottish to eliminate this threat. The attack was launched at first light on April 13. A short sharp engagement ensued, where the Canadian infantry had to cross a thickly sown minefield and were then met by heavy artillery and machine-gun fire which pinned down the right-hand platoon.

On 13 April 1945, "B" Company of the 1st Battalion, The Canadian Scottish, was given the task of taking the town of Olst in Holland. After sending out reconnaissance patrols, the company went into the attack with Corporal Wilfred Paradis as acting platoon sergeant.

The platoon proceeded up the road leading to the village, crossed an anti-tank ditch and, in extended line, started clearing the orchard on the right–hand side of *the road. Here they came under heavy artillery and machine-gun fire. To silence the machine-gun post, it was necessary to crawl near enough to throw a 36-Grenade.* This was done, killing one of the crew and wounding another who later died.*

With the machine-gun silenced, Number 12 Platoon continued the attack, proceeding another five hundred yards before they were again pinned down by heavy machine-gun fire coming from the left flank. Here, with disregard for his own safety, armed with his Sten gun, Corporal Paradis advanced up the road by himself. He encountered a German with a Schmeisser** whom he immediately fired on and killed. He then threw another 36–Grenade which effectively routed the crew of the second machine-gun post, thus clearing the way for the platoon to advance into the town.

Corporal Paradis then placed his men in strategic positions in the town and himself, with a few men, occupied a house on the corner of the cross roads in the centre of the town. Here they took up a position in the basement with a borrowed Bren gun. A German sniper, who had already inflicted one casualty on the platoon, then came down the road. Corporal Paradis opened fire on the sniper, hitting him five times and fatally wounding him. The platoon then continued their advance and consolidated on the dykes, thus accomplishing their objective.

Corporal Paradis' coolness under fire, undaunted courage, keen leadership and devotion to duty have been a source of inspiration to his men throughout. He was, in no small measure, personally responsible for the successful completion of his platoon's tasks and this non-commissioned officer played a part which assisted materially in the liberation of Holland.

For his actions, Corporal Wilfred Paradis was awarded the Netherlands' Bronze Lion.

After the fall of Deventer, the Germans withdrew the main body of their troops either across the Ijssel River or north to Zwolle. This town of about 50,000 people was a main transportation centre of the province of Overijssel and the last bastion of the Germans' Ijssel Line. The 7th Canadian Infantry Brigade had now been rushed up behind the 9th Brigade and, on April 13, prepared to make an assault on the defences the next day. The brigade had little information about the German defences and wanted a night patrol to make contact with the local resistance movement. Leo Major and Wilfrid Arsenault of Le Régiment de la Chaudière volunteered.

At about 2300 hours on April 12, the two scouts attempted to slip into the suburbs but unexpectedly encountered a German outpost which resulted in the death of Corporal Arsenault. Despite this, Private

---

*   The standard Canadian anti-personnel hand-grenade.

**   A German rapid-firing 9 mm Parabellum submachine gun.

Major decided to carry on with his mission carrying two Sten guns with a large quantity of ammunition and a sack of grenades. He arrived in the centre of Zwolle at about 0100 hours, finding the streets silent and deserted. Here, he spotted a German machine-gun nest which, since the crew was sleeping, he promptly attacked and eliminated. He then found a German scout car and forced one of the Germans, who he had captured, to drive through the streets with the lights on, flying a white flag. For several hours, Major moved through the streets, shooting up any targets he could find, attempting to make an impression that a large Canadian force had arrived.

The citizens were awakened but were afraid to come out of their houses. By a stroke of good luck, Private Major came across the head of the resistance, Frits Kuiper, and four of his men. By now the Germans appeared to have fled the city in panic. The group therefore returned to the town hall, the resistance fighters bringing the citizens out into the streets. The local radio station was able to announce that they had been liberated.

By now, Private Major was exhausted. But he had to return to his lines and bring back the body of his comrade, Corporal Arseneault. The resistance fighters arranged for a car to transport the body back but found that the outposts of the Chaudières fired on them. Major was furious and climbed onto the top of the car so that he could be easily seen from a distance. In this manner, he returned to the Canadian lines to report the result of his mission to Lieutenant-Colonel Taschereau.

On 13 April 1945, Le Régiment de la Chaudière was deployed and in position preparing to launch an attack on the town of Zwolle Holland. To save as many Dutch lives as possible, it was necessary to know exactly

Private Leo Major of Le Régiment de la Chaudière was awarded the Distinguished Conduct Medal for his actions at Zwolle, the Netherlands.
Printed with the permission of Leo Major.

the location of the enemy positions which had not been clearly identified. Private Leo Major and a corporal from the scout platoon volunteered to enter the town and contact the underground movement to obtain the necessary information.

A road–block was located at the entrance of the town, guarded by a small group of the enemy. The patrol was discovered and the corporal killed. Private Major killed two Germans and scattered the others. Undaunted by the death of a friend and comrade, he continued alone with the patrol's mission for six hours, contacting the underground and forming patrols of local Dutch civilians, with the result that by morning the enemy garrison, menaced from inside and outside, were forced to withdraw as their position became untenable. To urge them on, Private Major had the Gestapo headquarters set on fire.

At 0500 hours, 14 April 1945, this gallant soldier waded across a canal, after posting numerous patrols of the Dutch resistance movement at strategic points. On his way back, though wet and tired, he picked up the body of his corporal and brought it in.

The gallant conduct of this soldier, his personal initiative, his dauntless courage and entire disregard for his personal safety, was an inspiration to all. His gallant action was instrumental in enabling the mopping up, on 14 April, to be done without a shot being fired.

For his action, Private Leo Major was awarded the Distinguished Conduct Medal.[5]

On 13 April 1945, Le Régiment de la Chaudière was deployed on the south and east of Zwolle Netherlands. During the night of 13/14 April, Corporal Wilfrid Arseneault displayed a high standard of bravery, devotion to duty and utmost gallantry, paying the supreme sacrifice.

It was necessary to ascertain the exact location of enemy defences in order to save as many Dutch lives as was possible. This gallant non-commissioned officer volunteered to go with another soldier on reconnaissance. Near the town, an enemy outpost was found manned by four Germans. Ordering his companion to take cover, this brave non-commissioned officer charged the position alone, being mortally wounded doing so, but keeping on firing until he had no more ammunition. He personally killed two Germans and wounded another before he died. The enemy outpost was routed and his companion went on alone to finish the task.

The utmost gallantry, personal bravery and high standard of devotion to duty displayed by Corporal Arseneault was an inspiration to all, and was instrumental in the capture of Zwolle on the morning of 14 April 1945, without a civilian casualty.

For his action, Corporal Wilfrid Arseneault was posthumously awarded the Netherlands' Bronze Lion.

Twenty-five years later, Leo Major and his wife were invited back to the city of Zwolle where he was honoured as the liberator of Zwolle. He was presented to Queen Juliana and awarded a special medal struck by the city of Zwolle. The local newspaper wrote:

Leo Major and his wife were given a great welcome . . . Thousands of people were standing alongside the road that Zwolle's first liberator followed in 1945 . . . Thank you Canada! And let's not forget Willy Arseneault. He rests in the Canadian War Cemetery in Holten. Please put flowers on his grave.[6]

With the capture of Zwolle, the German resistance fell apart. Once again, the 7th Reconnaissance Regiment led the way towards Leeuwarden. Speeding northwards:

town after town was liberated as the far-flung patrols passed Meppel, Stenwijk and approached Heerenveen. Only small parties of enemy were encountered and they looked so meek and subdued that they were simply left for the infantry to pick up later.

It is very difficult to describe the excitement and thrill of liberating these small communities. As an armoured car patrol would approach one of these little towns, the patrol leader would peer at it through his binoculars wondering if, perchance, there were still some of those fanatical Nazis left about. Suddenly, there would be a flash of colour as hundreds of flags began to wave in the sun. Then, a few seconds later, the sound of a great cheering crowd would reach his ears and he would put his microphone to his lips, ordering the driver to move on into town.

Grateful Dutch citizens celebrate after being liberated by the 3rd Canadian Infantry Division
Donald I. Grant. NAC, PA-145972

As the cars began to near the place the people would spill out
on the road and start running towards them. There were thousands of them . . . all blond and cheering.[7]

But those "fanatical Nazis" still lurked in some places.

*On 14 April 1945 at Ildhuizen on the Ijssel River, the Troop of the 7th Ca-
nadian Reconnaissance Regiment in which Corporal Kenneth Amos Chapman
was section leader reached the outskirts of Ildhuizen where they came under heavy
machine-gun fire and air bursts. After trying to work their way around this position, the enemy launched a counter-attack. Corporal Chapman, completely disregarding the enemy fire, dismounted from his vehicle and advanced up the street
alone, firing the Bren gun from the hip. He broke up the enemy counter-attack,
killing three Germans and wounding seven others, causing the enemy to withdraw
in disorder. It was through the initiative, coolness and courage shown by Corporal Chapman that the squadron continued their advance and occupied Ildhuizen,
thus protecting the 7th Canadian Infantry Brigade in their advance to the
Zuider Zee.*

For his action, Corporal Kenneth Amos Chapman was awarded the Military Medal.

*On the evening of 15 April 1945, Number 13 Platoon of "D" Company,
Cameron Highlanders of Ottawa (MG) were ordered to advance in support of Le
Régiment de la Chaudière in the area north of Winschoten. Starting off at
1800 hours, the platoon advanced to take up a mortar position in the midst of
heavy enemy shell fire. Le Régiment de la Chaudière was meeting very heavy resistance and it was approximately 2330 hours before Number 13 Platoon was
able to take up a position. Enemy heavy and medium artillery fire intensified and
two carriers from Number 13 Platoon were knocked out.*

*Corporal Floyd Edison Webb proceeded calmly to get the mortars into posi-
tion. In their advance, the Chaudières had passed a German Panzerfaust crew
who were about one hundred yards to the front and right of the platoon position,
and these kept firing their bombs into the platoon area. It was now absolutely
pitch dark and Corporal Webb realized that, if something were not done about
the Panzerfaust crew, the Platoon would suffer many casualties. He therefore took
up a Bren gun and went out alone to deal with the enemy. He fired a full maga-
zine, killing the two members of the Panzerfaust crew and was back to his duties
on the mortar line in fifteen minutes. The heavy shelling continued all night but
the platoon managed to fire one thousand mortar rounds, thus assisting the
Chaudières to reach their objective. The success of this operation was due in no
small measure to the outstanding leadership and high courage of Corporal Webb.*

For his action, Corporal Floyd Edison Webb was awarded the Netherlands' Bronze Cross.

As the division raced northwards, its left flank along the Ijssel River
became exceedingly long but had to be covered in case the Germans
tried to cross over. The task of patrolling fourteen miles of river line was

assigned to the Cameron Highlanders of Ottawa. On April 17, "A" Company sent out two patrols, one of which under Sergeant H. E. Bird penetrated deeply into enemy territory and returned with four prisoners.

Sergeant Howard Edward Bird commanded Number 2 Section of Number 5 Platoon, "A" Company, Cameron Highlanders of Ottawa (MG) from 6 June 1944 to the end of hostilities. Throughout Sergeant Bird's service with "A" Company, he constantly displayed great personal courage, and magnificent leadership. This non-commissioned officer, by his fearless actions, created an esprit de corps within his section that proved a source of strength under the most trying conditions. His men would follow him anywhere. Not once throughout the campaigns in France, Belgium, Holland and Germany did Sergeant Bird's section falter or fail. On the contrary, they always displayed a keen offensive spirit, a spirit which in large part was created by their sergeant's example.

On 17 April 1945, "A" Company was containing the enemy along the line of the Ijssel River near the town of Wijhe Holland. Sergeant Bird and two men from his section were given the task of patrolling across the Ijssel for the purpose of ascertaining the strength and disposition of the enemy troops opposite Number 5 Platoon's position. Under cover of darkness, Sergeant Bird and his party slipped across the river. Having successfully penetrated the enemy lines, Sergeant Bird pushed on a distance of five miles to the northwest of the river. Here he decided to investigate a farmhouse which showed signs of military occupation. Going forward alone Sergeant Bird entered the house and found it occupied by four German soldiers. These he quickly disarmed and took prisoner and brought them back through the enemy lines, across the river, and into Number 5 Platoon's position. These pris-

Machine-gun platoon of the Cameron Highlanders of Ottawa (MG) at their carrier. Sergeant Howard Edward Bird, seated in the second row, left side, was awarded the Netherlands' Bronze Cross for his actions in Holland.
NAC, PA-138357

oners, together with Sergeant Bird's report, yielded valuable information concerning the enemy's positions. This is one example of the initiative and personal courage which were the prime characteristics of this non-commissioned officer.

For his action, Sergeant Howard Edward Bird was awarded the Netherlands' Bronze Cross.

On the afternoon of April 15, Canadian reconnaissance patrols reached Leeuwarden and the next day the Highland Light Infantry of Canada occupied Harlingen on the coast. On April 17, the 7th Canadian Infantry Brigade advanced against the eastern end of the great causeway that separated the Ijsselmeer (sometimes called "Zuider Zee") from the North Sea, to seal the final exit left to the German Army in western Holland. The North Shore (NB) Regiment was to take the town of Makkum on the southern approach to the causeway while the Queen's Own Rifles of Canada took the town of Pingjum on the north. The attack was expected to be difficult as the approaches were over low, flat fields intersected with canals.

At Makkum, prior to the North Shore's attack, a patrol was sent out by the Cameron Highlanders to gain information on the defenders' strength. The patrol unexpectedly ran into a strong German patrol. The patrol leader, Sergeant W. E. G. Coburn, managed to extricate his men, with support from "B" Company of the Camerons, from the resulting fire fight. The next day, fifty enemy dead were counted where this action had occurred.[8]

Sergeant William Edward George Coburn was a section commander of Number 6 Platoon of the Cameron Highlanders of Ottawa (MG). The company was assigned a holding role near the town of Makkum. On the night of 17/18 April 1945, this non-commissioned officer led a reconnaissance patrol of four men to gain information about the enemy strongpoint guarding a vital approach to the town. When within fifty yards of his objective, he ran into an enemy fighting patrol, approaching his position, fifteen men strong and led by an officer. He was challenged in German and fired on by three Maxim machine-guns and one Machine-gun 42. In the melee which ensued, he killed three of the enemy, including the officer, and led his patrol back safely to his own lines. He was able to accurately pin-point each of the enemy defences. Sergeant Coburn was interrogated by the commanding officer of the North Shore (NB) Regiment the next day and was able to supply detailed information vital to his plans for the assault on the town which was carried out without casualties after the enemy position had been neutralized by artillery fire.

Not only did the information obtained by this non-commissioned officer directly contribute to the success of the attack, but his vigorous interception of the enemy patrol probably saved a surprise attack on our own lightly held position.

For his action, Sergeant William Edward George Coburn was awarded the Military Medal.

On 18 April 1945, "C" Company of The North Shore (New Brunswick) Regiment, with the carrier platoon and two anti-tank guns under command, were acting in the role of a mobile battle group with orders to make a reconnaissance of the bridge on the approaches to Makkum. The company was embussed on carriers and were proceeding along when a huge crater was blown in the road. One carrier was blown up and all the troops on the carrier were killed. Nevertheless, the company established a firm base around a farm and returned the enemy fire which consisted of two 88-mm guns, small arms and Panzerfaust fire. Several casualties occurred in the consolidation area.

One anti-tank gun ran out of ammunition and Private James Benedict Lynch, whose gun was in the open and under severe fire from the enemy, handled his gun alone and returned the enemy fire. This soldier did superb work and silenced one of the 88-mm guns. This allowed the forward platoon of the company, which was trapped in the crater, to crawl back approximately three hundred yards to the company area without casualties. This was due to the efficient and courageous manner in which Private Lynch handled his anti-tank gun.

It was a brave example to all to see this soldier handle his six-pounder anti-tank gun alone while all enemy fire was directed at him.

For his action, Private James Benedict Lynch was awarded the Netherlands' Bronze Lion.

At 1400 hours, "A" and "C" Companies of the North Shore Regiment moved off in a two-pronged attack from the east and west against Makkum. They crossed the start line without any opposition and crossed the open fields so quickly that the enemy were surprised in their foxholes. With good coordination between fire and movement, the attacking platoons soon had taken possession of Makkum.[9]

While the North Shores were attacking Makkum, the Queen's Own Rifles were moving against the access to the causeway from the north.

Dutch women, wearing their national costume, welcome personnel of "C" Company, Highland Light Infantry of Canada, as the Canadians pass through Dalfsen, Netherlands.
Donald I. Grant, NAC, PA-130236.

On 17 April 1945, "D" Company, 1st Battalion, The Queen's Own Rifles of Canada, was ordered to attack and consolidate in the town of Pingjum Holland. Civilians provided information that the objective and its approaches were defended by approximately one hundred and forty enemy troops armed with automatic weapons, Panzerfausts, and one 88-mm artillery piece.

In order to make plans for the attack, it was necessary for "D" Company to ascertain if the crossroads were held by the enemy and Sergeant John Sterling Cameron was ordered to take out a reconnaissance patrol to determine the possibility of establishing a start line at the crossroads for an attack on the town. The patrol's task was two-fold: firstly to check a house near the crossroads; and, secondly, to investigate the crossroads itself. When the patrol reached their first objective and found it be unoccupied, Sergeant Cameron very courageously proceeded ahead of his companions to the second objective, leaving them to give covering fire if necessary.

Sergeant Cameron reached the crossroads and met no opposition. He then, on his own initiative, proceeded up the road toward the town, still keeping approximately one hundred and fifty yards ahead of his men. At a point on this road, he came under enemy fire from a barn on his right. Sergeant Cameron engaged this threat single-handedly, killing two of the enemy and wounding one, whom he took prisoner. During this action, he observed an enemy force with an estimated strength of thirty to forty troops, dug in astride the road.

At this time, Sergeant Cameron decided to withdraw and did so under heavy enemy fire, carrying the wounded prisoner with him for questioning. While retiring up the road, he observed enemy troops, previously unnoticed, in the area immediately southwest of the crossroads. He was therefore forced to make his withdrawal across country and continuously under heavy enemy small arms fire. He did so successfully and without harm befalling him.

For his action, Sergeant John Sterling Cameron was awarded the Military Medal.

The Queen's Own Rifles' attack concluded in an unusual way, as the hopelessness of the German situation was made apparent:

> Lieutenant J. L. Hancock, who spoke fluent German—and idiomatically—calmly walked down the road and roared out to the enemy that it was idiotic to resist. It only caused needless loss of life; the result was inevitable.[10]

On 17 April 1945, "D" Company, 1st Battalion, The Queen's Own Rifles of Canada, was ordered to attack the town of Pingjum Holland. By 1900 hours, Number 17 Platoon of "D" Company had secured a start line along a road through the crossroads, meeting with very heavy opposition from enemy small arms fire. The plan called for Number 18 Platoon led by Lieutenant John Leslie Hancock to pass across the start line and attack straight up the road to the town. Lieutenant Hancock and his men encountered heavy enemy small arms fire as they started their task and the tanks supporting their company were called up.

However, the enemy were so firmly entrenched that the effect of the fire from the tanks was minimized.

Lieutenant Hancock made a quick appreciation of the situation and decided to take his platoon up the road. He deployed his men on either side of the road while he, with great courage and under a hail of enemy small arms fire, walked up the road, well in advance of his men, encouraging and inspiring them. As Lieutenant Hancock neared the enemy position, he called upon the enemy to surrender and they, impressed by this officer's magnificent display of courage, disorganized by the boldness and directness of his actions, surrendered themselves, thirty-seven strong including one officer and one warrant officer. No casualties were suffered by "D" Company. Lieutenant Hancock then led his platoon into the town of Pingjum and there established a firm base.

Throughout the entire action, this officer conducted himself with great courage and displayed a high degree of initiative. His coolness, daring and audacity, under extremely heavy enemy fire, plus his regard for the safety of his men, were the deciding factors in the success of the company operations.

For his action, Lieutenant John Leslie Hancock was awarded the Military Cross.

On the morning of 18 April 1945, 1st Battalion, The Queen's Own Rifles of Canada, was committed to the attack on the strongpoint at the road junction at the northeast of the great causeway which crosses the Zuider Zee. The attack was to be launched from the village of Kornwerd. The success of this operation was vital as it meant the sealing of the final escape route across the Zuider Zee to the Germans still in western Holland.

Major John Douglas Pickup was in command of "C" Company, 1st Battalion, The Queen's Own Rifles of Canada, which was the company assigned to carry out this attack. Due to the open nature of the country and the exposed lines of approach to the objective, the matter of reconnaissance for the attack was extremely difficult.

Major Pickup, in spite of the heavy small arms and 20-mm fire directed against him by the German strongpoint, carried out a close personal reconnaissance of the ground over which "C" Company had to approach the objective. On completion of this, Captain Pickup personally led his company into the attack. His courage and leadership inspired his men so that, despite the heavy fire directed at them by the defenders as they approached across the coverless country, "C" Company quickly overran the enemy positions.

Major Pickup's personal courage and lack of regard for his personal safety was an inspiration to his men who followed him to steadily and quickly overcome a position which showed every sign of being a very difficult one to capture.

For his action, Major John Douglas Pickup was awarded the Netherlands' Bronze Lion.

With the capture of Makkum and Pingjum, the immediate task of the 3rd Division was successfully completed after a breathless drive through central Holland. As described by Col Stacey:

> In the course of their advance from the Rhine to the North Sea, General Keefler's men had fought forward 115 miles in 26 days, built 36 bridges and captured 4600 prisoners.[11]

A job well done to the satisfaction of thousands of grateful Dutch people.

NOTES

1. National Archives of Canada Record Group (RG) 24, Vol 15123, North Nova Scotia Highlanders War Diary, 8 April 1945.

2. Capt W. G. Pavey, *An Historical Account of the 7th Canadian Reconnaissance Regiment in the World War 1939 - 1945* (Montreal: privately published, 1948), p. 112.

3. RG 24, Vol 15123, Nth NS Hghrs W.D., April 1945, Report on Bathmen by Maj. L.C. Winhold.

4. Col C. P. Stacey, *The Victory Campiagn* (Ottawa: The Queen's Printer, 1966), p. 556.

5. Leo Major subsequently was awarded a Bar to his DCM for his actions on November 1951 on Hill 227 in Korea.

6. Correspondence from Leo Major, 11 October 1994.

7. Pavey, p. 116.

8. Lt Col R. M. Ross, *The History of the 1st Battalion Cameron Highlanders of Ottawa* (MG) (Ottawa: privately published, 1946), p. 88.

9. Will R. Bird, *North Shore (New Brunswick) Regiment* (Fredricton: Brunswick Press, 1968), p. 552.

10. Lt Col W. T. Barnard, *The Queen's Own Rifles of Canada 1860 - 1960* (Don Mills: The Ontario Publishing Co. Ltd., 1960), p.259.

11. Stacey, p. 557.

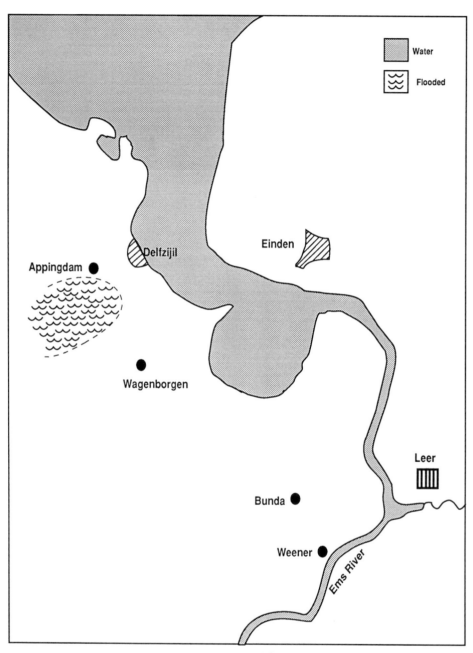

Flooded

Einden

Delfzijl

Appingdam

Wagenborgen

Leer

Bunda

Weener

Ems River

Northwest Holland and Germany.

-12-
CLEARING NORTHWEST HOLLAND

> The war is an ideological conflict of the greatest magnitude. Only fanatical fighters will achieve victory in it. Unit commanders must therefore radiate faith and confidence in victory . . . The battle of destiny of the Reich demands that every commander of a threatened position does his duty to the utmost. Unit commanders who leave their units when in danger and seek personal safety are to be sentenced to death.
>
> Generalfeldmarschall Model
> Commander-in-Chief West[1]

While the 3rd Canadian Infantry Division was heading north toward Leeuwarden, the other divisions of II Canadian Corps were heading in a westerly direction. On April 15, the 1st Polish Armoured Division reached the Ems River estuary on the border between the Netherlands and Germany. This cut off all German troops in the western part of the Netherlands from escaping to Germany. As a result, a little port northeast of Groningen, called Delfzijl, now became a magnet for these German forces. From here, they could escape by sea to Emden. It now became a question of how stubbornly the German defenders could hold the perimeter of this area to gain time for the evacuation to take place. It was Dunkirk in reverse.

Delfzijl had some natural features which favoured the defence. The ground was flat with very little cover, and a network of ditches and canals made cross-country movement impossible. The ground to the west was flooded so that the town could only be reached from either the north or south. The key to the northern approach was the town of Appingdam, while Wagenborgen covered the southern approach. The German commander, determined to make a strong stand, prevented fighting troops from getting on the ferries so that they could be used as reinforcements for the marine forces holding the perimeter.[2]

On April 20, the Royal Winnipeg Rifles launched an attack on the village of Loppersum which lay about six kilometres to the west of Appingdam.

On 20 April 1945, The Royal Winnipeg Rifles were ordered to take the town of Loppersum Holland. In the plan of attack, "B" Company was given the task of entering the town from the north, while "D" Company approached from the southwest. Before "B" Company could get into the town, it was necessary to clear a group of farm buildings which were situated on the only accessible road.

Lance Corporal Walter Bruce Carstairs, in command of the leading section, had successfully cleared most of the opposition from this obstacle when he was forced to take cover from the fire of determined enemy at one point. Rather than hold up the advance of the main body upon the town while he went back for assistance, he positioned his men so that they could give covering fire and take advantage of the success of his scheme. Since none of his men had sufficient battle experience to tackle such a perilous task, Lance Corporal Carstairs crept forward alone until he was within twenty yards of the enemy. One grenade, followed by his sudden appearance in their midst with his Sten gun at the ready, resulted in the surrender of the strongpoint. The Lance Corporal emerged with five prisoners. This action was completed under heavy small arms fire.

The quick thinking and dash and the very courageous action of this soldier undoubtedly assured the rapid advance of the company and the attainment of their objective, the capture of Loppersum.

For his action, Lance Corporal Carstairs was awarded the Military Medal.

On April 21, the regiment moved on Appingdam, attempting to capture the main bridge crossing the canal in front of the town. The Germans managed to blow it up before it could be taken, but patrols found a small alternate bridge which just managed to bear the weight of a jeep. "A" and "C" Companies crossed over the bridge early on April 22, but their advance was contained by minefields and mortar fire. Early the next morning, the Winnipegs resumed their attack before dawn, gaining a foothold before the enemy could recover and cleared the town before night.[3]

Captain Thomas Johnston Bell of the 12th Canadian Field Regiment RCA was forward observation officer with "A" Company of The Royal Winnipeg Rifles when that battalion was ordered to capture Appingdam on 22 April 1945. "A" Company was to secure the left flank by capturing and holding the town of Jukwerd. Throughout the whole day of 21 April, the company was under incessant enemy shell fire in the town of Oosterwijtwerd. Several casualties resulted which were impossible to evacuate due to the heavy observed fire of the enemy. The situation was further aggravated by the lack of sleep and the fact that it was impossible to bring up food.

Realizing the acute necessity for counter-battery fire to silence the enemy guns, Captain Bell waded a canal which was under direct observation by the enemy and set up an excellent observation post from which he was able to materially reduce the enemy fire. During the early hours of 22 April, as the main attack was being mounted, the company commander was mortally wounded. Captain Bell, under heavy shell fire, supervised the dressing of his wounds and his evacuation. He also realized that a firm grasp had to be taken to maintain control and keep up morale. Captain Bell was able to do this and it was undoubtedly largely due to his courage and leadership that the company was able to successfully reach and hold their objective which, in turn, enabled the battalion to capture Appingdam.

For his action, Captain Thomas Johnston Bell was awarded the Military Cross.

The Royal Winnipeg Rifles were ordered to capture the town of Appingdam on 22 April 1945. At one point during the attack, "B" Company's position became almost untenable due to the concentration of heavy artillery and machine-gun fire. While pinned down by some very accurate enemy fire, one of the platoons had an important message to send to company headquarters. Knowing full well that it was an extremely hazardous trip, Rifleman John Gingras volunteered to take the message. As he was bravely making his way along, he was wounded in both legs, first by a bullet and then by shrapnel from enemy shell fire. Regardless of his wounds, he not only delivered this message safely to company headquarters, but he returned to his platoon and carried on until the action was successfully completed before allowing himself to be evacuated.

It was a determined enemy that held the town, but the fine example of courage and devotion to duty displayed by Rifleman Gingras raised the men's sprits and gave them heart to carry on and defeat the enemy and capture Appingdam.

For his action, Rifleman John Gingras was awarded the Military Medal.

On 23 April 1945, The Royal Winnipeg Rifle Regiment was ordered to take and hold Appingdam Holland. A section of carriers, commanded by Sergeant Francis Jeremia Thomas Ryan was attached to "B" Company which had the role of clearing the northern outskirts of Appingdam. On the approach march, Sergeant Ryan was sent out ahead of the company to make reconnaissance of enemy positions. On approaching a group of buildings, the section was fired on by two Panzerfausts and an enemy machine-gun. Without waiting for the rifle company to deploy, Sergeant Ryan ordered his section into action and was personally responsible for silencing the machine-gun. The enemy outpost was cleared, more Germans were killed and five taken prisoner. By Sergeant Ryan's quick thinking and courageous action, the enemy outpost was neutralized and the rifle company was able to proceed without delay.

On the direct attack on Appingdam, Sergeant Ryan's task was to protect the right flank of the battalion. The section came under heavy shell fire as they occupied a group of buildings on the right flank. Sergeant Ryan, disregarding the shell fire, moved from house to house, positioning his Bren guns until he was confident the battalion's right flank was protected.

During the afternoon, small enemy patrols tried to penetrate his position but all were repulsed. His position was under constant shell fire all afternoon, yet he personally supervised all defensive measures. During his last visit, Sergeant Ryan was seriously wounded and evacuated. The perseverance and courage displayed by Sergeant Ryan resulted in the battalion having its right flank protected whilst attacking Appingdam, thereby assisting in the success of the operation.

For his actions, Sergeant Francis Jeremia Thomas Ryan was awarded the Military Medal.

On 22 April 1945, Lance Sergeant James William Bryan of the 6th Canadian Field Company RCE, with his section, was in support of the 7th Canadian Infantry Brigade in an attack on Appingdam. He was with the leading company of The Royal Winnipeg Rifles and responsible for the clearance of mines and other obstacles along their axis.

They came across a road–block at the southern approach to the town. While the infantry provided covering fire, Lance Sergeant Bryan's party proceeded to clear the obstacle. The task was half–completed when direct enemy shell and mortar fire came down on the site. Lance Sergeant Bryan ordered his men to take cover and then alone, under the same persistent fire, continued to prepare the road–block for demolition until he was wounded. At the same time, his platoon commander and another sapper were wounded and Bryan insisted on aiding them, until all three were evacuated. The remainder of the section, inspired by this non-commissioned officer's gallant action, completed the job and the route was opened, allowing supporting armour to move up without serious delay.

It was this non-commissioned officer's cool determination and brilliant leadership which on this occasion resulted in the clearing of a road–block, allowing tanks to take part in the capture of Appingdam—an operation vital to the liberation of northern Holland.

For his action, Lance Corporal James William Bryan was awarded the Netherlands' Bronze Lion.

On 22 April 1945, The Royal Winnipeg Rifles were ordered to capture Appingdam Holland. The attack went in shortly after noon, but mopping up was not completed until the evening of 24 April at which time the objective had been completely cleared of the enemy.

During the early stages of the attack, enemy shell fire knocked out all the battalion's ambulance jeeps except the one driven by Rifleman William Chapman. In order to evacuate all the casualties, he made trips continuously for thirty-eight hours, often under observed artillery fire. At one point, the road over which he had to travel was observed by the enemy for a distance of four hundred yards. On several occasions, shells landed close enough to splatter the jeep with mud and puncture the frame with shrapnel. However, Rifleman Chapman continued his task without flinching.

His determined devotion to duty and his superior courage gave the casualties he carried the strength and will to live. He never hesitated when there were casualties to be evacuated, and he refused relief until ordered down by the commanding officer. His complete disregard for his personal safety saved many lives and materially assisted in the successful attack on Appingdam.

For his action, Rifleman William Chapman was awarded the Military Medal.

Gunner Donald Wright of the 12th Canadian Field Artillery was an artillery signaller transmitting orders for the artillery forward observation officer advancing with the forward infantry company in Bierns Holland on 22 April 1945. During a heavy shelling of the town and the company area by enemy self-

propelled and coastal guns, the telephone line between the artillery observation post and the radio set was cut many times. New lines had to be laid over the distance of one hundred and fifty yards three times. The coolness and courage shown by Gunner Wright in repairing and relaying line in the open, under fire, was responsible for the forward observation officer being able to engage and silence the enemy guns. Gunner Wright's cool behaviour and leadership throughout the whole campaign was an example to all and in keeping with the best traditions of the Royal Canadian Artillery.

For his actions, Gunner Donald Wright was awarded the Military Medal.

On the right of the Brigade front, units of 1st Battalion, The Canadian Scottish fanned out over a thirty-kilometre sector between Groningen and the German border. Patrols of the 7th Reconnaissance Regiment had reported that the village of Wagenborgen was occupied by the Germans. Since the garrison was estimated at about 200 men, it was felt one company could deal with them. Thus, "D" Company of the Scottish was ordered to capture the village on April 21. The intelligence estimates were, however, incorrect as Wagenborgen was held by the 360th Marine Fortress Battalion with at least 600 naval troops well-equipped with machine-guns, mortars and 20-mm guns.

"D" Company advanced from the southwest on Wagenborgen before dawn, but were met by heavy small arms and 20-mm gun fire from the fully alert defenders. Unable to advance along this route, "D" Company pulled back, reorganized and, in the afternoon, attempted to attack from the south. As the forward elements reached the outskirts, the Germans counter-attacked and cut off one platoon. Heavy shell fire came down and the building in which the company headquarters was located received a direct hit. The building collapsed in flames, trapping the personnel, including the company commander, the pioneer officer and the forward artillery observer. The company became temporarily disorganized and Support Company played an invaluable role in holding off the enemy with mortars and anti-tank guns.[4]

On 21 April 1945, Corporal William Knowles was commanding a section of the anti-tank platoon, Support Company, 1st Battalion The Canadian Scottish Regiment, which was supporting "D" Company in an attack on Wagenborgen Holland. The area in which Corporal Knowles had his gun was under extremely heavy enemy shell and machine-gun fire. He continued firing until he had used up all his ammunition. Just at this time, one platoon of "D" Company was forced to withdraw to the vicinity of Corporal Knowles' position and, when he observed that the company commander and several others had been wounded, he organized and assisted in their evacuation with his carrier. This non-commissioned officer then organized the platoon of "D" Company and, together with his own detachment, occupied a new position with a view to preventing any further enemy penetration.

As a result of the leadership and exceptional personal courage displayed by Corporal Knowles, a firm position was held, thus permitting another company to pass through to complete the battalion's task.

For his action, Corporal William Knowles was awarded the Military Medal.

Sergeant George Hugh Jackson of Support Company, 1st Battalion, The Canadian Scottish Regiment, landed on 6 June 1944 as a Lance Corporal. He participated in every engagement of the unit from D-day to the cessation of hostilities, working his way quietly and efficiently until he held the rank of senior non-commissioned officer in the anti-tank platoon. He proved himself a reliable and resourceful leader and, during the many actions of the battalion, often was with the leading rifle companies at the head of his detachment during the attack.

On 21 April 1945 during the attack on the town of Wagenborgen Holland, his detachment was with "D" Company. The company was hotly engaged prior to reaching its objective and many casualties suffered. Here Sergeant Jackson displayed great initiative in using his detachment as infantry to give covering fire to a forward platoon which was pinned to a single axis by strong enemy small arms fire. Sergeant Jackson was everywhere, encouraging his men fearlessly in their self-appointed infantry task. Later, this non-commissioned officer carried wounded back to his own carriers to assist in their evacuation under fire. When enemy artillery set "D" Company Headquarters' building on fire and all was a raging inferno, Sergeant Jackson, disregarding his own safety, continued to remove wounded from the building and to reach safety, until all further aid had to be abandoned.

Throughout his service, Sergeant Jackson inspired confidence in his abilities and was an inspiration to the men he commanded. His utter disregard for his personal safety and his able leadership in action were a credit to the regiment and will continue to be held as an example by all the personnel with whom he has been associated.

For his actions, Sergeant George Hugh Jackson was awarded the Military Medal.

Gunner William Clifford Ace of the 12th Canadian Field Regiment RCA acted as signaller to a forward observation officer with The Canadian Scottish Regiment throughout the entire period prior to and after the crossing of the Rhine. Always right up with his officer, Gunner Ace was continually under mortar, small arms and artillery fire. However, throughout this long exhausting period, he was always cheerful and willing to do any and all tasks required.

On the afternoon of 21 April 1945, Gunner Ace was in an observation post in a barn near the village of Wagenborgen Holland when the barn was very heavily shelled. As his radio set was the only communication for both the artillery and the infantry, he manned his set until long after the barn was well ablaze and his officer missing in the ruins. Gunner Ace then helped tend the wounded, even in the face of an enemy counter-attack, and was finally one of the very last to leave the position.

One of the observation officers with Gunner Ace during this long period was killed and one wounded, but he always stuck to his job and kept the all-necessary communications open as long as was humanly possible.

For his actions, Gunner William Clifford Ace was awarded the Military Medal.

As news of "D" Company's repulse arrived at the battalion headquarters, Lieutenant-Colonel Henderson immediately realized that the attack would have to be reinforced. The scattered companies were rushed up to Wagenborgen, with "B" Company relieving "D" Company. Patrols were sent out during the night to better identify the enemy positions. That evening, a new attack was launched, with "A" Company coming from the west at 2150 hours to seize the north part of the village. "B" Company then gained a foothold on the south part of the village an hour later. "C" Company established its platoons on some dykes east of the village to cut off the garrison.

Confused fighting continued through the night, along with shelling from self-propelled guns. Although the forward Canadian Scottish companies were well established, they were isolated from the rear by snipers who controlled the access routes. During the day of April 22, the Germans continually attempted to infiltrate and counter-attack. At mid-morning, word was received that the Germans were preparing a major counter-attack. Carriers were therefore called to come forward to cover the gap between the two forward companies. However, Germans had infiltrated the area and knocked out a number of carriers with Panzerfausts. An attempt was made to try to bring up some tanks from the Governor General's Foot Guards, but these too were knocked out.

Fighting continued throughout the day. Although the Canadian Scottish forward companies were outnumbered, they held commanding positions and made skilful use of their weapons. A platoon from "D" finally managed to come up and help clear the gap between the other two companies. By nightfall, April 23, the Canadian Scottish were finally firmly in control of Wagenborgen. The victory had been costly, with a loss of 60 men, but it was estimated that the enemy had lost 200.[5]

On 21 April 1945, Captain Stewart Leslie Chambers was commanding "A" Company, 1st Battalion The Canadian Scottish Regiment in the attack on Wagenborgen Holland. Patrols from the company had determined that the enemy was holding the northern outskirts of the town in considerable strength. By evening, the company, which was advancing along the railway tracks, was in position and launched an attack. Against stiff opposition, a wedge was driven into the town, extending to the eastern limits, thus cutting off any possible withdrawal. Captain Chambers' company then proceeded to clear the remainder of the town and pushed south to join up with "B" Company.

During the night, the enemy counter-attacked from the north in force and succeeded in knocking out four of the tanks supporting Captain Chambers' company.

This officer directed his men in a most able manner against an enemy force considerably stronger than his own. The commander of one of his platoons was a casualty and Captain Chambers kept continual personal contact with this platoon, giving the non-commissioned officer in command very valuable guidance and assistance, and encouragement to the men by his cheerful and confident bearing.

The leadership, undaunted courage and devotion to duty, shown by Captain Chambers in this difficult battle, which was his first as a company commander, gave the men courage and helped to a great extent in the successful capture of Wagenborgen.

For his actions, Captain Stewart Leslie Chambers was awarded the Military Cross.

On the evening of 21 April 1945, "B" Company, 1st Battalion The Canadian Scottish Regiment, commanded by Major Earl Grey English, was ordered to capture the town of Wagenborgen Holland. Leading his Company under cover of darkness against the town, held by a strong force of determined and well dug-in enemy, he skilfully directed his platoons through mines and heavy fixed-line machine-gun fire to the outskirts of the town.

As the attack progressed into the built-up area, the fighting became fluid and furious. With utter disregard for his personal safety, Major English moved from platoon to platoon, giving a word of direction here and encouragement there. After some very heavy fighting, the town was captured but, during the night, the fanatical enemy launched three counter-attacks which were beaten off. By morning, the company had linked up with "A" Company on the other side of the town and the position was secure.

The success of this attack was largely due to the leadership and skill displayed by Major English. His actions in this engagement were an inspiration to all his men and were in accord with the highest traditions of the Canadian Army.

For his actions, Major Earl Grey English was awarded the Distinguished Service Order.

On 21 April 1945, during the attack on Wagenborgen, Corporal William Lawrence, of the 1st Battalion The Canadian Scottish Regiment, took over command of his platoon when the platoon officer was killed. He carried on in this capacity for that night and the following day during the heavy fighting.

During a heavy German counter-attack, the building in which his platoon was situated was set afire by exploding shells. Corporal Lawrence quickly and efficiently removed his men from the burning building to move to a new position of defence with no loss of men or equipment. He maintained and held his new defensive positions throughout the night and day of repeated German counter-attacks in which the enemy used mortars, machine-gun fire and Panzerfausts in an effort to dislodge the defenders from their positions. Corporal Lawrence's ability to inspire and encourage his men was outstanding and helped greatly in bringing his platoon through this heavy fighting.

Corporal Lawrence's coolness under fire, undaunted courage, keen leadership and devotion to duty have been a source of inspiration to his men throughout, and assisted greatly in the successful completion of his platoon's tasks. He assisted materially to achieve the ultimate liberation of Holland.

For his actions, Corporal William Lawrence was awarded the Netherlands' Bronze Lion.

On 23 April 1945, Lance Sergeant Armond Thomas Patterson Connell, as Number 3 Troops leader of "C" Squadron, 27th Canadian Armoured Regiment (Sherbrooke Fusiliers), was allotted the task of supporting The Canadian Scottish Regiment into the town of Wagenborgen Holland, and of breaking up an enemy counter-attack.

In the market square of the town, his troop suddenly met the enemy force. In a matter of seconds, the second and third tanks of Lance Sergeant Connell's troop were destroyed by enemy Panzerfaust teams. He quickly assessed the critical situation and realized that he had the alternative of retiring from an overwhelming force or accepting the difficult and very dangerous task of holding his ground. Without hesitation or consideration of his own safety, he chose the latter.

In quick succession, he destroyed two enemy Panzerfaust teams and several infantrymen. So accurate and deadly was his fire that he not only held the counter-attack but caused the enemy to become so inextricably disorganized that they were forced to withdraw.

At this moment, an enemy mortar bomb fell so close that it knocked out the wireless set in the tank. Realizing that information about the enemy withdrawal must be sent to the infantry battalion headquarters immediately, Lance Sergeant Connell dismounted, disregarded the heavy enemy snipers and mortar fire and on foot guided his tank towards the rear. While passing his burning third tank, exploding ammunition knocked him against a wall with such force that he became unconscious. He recovered in less than a minute and, with amazing fortitude, guided his tank to a fire position covering the main street in the vicinity of battalion headquarters. The information he brought was of vital assistance in making new plans for continuing the attack.

Through Lance Sergeant Connell's actions, the enemy counter-attack force completely failed to take the town. His example is of an exceptionally high standard, and his initiative and bravery are worthy of the highest praise.

For his actions, Lance Sergeant Armond Thomas Patterson Connell was awarded the Military Medal.

Lieutenant Kenneth Frederick Prueter was the platoon commander of Number 14 Platoon (Heavy Mortar), "D" Company of The Cameron Highlanders of Ottawa (MG). His platoon was under command of 7th Canadian Infantry Brigade and were holding part of the line near Finsterwolde which was north of Winchoschen. On the afternoon of April 25, the platoon was suddenly called upon to bring down mortar fire by the Canadian Scottish Regiment, who were being counter-attacked by the enemy. Lieutenant Prueter proceeded up to his ob-

servation post which afforded an excellent view but was very exposed to enemy small arms and artillery fire. He succeeded in a very few minutes to engage the enemy. By his excellent observation and direction he caused many casualties and great confusion in the enemy's ranks and was largely responsible for breaking up the counter-attack. His mortar fire kept the enemy pinned down for some hours and, under cover of darkness, the Germans withdrew.

During the action the Canadian Scottish communication system broke down and Lieutenant Prueter organized his platoon communications in such a way that he was able to relay all messages from the infantry companies to their battalion headquarters. By Lieutenant Prueter's quick and thoughtful action, he was able to turn a possible setback into a successful action.

For his actions Lieutenant Kenneth Frederick Prueter was awarded the Netherlands' Bronze Cross.

With the immediate objectives of Wagenborgen and Appingdam now secured, the 8th Brigade was relieved by units of the 5th Canadian Armoured Division which would take care of the final elimination of the Delfzijl pocket. The 3rd Division now prepared to move towards the German border.

Just a few kilometres from the border, a German heavy coastal battery remained to be cleared. The Regina Rifles launched an attack towards this position at 0100 hours on April 25. Heavy enemy shelling

Troops of "C" Company, The Highland Light Infantry of Canada, advancing through central Holland
Donald I. Grant, NAC, PA-112640

caused the advance to become temporarily disorganized. However, the Reginas pressed on and, by 0930 hours, all objectives had been taken.

On the afternoon of 24 April 1945, Captain John Douglas Crowe of the 12th Canadian Field Regiment RCA was performing the duties of artillery forward observation officer in support of The Royal Winnipeg Rifles and Regina Rifle Regiment. He established his observation post in a windmill on the edge of the village of Ganzendijk Holland. From this vantage point, he was able to observe the enemy battery of four 10-cm dual purpose guns on a dyke dominating the ground over which the Regina Rifle Regiment was to attack during the night.

The village and the windmill were in full view of the enemy's guns which subjected them to intense shelling throughout the afternoon. Captain Crowe remained at his post, directing the fire of his own guns on the enemy position. His coolness, determination and skill resulted in two of the 10-cm guns being destroyed and the other two being neutralized. Later that night, the battery surrendered without having to be assaulted by the infantry.

There is no doubt that Captain Crowe's efforts considerably assisted the two battalions in their task of clearing the enemy from the west bank of the River Ems with a minimum of casualties. His skill, devotion to duty, in complete disregard of his own personal safety, provide an example to the army as a whole and were in keeping with the best traditions of the Royal Canadian Artillery.

For his action, Captain John Douglas Crowe was awarded the Military Cross.

On 25 April 1945, The Regina Rifle Regiment was engaged in executing a daring plan to capture an enemy strongpoint containing several active artillery guns north of Oudedijk Holland. At 0100 hours, "A" Company, commanded by Captain John Ivan Nicholson, moved forward until the leading platoon came under very heavy machine-gun and rifle fire. The platoon commander was a casualty, the platoon became disorganized and the advance was halted. Without thought of his own safety, Captain Nicholson went forward as quickly as possible, contacted the leading section, and under point-blank fire reorganized the entire platoon as a fire group. He personally silenced much of the enemy fire with grenades and then led the remainder of his company into the assault.

Inspired by this officer's actions, the company went forward quickly and overran the enemy strongpoint, killed many, capturing one hundred and thirty prisoners and four 105-mm guns

Through Captain Nicholson's exceptional courage, leadership and inspiration, this enemy strongpoint was eliminated quickly and "A" Company of The Regina Rifle Regiment accomplished their task with a minimum of casualties to themselves.

For his action, Captain John Ivan Nicholson was awarded the Military Cross.

NOTES

1.   National Archives of Canada Record Group (RG) 24, Vol 10565, 2 British Army Intelligence Summary No 328, dated 26 April 1945.

2.   RG 24, Vol 15042, 1st Battalion, The Canadian Scottish War Diary for April 1945, 3 CID Intelligence Summaries No. 98 and 100, dated 18 and 23 April 1945 respectively.

3.   Bruce Tascona and Eric Wells, *Little Black Devils: A History of the Royal Winnipeg Rifles* (Winnipeg: Frye Publishing, 1983), p. 188.

4.   RG 24, Vol 15042.

5.   RG 24, Vol 15042; R. H. Roy, *Ready for the Fray* (Vancouver: The Canadian Scottish Regiment, 1958), pp. 421 - 427.

Conquerors' not Liberators (From a painting by D. K. Anderson Canadian War Museum)

-13-
THE END IN GERMANY

Corps HQ, 20 April 1945

The enemy believes that he is near victory. He deceives himself, as so often before. Never yet in history has a people been
beaten unless it gave itself up as lost . . . We do not allow
events to overwhelm us, nor do we stare hypnotised at the
map. So long as we fight, everything can be achieved! Full of
confidence we look to our Führer, who places firm and unshakable reliance upon us soldiers. Today, on his birthday, we vow
to our Führer once again that we will fight to the last drop of
blood, in loyalty to our oath, for our freedom and honour, for
our National-Socialist Reich, until at the end, in defiance of
circumstances, victory is ours.

Signed (Rasp) General der Infanterie
General Officer Commanding
Ems Corps[1]

The task assigned to II Canadian Corps in the invasion of Germany was
to clear the East Friesland Peninsula, the Emden-Wilhemshaven promontory on the north coast. The 1st Polish Armoured Division led the way in
attempting to seize the nearest approaches to the area. Upon meeting stiff-
ening resistance, however, General Simonds assigned to the 3rd Canadian
Infantry Division the job of capturing Leer, the western gateway to the
promontory. Once Leer had been secured, the 3rd Division would advance
north and attack the major port of Emden from the rear.

The small port of Leer lay on the east bank of the Ems River, about
twenty kilometres down river from where it exited into the main estuary.
Here, the junction of the Ems River with the Leda River covered the town
on both the west and south sides, providing a strong natural defensive position. In addition, the surrounding terrain was flat and wet, crossed by numerous ditches which could limit the movement of the tanks of the
Sherbrooke Fusiliers, assigned to support the 3rd Division. The town
was a key communications centre, with highways radiating north to the
port of Emden, close by, and northeast to Wilhemshaven. The German
commander, Fregatten-Kapitain Frey determined to use his troops from
the 18th Marine Reinforcement Unit and 747th Flak Battery along the
river lines to block the Canadian advance as long as possible.[2]

Clearing the Approaches to Leer

The advance began in late April with two brigades pressing in towards the rivers from the positions taken over from the Polish Division —the 8th Brigade on the left advancing eastward from near the German-Dutch border towards the Ems River and the 7th Brigade on the right advancing northward towards the Leda. In the 8th Brigade sector, The North Shore Regiment advanced along the highway leading to Leer and attacked Weener on April 23. The leading platoon of "C" Company received heavy casualties and the supporting tanks were held up by Panzerfaust and anti-tank fire. However, after a well-directed artillery concentration brought down on the defences, the town was quickly taken. During this battle, Sergeant H. L. Hennigar, who had been awarded the Military Medal at Millingen, was wounded by a Panzerfaust.[3]

On the morning of 23 April 1945, the 3rd Canadian Infantry Division with the 27th Canadian Armoured Regiment in support, attacked a strongly held enemy defence line hingeing on Weener in Germany. The task of forcing the hinge was allotted to the 7th Canadian Infantry Brigade with "A" Squadron in support. The attack proceeded satisfactorily until the tanks were held up by mines and demolitions. At this point, the infantry were unable to advance further due to enemy machine-guns and mortars. Consequently the attack stalled.

Lance Corporal Milton David Davis, scout car driver of "A" Squadron, without hesitation, volunteered to make a reconnaissance for a route through the minefields for the tanks. He dismounted from his scout car and, despite the small arms fire directed at him, and despite the inevitable anti-personnel mines always found in the vicinity of demolitions, successfully found a route through which the tanks could go. He returned to the tanks and, on foot, personally led them through the mines and crated area. Almost immediately the tanks found targets: one 75-mm infantry gun crew and at least two machine-gun crews were promptly destroyed.

Later the same day, in the final stages of the town clearing, the tanks were again held up by mines in and around demolitions and obstacles. On this occasion, Lance Corporal Davis took his scout car and, quite regardless of the mines, attempted to find a route bypassing the danger area. On several occasions, he drove through streets and back alleys where street fighting was in progress and, in doing so, exposed himself to the fire of both enemy and our own weapons. Unfortunately, just as his reconnaissance was completed, Lance Corporal Davis was severely wounded when his vehicle struck a Teller* mine.

For his contribution towards maintaining the speed of the attack, for his great courage and, above all for the complete disregard for his own life, Lance Corporal Davis is worthy of the highest honour.

---

*   A large German anti-tank mine weighing fifteen pounds and shaped like a plate (from the German word Teller, meaning "plate").

For his actions, Lance Corporal Milton David Davis was awarded the Military Medal.

In the centre of the 8th Brigade front, Le Régiment de la Chaudière began their advance early on April 22, on a one-company front, with each company taking its turn in the lead. The Germans conducted a frustrating delaying action in which their rear guard held firm just long enough to force the battalion to deploy before withdrawing again. Lt Col Taschereau ordered that his forward company should not lose contact, but to continue pressing the enemy. However, on April 24, "D" Company was struck by a violent artillery bombardment at a crossroads near the village of Bunde. They had come within range of the heavy German coastal artillery in the naval base at Emden. Major Rochon, who had been awarded the Military Medal at Hollen, was killed, the company thereby losing "not only its chief but a friend of all whom he commanded." "A" Company was called upon to take over the lead. Shortly thereafter, Major C. R. Lamoureux was then badly wounded in the head and legs, although his company managed to make good progress. Finally, "C" Company moved up and the enemy could no longer hold their position.

The regiment reached the edge of the Ems River north of Leer on April 25 and, continuing to fight against stubborn resistance for a number of villages, finally cleared the area of the peninsula west of the Ems River by April 27. The operations had lasted six days during which forty-two casualties had been suffered.

Major Charles Roch Lamoureux, Le Régiment de la Chaudière, landed on 6 June 1944, as liaison officer with the 8th Canadian Infantry Brigade. From this early date he set a very high example of personal courage, devotion to duty and utter disregard of danger. His duties as liaison officer were performed in a most excellent manner despite danger. In November 1944, after many requests, he returned to regimental duties as a company commander of his unit. Once in this new post, he was recognized as a superb leader, constantly visiting the most exposed positions of his company encouraging his men and boosting their morale.

On 24 April 1945, he particularly distinguished himself at Hammrich, near Bunde Germany. The battalion was attacking an important and vital crossroads, well defended by a stubborn enemy trying to delay the advance. Major Lamoureux was leading the advance with his company. The enemy suddenly opened fire with an intense concentration of fire from all types of weapons.

The intensity of the fire forced the company to take cover. After a few minutes, this company commander realized that the attack was in danger of bogging down. Taking immediate action, he stood up on the shell-swept road and rallied his company, encouraging his men on and, taking the lead, personally led a gallant charge. He was wounded once but carried on nevertheless. He finally reached the enemy position where he fell severely wounded a second time. Inspired by this gallant display of leadership, his men charged on and cleaned out the position, routing the enemy.

It was due to the superb and gallant display of high devotion to duty on the part of Major Lamoureux, his personal bravery, utter contempt of danger and utmost gallantry that the position was taken, allowing other companies to go through and capture a sizable portion of enemy territory.

For his action, Major Charles Roch Lamoureux was awarded the Distinguished Service Order.

On 24 April 1945, early in the morning, Le Régiment de la Chaudière in its third day of continuous fighting was proceeding from the village of Bunde in Germany, clearing the road leading to Ditbumer Verlaat. During the stiff fighting of this day, Sergeant George Etienne Deschenes of "D" Company, particularly distinguished himself by his personal bravery and unusually high standard of leadership.

The advance was limited to the road due to the numerous canals and ditches. The enemy had appreciated the fact and the road was under heavy fire from artillery, machine-guns and rifle fire. This company was particularly unlucky in that the company commander and several other officers were killed or wounded. Enemy defensive fire from artillery supplemented by machine-gun fire from close range forced the new company commander to give the order to take cover.

Sergeant Deschenes, commanding Number 18 Platoon, divided his platoon in small groups and taking the lead conducted each of his Major Charles Roch Lamoureux, Le Régiment de la Chaudière, was awarded the Distinguished Service Order for his actions at Leer, Germany

NAC, PA-192248

groups in turn through the enemy defensive fire and launched an attack on a series of five houses from which machine-gun fire was directed at the company. He succeeded in clearing out these machine-gun nests, his platoon suffering many casualties. Once the position was firmly in his hands, he returned coolly to company headquarters, asking for further orders. The superb display of leadership on the part of this non-commissioned officer permitted the company to reach its objective which was to secure a Start Line for the battalion.

The initiative, coolness under fire, personal bravery and superb leadership of Sergeant Deschenes was largely instrumental for the successes of the battalion that day.

For his actions, Sergeant George Etienne Deschenes was awarded the Distinguished Conduct Medal.

Meanwhile, 1st Battalion, The Canadian Scottish Regiment, was given the task of clearing the southern approaches to the Leda River. The attack began on April 26, with two companies working their way north along the dykes lining the east bank of the Ems River, moving cautiously to avoid the mines and booby traps. The defenders put up determined resistance at selected villages and fortified farmhouses, with artillery support from north of the Leda. The Canadian Scottish pushed forward, however, assisted by counter-battery fire and an effective strike by Typhoon and Mustang aircraft. By the evening of April 27, all the river banks had been cleared on schedule for the assault on Leer.[5]

On 27 April 1945 during the battle to gain possession of the ground immediately across the river from Leer Germany, Captain Peter Ferguson McDonnell commanded "A" Company, 1st Battalion, The Canadian Scottish Regiment.

Under the leadership of this officer, "A" Company cleared small pockets of resistance on the approach to the river. The enemy had established themselves in some force along the banks of the River Leda to give their troops covering fire whilst crossing in boats. The whole area was under intense enemy mortar fire as well as heavy and accurate 20- and 88-mm gun fire, during which a direct hit was scored on the building being used as "A" Company headquarters. Captain McDonnell was wounded by this fire but he continued to command his company until the operation was successfully completed and the platoons were firmly established. It was only then that he allowed himself to be evacuated.

The undaunted courage, keen leadership and devotion to duty of this officer was inspiring to all ranks in the company, and his actions were instrumental in the success attained by those under his command.

For his action, Captain Peter Ferguson McDonnell was awarded the Military Cross.

The Battle for Leer

The plan for the advance into the East Friesland Peninsula envisaged the 9th Canadian Infantry Brigade assaulting across the Ems and Leda Rivers, then being joined by the 7th Canadian Infantry Brigade to develop a secure bridgehead. However, the Ems and Leda Rivers presented major problems because they were tidal. If the crossing were to be made on an outgoing tide, the turbulent currents at the confluence of the rivers would make navigation very hazardous; a crossing at low tide, however, would force the troops to land in deep mud far from the actual river bank. The river was furthermore lined with dykes into which the Germans had dug their slit trenches and machine-gun posts. It was important to bridge the river as soon as possible after the assault troops had crossed in order to get supporting weapons and supplies across. With this stretch of the river within range of the heavy German naval guns at Emden, establishing a bridge in daylight could be difficult.

Major-General Keefler and his corps commander, Lieutenant-General Guy Simonds, solved these problems with a creative plan which required good staff work and clear understanding by all arms. The crossing would be made late in the day so that the engineers could immediately begin work on the bridge under cover of darkness. The crossing would therefore be made at 1600 hours, one hour before high tide. This would allow about three hours during the cresting of the tidal effect when the river would be relatively calm and would allow the assault boats to land against the actual river bank.[6]

H-hour was set at 1500 hours for the North Nova Scotia Highlanders to make the southern advance on Leer by crossing the Leda River. Twelve minutes before the crossing, Canadian artillery began a mixed bombardment of smoke and high explosive shells, while heavy machine-guns of the Cameron Highlanders of Ottawa swept the top of the far dykes. At H-hour, under a cold, heavy rain, two platoons of "D" Company hauled their storm boats over the near–bank dyke and raced across the river. The speed of the crossing and the effectiveness of the artillery support allowed the Canadians to surprise the defenders and the initial objectives were quickly taken. Unfortunately, one boat capsized and five men were reported "missing, believed drowned."

As soon as the initial bridgehead was consolidated, the forward elements began to advance towards the southern part of Leer.[7]

On 28 April 1945, when commanding "D" Company, North Nova Scotia Highlanders, Major Kenneth Nelson Webber showed leadership and bravery of the highest order which influenced the brigade attack on Leer (the key to the East Friesland Peninsula) Germany by protecting the right flank.

In the initial assault on Leer, "D" Company was detailed to cross the Leda River, land on the exposed right flank and cover the assault of the Highland Light Infantry of Canada, and the Stormont, Dundas and Glengarry Highlander. The enemy was dug in on the dyke seventy-five yards from the river bank in strength and had four 20-mm guns covering the river. Under a partial smoke, screen the company landed and, while under fire, rushed the dyke. There were approximately six hundred yards of dyke and Major Webber, in spite of the fire they were under, proceeded to direct his men until the whole of the position was captured and all the enemy either killed or captured. The company then came under shell and increased small arms fire, and a counter-attack came in. Major Webber personally directed the smashing of this with great disregard for personal safety. He then called down artillery fire on a sector that was shooting up The Highland Light Infantry of Canada and conducted a mopping up along the right flank of his own position.

The inspired leadership and utter disregard of personal safety shown by Major Webber in leading his company, first in assault boats and secondly over the bullet-swept dyke was the means of establishing the right flank and allowing ensuing troops to go into and take the town.

For his action, Major Kenneth Nelson Webber was awarded the Distinguished Service Order.

On 28 April 1945, "C" Squadron of the 27th Canadian Armoured Regiment supported, with indirect fire from their 75-mm guns, the North Nova Scotia Highlanders in an assault across the River Leda. Captain John Paul Brennan was the forward observation officer and, as such, landed with the forward elements of the assaulting infantry on the enemy-held river bank. On the right flank of the battalion bridgehead was an enemy-held woods, from which small arms fire was causing casualties to the assaulting infantry. From his first post, Captain Brennan was unable to effectively observe the enemy, but any location further forward was inside the field of fire of our own medium artillery.

With utter disregard for his own safety and knowing full well the danger involved, Captain Brennan moved forward to a position from which he could effectively control his guns. In the barrage of medium artillery fire that followed, Captain Brennan's right arm was badly gashed by flying shrapnel. Despite his injury, he remained at his post and, by doing so, continued to bring down such effective fire from his guns that the infantry were able to complete the final assault with little or no opposition from the right flank.

Captain Brennan's decision to accept the risk of taking up a very dangerous observation post resulted in not only saving lives but in considerably accelerating the

The Highland Light Infantry loading into assault boats, getting ready to cast off on the reedy flat shore of the Ems River to start the attack on Leer
Donald I. Grant, NAC, PA-192263

operation. His exceptional bravery and his fortitude in continuing his work though painfully wounded had a direct bearing in the success of the operation. His contribution was worthy of the highest praise.

For his action, Captain John Paul Brennan was awarded the Military Cross.

The Highland Light Infantry of Canada, attacking in the centre of the brigade front, launched their boats twelve miles up the Ems River, moving down to land just past the confluence of the Ems and Leda. The artillery barrage was so effective that many of the German marines were still crouching in their slit trenches when the Canadians landed. The initial objectives were again taken in record time and the troops pushed on into Leer.

In order to have armoured support available in the bridgehead, the assault plans included the transportation of tanks of the Sherbrooke Fusiliers across the Ems to land with the Highland Light Infantry of Canada. Number 3 Troop of "B" Squadron was to cross on rafts. However, the crossing did not happen as planned and the tanks were not available to assist in the initial assault.[8]

On the night of 28 April 1945, Lieutenant George Douglas Goodwin, as Number 3 Troop Leader in "B" Squadron, 27th Canadian Armoured Regiment, was given the task of supporting the Highland Light Infantry of Canada in the assault across the River Ems. The tanks were to be loaded on rafts, floated down the river and landed at Leer Germany.

Whilst going down the river, the rafts became widely separated and Lieutenant Goodwin found his raft was the only tank approaching the enemy-held river bank. Regardless of enemy machine-gun, mortar and 20-mm fire, he dismounted and, on foot, guided his tank from the raft to the bank. Under extreme danger and quite regardless of sniper and mortar fire, Lieutenant Goodwin proceeded on foot to find places where his other tanks could land. By darkness, Number 3 Troop was across the river and concentrated at battalion headquarters.

At 0500 hours the following morning, the infantry were held up by machine-guns and the tanks by an anti-tank gun. Lieutenant Goodwin, by careful though dangerous manoeuvring of his tank, was able to draw fire from the anti-tank gun, enabling his troop sergeant to neutralize its fire. This allowed Lieutenant Goodwin to move to an advantageous position and destroy the machine-guns, thus allowing the infantry to gain their objective.

Lieutenant Goodwin, by sheer determination and despite heavy enemy fire, organized his troop against great odds and was thus able to not only inflict heavy casualties on the enemy, but lend great moral support to our own troops during an assault. He consistently showed initiative, courage, coolness and determination, and proved himself worthy of great commendation.

For his actions, Lieutenant George Douglas Goodwin was awarded the Military Cross.

The crossing of The Stormont, Dundas and Glengarry Highlanders was, however, a different story from the other two landings. In the northern stretch of the Ems, where the river was four-hundred-yards wide, German guns opened up as the boats were still in mid-stream. Enemy shell fire caused the commander of "B" Company, Major Forman, to be thrown into the water along with the company wireless set. The remainder of "B" Company bore the brunt of the enemy small arms fire and the other assault company, "A" Company, landed bunched up in "B" Company's sector, waist deep in water. On the near bank, Captain D. Stewart observed the loss of the company commander and immediately crossed over in a spare boat to avert a developing crisis.

During the assault landing on 6 June 1944, breakout of the bridgehead, the advance through France and subsequent actions, Captain Donald Charles Stewart, second in command of "B" Company of The Stormont, Dundas and Glengarry Highlanders, showed such courage, devotion to duty and exceptional leadership as to set an example of the highest standard to the officers, non-commissioned officers and men of his battalion.

On 28 April 1945, Captain Stewart showed extreme courage and resourcefulness during the water-borne assault on Leer. When the storm boats set out with "B" Company, they came under intense machine-gun fire and several were sunk, among them "B" Company Headquarters boat, with the company commander, signallers and runners. Captain Stewart was observing the crossing from

Three officers of The Stormont, Dundas and Glengarry Highlanders just after receiving their decorations from the King at Buckingham Palace. From left to right: Captain Donald Stewart was awarded the Military Cross for his actions during the crossing of the Ems River; Major James Wallace Braden was awarded the Distinguished Service Order for his conduct at Emmerich; Captain Alexander Stephen was awarded the Military Cross for his action in the Hochwald.
NAC, PA-192260

the embarkation point on the near bank. Realizing that his company had no commander on the spot and the extreme gravity of the situation, he immediately called up a spare boat and ordered that he be ferried across the bullet-swept river without delay. On reaching the far bank, he quickly reorganized his depleted company and gave orders to his platoon commanders for the advance of "B" Company across one thousand yards of bullet-swept open country. Displaying bravery and courage of the highest order, Captain Stewart led his dwindling company to his objective on the outskirts of Leer, and consolidated his position clearing the area of snipers.

Through all the actions in which he took part, Captain Stewart commanded his men with such continuous gallantry as to be worthy of the highest traditions of the Canadian Army.

For his actions during the crossing of the Ems River and in Normandy, Captain Donald Charles Stewart was awarded the Military Cross.

April 1945, Sergeant Frederick Howarth was commanding Number 8 Platoon, "A" Company of The Stormont, Dundas and Glengarry Highlanders in the storm boat crossing of the River Ems at Leer Germany. By outstanding courage, leadership and initiative, he led his platoon onto their objective despite stiff opposition, early losses and the upsetting of initial plans.

Sergeant Howarth, commanding the lead platoon of the left forward company was given the task of storming the dyke one hundred and fifty yards inland and providing covering fire for other following platoons. The river crossing proved difficult. As soon as the boats had entered the main stream, they came under heavy rifle and machine-gun fire, causing many casualties. The engineer personnel manning the boats were unable to reach the planned landing point and landed the entire assault force of two companies, badly bunched and under heavy fire, in the right company area.

Sergeant Howarth lost no time in organizing and leading his men out of the confusion, deploying them on the left flank, though it was from this direction that the most troublesome fire came. Despite the fire, he pressed his platoon forward, using fire and movement to advance. By leading first one section and then another, he reached one side of the dyke. The enemy on the other side of the dyke were assaulted with speed. Sergeant Howarth was again in front, leading his men with mastery and courage. He was the first man to cross the dyke, closing with such dash and fury that he surprised one German machine-gunner from behind and hurled him bodily into a deep ditch full of water. Emulating their leader, his men made short work of the remaining enemy in their area.

The objective taken, it was soon apparent that the platoon would be short of ammunition for their fire task. Realizing this and with complete disregard for his personal safety, Sergeant Howarth went back under fire along both sides of the dyke and towards the landing point, collecting ammunition from the packs and equipment of casualties. This enabled his platoon to maintain adequate fire support until the other platoons were on their objectives. Then he went out to bring in wounded. In the face of vicious sniping, he organized parties to carry casualties back to the dug-out on the dyke.

For his actions, Sergeant Frederick Howarth was awarded the Distinguished Conduct Medal.

Private Gerald Robert Campbell was a stretcher bearer in "B" Company of The Stormont, Dundas and Glengarry Highlanders, during the assault on Leer on 28 April 1945. Although himself wounded and under intense shell, mortar and machine-gun fire, he attended seventeen wounded men.

On 28 April 1945 during the crossing of the River Ems, "B" Company was advancing over open ground when they were met with very heavy concentration of artillery and mortar shelling, along with heavy machine-gun and small arms fire. During this barrage, "B" Company suffered seventeen casualties, among them two of the four stretcher bearers. Private Campbell and the remaining stretcher bearer started to evacuate the wounded. While they were moving back with a stretcher case, a shell landed and exploded directly under the stretcher, wounding the patient and two stretcher bearers. Private Campbell, neglecting his own wounds, immediately applied first aid to the other two men and, summoning an additional man, proceeded once again to evacuate wounded. Being the only stretcher bearer left in the company and, disregarding his own safety, Private Campbell worked incessantly and speedily until the last wounded man was evacuated. Only then did he stop long enough to dress his own wound and proceed on with his company under heavy fire.

Private Campbell stayed with his company and carried on his magnificent work with cheerfulness until his company consolidated. Only then did he go to the Regimental Aid Post to have his own wounds attended. The bravery and devotion to duty shown by this stretcher bearer was an inspiration and example to all about him.

For his action, Private Gerald Robert Campbell was awarded the Military Medal.

At 1500 hours, 28 April 1945, Sapper Hakon Ingeman Bredeson of the 20th Canadian Field Company RCE was motor operator on one of the storm boats taking assaulting infantry of The Stormont, Dundas and Glengarry Highlanders from the west to the east bank of the Ems River. The Forming Up Place for the boats was under enemy shell fire and, while waiting at the start point, Sapper Bredeson was wounded in the leg by shrapnel. There were no spare boat crews, so Sapper Bredeson realized that, if he had his wound attended to, his boat would be lost to the operation. He therefore carried on with the job, making two trips with boats of infantry under heavy small arms fire. He was wounded again on the second trip and brought his boat safely back to the near bank before receiving medical attention. His desire to carry on in spite of a wound which needed attention showed devotion to his duty and helped the operation to be a success.

For his action, Sapper Hakon Ingeman Bredeson received the Military Medal.

At 1500 hours, 28 April 1945, Lance Corporal Arthur Charles Smith, of the 20th Canadian Field Company RCE, was in command of a storm boat taking assaulting infantry from the Stormont, Dundas Glengarry Highlanders from the west to the east bank of the Ems River under direct small arms fire from the enemy on the east bank. Two companies were taken in the first wave of the assault, the boats returning for a second trip to take across the remaining two companies. The boats came under heavy fire as soon as they left the near bank. Lance Corporal Smith was wounded by a bullet along his ribs early in the first crossing, but continued on with his job. Having disembarked the infantry on the bank, he returned to the near bank. Realizing that there were no spare storm boat crews available, in spite of his painful wound, and knowing that the crossing was still under heavy fire, he concealed the fact that he had been wounded and crossed again with a load of infantry in the second wave. During this crossing, he was again wounded in the shoulder but carried on to complete the crossing and bring his boat safely back to the near bank.

His gallant conduct helped to make the assault a success. Had he stopped, after the first assault wave, to have his wound dressed, his boat would not have been available for the second wave. His fine example was an inspiration to others.

For his action, Private Arthur Charles Smith was awarded the Military Medal.

"C" and "D" Companies crossed the Ems at 1530 in a second wave, still under continuing German fire which sank two boats and left fifteen men believed drowned.[9] Passing though "A" Company, these companies advanced toward the western edge of Leer. Passing over the flat, exposed terrain, they made the best use possible of the frequent drainage ditches to move forward in bounds from one to the next.[10]

On 28 April 1945, Private Peter Alexander MacLean, a Bren gunner in "D" Company of The Stormont, Dundas and Glengarry Highlanders, while under intense enemy fire, crossed open ground to an observed vantage point to bring point–blank fire on the enemy who were holding up the company's advance. By his action, he facilitated the capture of the enemy strongpoint and opened a line of advance for The Stormont, Dundas and Glengarry Highlanders.

On 28 April, after crossing the Ems River, "D" Company was held up on flat open ground by cross–fire from enemy small arms fire in the city of Leer. Immediately appreciating the seriousness of the situation, Private MacLean rose with his Bren gun in one hand, a case of ammunition in the other and, disregarding the heavy fire being brought to bear on himself and his company, ran forward to a rise in the ground near an irrigation ditch and opened fire on the enemy gun position. He was immediately spotted by the enemy and fire was brought to bear on his position. In spite of the heavy German fire, he silenced four enemy machine-gun posts and a section of enemy riflemen.

Due to Private MacLean's gallant actions, his company moved through the enemy on the outskirts of Leer and opened a line of advance into the city for the entire battalion.

For his action, Private Peter Alexander MacLean was awarded the Military Medal.

Lance Bombardier Roy William Hammond was the wireless operator for the battery commander of the 81st Battery, 14th Canadian Field Regiment, on the morning when this battery was supporting the Highland Light Infantry of Canada's attack across the River Ems against Leer. During the assault, battalion headquarters was situated in a farmhouse very well forward, and Lance Bombardier Hammond's wireless vehicle was hidden some distance away with a remote into the house.

Just before H-hour, the area of the headquarters was very heavily machine-gunned and mortared with the result that the wireless truck was hit and the set put out of action. It was essential that communications be re-established at once. Lance Bombardier Hammond immediately started back for his truck and, despite the heavy mortaring, managed to reach it and repair the damaged set. He then returned to battalion headquarters only to find that the remote line had been cut by shell fire. He again crossed the shell-swept area and calmly repaired the line under what was by that time direct enemy fire.

As a result of this man's bravery, communications were re-established and the infantry received the much-needed artillery support and the attack was able to proceed successfully.

For his action, Lance Bombardier Roy William Hammond was awarded the Military Medal.

Fighting continued through the night in the town with units of all three Canadian battalions methodically clearing stubborn resistance block by block. The Germans had converted cellars into strongpoints and positioned 20-mm anti-aircraft guns to fire straight down streets. In the darkness and in the strange and narrow streets, much of the fighting was confused with sudden confrontations and Germans attempting to infiltrate back into areas thought to have already been cleared. As a result, early in the morning of April 29, infiltrating Germans cut off the command post of The Highland Light Infantry of Canada and began to fire on it. A serious situation developed as the commander and his staff "were not able to make a move without drawing fire from machine-guns and Panzerfausts stationed in nearby windows."[11]

On 28 April 1945, Lance Corporal John James Wighton was a section commander in Number 16 Platoon of "D" Company, The Highland Light Infantry of Canada, when they, as part of the Canadian Infantry Brigade, crossed the Ems River and attacked the town of Leer Germany.

After nightfall, with the first objectives taken, The Highland Light Infantry of Canada passed though the North Nova Scotia Highlanders in the town itself, with the railway crossing northeast of the town as "D" Company's objective. The ensuing fighting was sharp and at close quarters and, due to the nature of the town, the problem of control was most difficult. "B" Company of the Highland

Light Infantry of Canada was pinned down by heavy automatic and Panzerfaust fire emanating from the area of its objective and the Germans, in addition to carrying out extensive infiltration tactics, were counter-attacking heavily.

At approximately 0300 hours on 29 April 1945, the command post of The Highland Light Infantry of Canada was seriously threatened by a strong group of enemy which had successfully infiltrated through the town. In answer to an SOS call from the command post, the rifle companies despatched relieving forces that could be spared. Lance Corporal John James Wighton, who had been appointed section leader the previous day, led his section in an attempt to get through to the command post, requiring extensive house-to-house fighting.

In one position, the enemy had set up a 20-mm gun and were directing heavy fire on our troops. Lance Corporal Wighton, appreciating that relief could not be accomplished if this gun remained in action, led his section into the attack and killed the gun crew. Other elements of the enemy force had positioned themselves in houses opposite the command post and these Lance Corporal Wighton again attacked without hesitation. In the ensuing fight, he killed several of their number with his automatic weapon and the remainder were driven into a killing ground covered by a flanking company, after which he contacted the battalion headquarters and effected their relief.

Throughout this action, which took place in darkness and under the most adverse conditions of street fighting, the personal qualities of leadership exhibited by this junior non-commissioned officer, and his determination and unswerving devotion to duty, were the factors which were responsible for the relief of the headquarters, which ultimately enabled the battalion's battle to be directed to a successful conclusion. This established a clear start line for battalions of a succeeding brigade in their subsequent drive eastward.

On many occasions, this non-commissioned officer led his men with great dash and ability, encouraging them by his own fearless example to close with the enemy, capture and consolidate their objectives.

For his actions, Corporal John James Wighton was awarded the Military Medal.

By dawn, Leer had been cleared to the east side and only mopping up remained to be done on April 29. On April 30, the Germans launched a strong counter-attack, destroying three carriers of the Glens in the fighting. Machine-gunners of the Cameron Highlanders of Ottawa had arrived, however, and were able to provide valuable support to help drive off the attack.

Lieutenant Merrill Asal Ruiter was the commander of Number 11 Platoon, "C" Company, The Cameron Highlanders of Ottawa (MG), which was in support of The Stormont, Dundas and Glengarry Highlanders during the assault crossing of the Ems River by the 9th Canadian Infantry Brigade to capture the town of Leer.

At approximately 0500 hours on 30 April 1945, the enemy counter-attacked the Stormont, Dundas and Glengarry Highlanders with approximately a company in strength. The enemy advanced to the forward positions of the Stormont, Dundas and Glengarry Highlanders, experiencing considerable success with their Panzerfausts which accounted for three of the SDG carriers. Lieutenant Ruiter, called on for close support, moved his platoon while under heavy enemy small arms fire to an alternative position from which he engaged the enemy with such excellent effect that the enemy immediately withdrew leaving many casualties. Lieutenant Ruiter's platoon continued this much–needed support until the infantry were reorganized and once again firm. The platoon was the only supporting arm at the disposal of the infantry, our own artillery not being available. At this critical time, a serious reverse was prevented on the brigade front due to the determined leadership and courage of Lieutenant Ruiter.

For his action, Lieutenant Merrill Asal Ruiter was awarded the Military Cross.

On the evening of 29 April 1945, Signalman George Edward Thomas, of 3rd Canadian Infantry Division Signals, was a member of a cable detachment consisting of a corporal, three linemen and one driver, in two 5–cwt cars. The task of the detachment was to lay a cable from a point on the east bank of the River Ems opposite Weener to a point on the Leda River. It was known that the area was heavily mined, but the provision and maintenance of line communications to the 9th Canadian Infantry Brigade, which was across the River Leda at Leer, and the 7th Canadian Infantry Brigade which was to follow across shortly was imperative.

Before the line was completed, one of the cars blew up on a mine, killing the corporal in charge of the detachment and severely wounding the other two linemen in the vehicle. After seeing that his wounded comrades were attended to, Signalman Thomas took charge of the situation and carried on with the driver to complete the line.

However, upon testing through, it was found to be broken. By this time, darkness had fallen and it was raining heavily, making visibility very limited. Without regard to his personal safety, Signalman Thomas went back over the line through an area that he knew to be mined and repaired the breaks. He continued to maintain this line throughout that night and all the following day, thus assuring line communications from Headquarters, 3rd Canadian Infantry Division, to 7th and 9th Canadian Infantry Brigades at a time when it was most essential to the operation.

This soldier's courage, determination and devotion to duty was an example and inspiration to all ranks of his section and his actions are worthy of the highest traditions of his corps.

For his action, Signalman George Edward Thomas was awarded the Military Medal.

On the morning of April 30, the 7th Canadian Infantry Brigade had come into action with the Regina Rifles attacking west from Leer to expand the bridgehead toward the adjacent town of Loga. Stubborn resistance was again encountered at a German marine barracks where "B" Company had to call on flame-throwing Crocodile tanks "to persuade the Huns to give up. No signs of surrender here! Men were still being killed, still being wounded."[12]

On the morning of 30 April 1945, "B" Company, 1st Battalion The Regina Rifle Regiment was ordered to clear the area of the German barracks west of Leer Germany. Sergeant Elmer Milton Evoy was platoon sergeant of Number 10 Platoon. Their particular task was to search out along the dykes and road west and south of the barracks. The platoon successfully completed this task and were returning to assist in house clearing when they came under heavy .43 machine-gun fire. This fire sounds very similar to Bren gunfire and it was at first thought that it was one of our own troops firing at them. This non-commissioned officer quickly seized the initiative, contacted his company headquarters by wireless and established the fact that it was enemy fire.

Sergeant Evoy then pin-pointed the fire and, by the skilful use of fire and movement, worked the platoon to a position on the flank of the enemy. Using the covering smoke of several Number 77 Grenades, he took two men and went back under fire for as many 2-inch mortars and PIAT bombs as were available. With complete disregard for his own safety, Sergeant Evoy took up an exposed position and personally fired fifteen PIAT bombs into the enemy strongpoint in addition to directing the fire of the platoon. This accurate close–range fire had such an effect that Sergeant Evoy's platoon took one officer and thirty-four other ranks prisoner which completely silenced all opposition in the southern sector of this area.

In all this fighting, this non-commissioned officer only lost one man killed and two wounded. It was undoubtedly Sergeant Evoy's cool and skilful handling of the platoon plus his bravery and stubborn determination to fight which enabled "B" Company to take its objective quickly and with a minimum of casualties.

For his actions, Sergeant Elmer Milton Evoy was awarded the Military Medal.

The Final Advance

On the morning of May 1, it was clear that the enemy had withdrawn from the area. Late in the day, as described by Colonel C. P. Stacey:

> 3rd Division Headquarters issued instructions for the final phase of the campaign that had begun on the beaches of Normandy. While the 7th Brigade held the Leer bridgehead, the 8th was to drive on towards Aurich . . . The 7th would then take over and capture Aurich while the 9th Brigade, on the left, probed towards Emden. The 8th and 9th Brigades pro-

ceeded to advance steadily along their designated routes in the
face of scattered resistance and extensive demolitions . . .[13]

On May 1, The Stormont, Dundas and Glengarry Highlanders had
reached the village of Terborg, situated on the east bank of the Ems
River about a third of the way to Emden.

*Lance Bombardier John Russell Millar was a wireless operator for the forward
observation officer of the 66th Field Battery, 14th Canadian Field Regiment
RCA, on the afternoon of 1 May 1945 when the officer was supporting The
Stormont, Dundas and Glengarry Highlanders in their attack on the village of
Terborg. The infantry successfully entered Terborg only to immediately come under very heavy artillery fire prior to an enemy counter-attack. In order to keep
communications open, it was necessary for the carrier with the wireless set to
move forward to a very exposed position on one of the dykes south of the town.*

*Lance Bombardier Millar, realizing the danger, ordered his driver and other
members of his crew to stay back and personally took the carrier forward. He remained in this exposed position for five hours, despite his carrier being hit by shell
splinters on four occasions. As a result of his actions, communications were kept open
during this vital period and the forward observation officer was able to bring artillery concentrations down on the enemy's counter-attack and break it up.*

For his action, Lance Bombardier John Russell Millar was awarded the
Military Medal.

It was now evident to everyone that the end of the war was near. On
May 2, news circulated that the Germany Army in Italy had surrendered unconditionally and that Hitler was reported dead. Yet fanatic
groups still insisted on fighting a lost cause. At dawn on May 4, the enemy launched an attack on the two forward companies of the Stormont,
Dundas and Glengarry Highlanders, occupying the village of Riarchum.
The Canadians had taken up carefully prepared defensive positions with
interlocking lines of fire and, as a result, could immediately bring down
a storm of fire from artillery, mortars and machine-guns on the attackers. The regimental history reported that "the dead, including a couple
of officers, were piled in front of the Canadian lines."[14]

*Private Chelsey Roy Mathews, acting section commander in Number 7 Platoon,
"A" Company of The Stormont, Dundas and Glengarry Highlanders, showed outstanding courage, initiative and alertness in repulsing a strong counter-attack. On
the early morning of 3 May 1945, the enemy mounted a strong counter-attack of
about one hundred men on the village of Riarchum, held by "A" and "C" Companies, near Emden Germany.*

*Private Mathews' section first noticed the advance of the enemy, covered by in-
tense artillery fire, at about 0500 hours. Thirty enemy, led by an officer, tried to
storm the section position in the first house of the village by charging across a
small field. Private Mathews quickly organized his defence and the enemy were
halted by Bren gun and small arms fire. They were then compelled to withdraw,
leaving many dead and wounded on the ground.*

A few minutes later, Private Mathews noticed a German officer leading six or seven men up a deep ditch on the section's left flank. This ditch could not be effectively covered from the section's position. Private Mathews, without hesitation, left his covered position and dashed down a hedgerow and across a wide road. He came under heavy fire from his right as he moved but pressed forward and leaped into the ditch up which the enemy were advancing. He worked up this ditch, still under fire, until he was in a position to engage the enemy with his Sten gun. Then he opened fire at extremely close range, killing the German officer, wounding one other German and driving the remainder back. This vigorous and fearless counteraction completely demoralized the enemy who cowered under his fire for some time and then surrendered in batches.

In this action, nine enemy were killed outright and many were wounded. Twenty prisoners were taken. Private Mathews' aggressive spirit was largely responsible for this success, his alert defence having routed the first assault and his spirited single-handed sortie having struck fear into the hearts of the enemy.

For his action, Private Chesley Roy Mathews was awarded the Military Medal.

A typical scene of Germany in defeat, the wreckage of Emden in May 1945 and all that is left of the transportation system—the horse.
Donald I. Grant, NAC, PA-192262

Victory and the End of the Campaign

On 4 May 1945, a message was sent out from the 3rd Division Headquarters: "CEASE ALL OFFENSIVE OPERATIONS FORTHWITH. CEASE FIRE 0800 HOURS 5TH MAY. REMAIN PRESENT AREA." On May 5, terms were signed at Field–Marshal Montgomery's headquarters for the unconditional surrender of all German troops in Northern Germany, Holland, Denmark, the Friesien Island, and Heliogoland. Finally, two days later:

> During the evening, news came over the radio of the unconditional surrender of all German land, sea and air forces . . . By the troops, this news was received with the same calmness as the news of the collapse on the 21st Army Group front. There were no celebrations. One still sensed that feeling of unbelief and of relief that, after almost six long years of fighting, the self-styled Master Race who had set out to establish a new Order in Europe and the world had been beaten to their knees.[15]

The war was over. On 10 May 1945, 3rd Division Headquarters issued the following message to all units:

CONGRATULATORY MESSAGE

PRIME MINISTER OF CANADA

In the name of the Government, I desire at this hour to send you, the officers and men of the Canadian Army, wherever you are serving, heartiest congratulations upon the victory over the armed forces of Nazi Germany, to which you have all so greatly contributed . . .

Our country honours especially today those of you who have been in the thick of the conflict. By your valour, your skill, your endurance in the hardest fighting you have won battle honours of which Canada will never cease to be proud.

In tribute to those of our comrades who have made the supreme sacrifice, the whole nation reverently bows its head.

The record of achievements of Canada's fighting forces in the defeat and destruction of Nazi tyranny will constitute an immortal chapter in the history of our country.[16]

NOTES

1. National Archives of Canada Record Group (RG) 24, Vol 10565, 2 British Army Intelligence Summary No 333, dated 2 May 1945.

2. Col C. P. Stacey, *The Victory Campaign* (Ottawa: The Queen's Printer, 1966), p. 563, 595; RG 24, Vol 15042, 1 Battalion Canadian Scottish War Diary, April 1945, "3 CID Intelligence Summary No. 102," dated 28 April 1945.

3. Will R. Bird, *North Shore (New Brunswick) Regiment* (Fredricton: Brunswick Press, 1963), p. 555.

4. Jacques Castonquay and Armand Ross, *Le Régiment de la Chaudière* (Lévis: Le Régiment de la Chadière, 1983), p.359.

5. R. G. Roy, *Ready for the Fray* (Vancouver: The Canadian Scottish Regiment, 1958), pp. 428 - 430.

6. Maj-Gen. R. H. Keefler, "The Last Canadian Battle and the Suppression of Germany," *The Canadian Military Journal* April 1947, p. 11.

7. Bird, p. 377.

8. Lt-Col H. M. Jackson, *The Sherbrooke Regiment (12th Armoured Regiment)*, privately published, 1958, p. 176.

9. Stacey, p. 596.

10. W. Boss, *The Stormont, Dundas and Glengarry Highlanders, 1783 - 1951* (Ottawa: The Runge Press, 1952), p. 263.

11. Jack Fortune Bartlett, *1st Battalion, The Highland Light Infantry of Canada 1940 - 1945* (Galt: The HIghland Light Infantry Association, 1951), p.111.

12. Capt Eric Luxton, *1st Battalion, The Regina Rifle Regiment 1939 - 1946* (Regina: The Regina Rifles Association, 1946), p. 62.

13. Col C. P. Stacey, *The Victory Campaign*. Ottawa: The Queen's Printer, 1966,

14. Boss, p. 263.

15. RG 24, Vol 15123, Nth NS Highrs W.D., 7 May 1945.

16. RG 24, Vol 15170, The Queen's Own Rifles War Diary, May 1945.

EPILOGUE

So honour the men of the western plains,
Black Devils, Reginas too;
The Queens, North Shores and Chaudières,
And Scots from the Western blue.
Victoria, Winnipeg, Ottawa
Sent sons for the treacherous trail,
Who must feed the guns and the tanks and the men,
The men who dare not fail.
There were gunners and sappers from homes which range
From the east to the setting sun,
And many lie where the ripening rye,
Danced to the devil's fun.
They do not ask a golden casque,
Or a tower of graven stone,
But that men may live in a world set free
From guilt by their blood atoned.[1]

H/Capt. Stanley E. Higgs
October 21, 1944

1   Jane and Walter Morgan, ed., *Soldier Poetry of the Second World War* (Oakville: Mosaic Press, 1990), p.16.

GLOSSARY OF TERMS

Anti-Tank-Gun (6-pounder)   The standard towed anti-tank weapon for an infantry battalion, called a "6-pounder" because of the weight of the shell it fired. It had a range of 5,150 yards but had limited effectiveness against heavy German tanks.

Battalion   Each brigade was divided into three infantry battalions each totalling 35 officers and 786 other ranks and commanded by a lieutenant-colonel.

Bren gun   The standard Canadian light machine-gun, weighing 19 pounds, firing .303-calibre ammunition at a rate of 520 rounds per minute.

Bridgehead   The area on the far side of a river obstacle occupied by an advancing army immediately after crossing.

Carrier   A self-propelled tracked vehicle designed to transport personnel or heavy weapons of an infantry battalion. The Universal Carrier had 10-mm of armour, could travel at a speed of 30 miles per hour and most commonly carried a Bren gun. When modified to be used as a flame-thrower, it was called a "Wasp."

Companies   Each infantry battalion was made up of four rifle co panies, each totalling five officers and 122 men, and one support company, the latter equipped with heavy support weapons such as medium machine-guns and 3-inch mortars. The company was commanded by a major.

Support Company   Each infantry battalion included one support Support company which provided the heavy weapons for supporting the rifle companies in battle. It was made up of four platoons: the mortar platoon with six 3-inch mortars; the carrier platoon with 13 carriers; the anti-tank platoon with six 6-pounder guns; and an assault pioneer platoon.

Crocodile   A Churchill tank fitted with a flame projector in place of its bow machine-gun.

Panzerfaust	A German shoulder-held infantry anti-tank weapon. Designed to be discarded after one shot, its projectile could penetrate 200 mm of armour at 80 yards.
Platoon	An infantry company was made up of three platoons, each of 37 men. A platoon was commanded by a lieutenant with a sergeant as second in command.
PIAT	The British shoulder-held infantry anti-tank weapon (from Projector, Infantry Anti-Tank) firing a rocket-propelled charge weighing 3 pounds. It had a maximum range of 115 yards against tanks and 350 yards against houses.
Section	An infantry platoon was made up of three sections, each commanded by a corporal, with ten other ranks and equipped with one light machine-gun (Bren gun).
Schu-mine	A German anti-personnel mine designed not to kill a man but to blow off his foot. It was constructed of wood and therefore almost impossible to detect.
Spandau	Nickname given to the German light machine-gun.
Squadron	An armoured regiment was divided into three tank squadrons, of 19 tanks each, and a headquarters squadron.
Sten gun	A standard Canadian machine-carbine firing 9-mm bullets at a rate of 550 to 600 rounds per minute designed for close-range action.
Troop	Each tank squadron was divided into five troops of three tanks each, and a headquarters troop of four tanks.
Typhoon	A British single-seat single-engine fighter-bomber armed with eight 60-lb rocket projectiles and four 20-mm Hispano cannons. It was used most effectively in support of ground troops
Wasp	Universal tracked carrier fitted with a flame-thrower with a range of 100-200 yards. It carried a fuel tank of 80 gallons which allowed for only twenty one-second shots.

THE AWARDS*

A. British Orders and Decorations

During the Second World War, the Dominion of Canada, as part of the British Empire, followed the traditions for honours and awards which would be presented to officers and men of His Majesty's fighting forces to recognize outstanding service. The tradition for awarding decorations for gallantry began in the nineteenth century and gradually grew into an extensive system of military honours and awards.

The precedence of orders and decorations is regulated by the British Central Chancery of the Orders of Knighthood. Those awards mentioned in this book are defined as follows:

1. The Victoria Cross
2. Distinguished Service Order
3. Decorations:
   Military Cross
   Distinguished Conduct Medal
   Military Medal
4. Foreign Orders, Decorations and Medals

The Victoria Cross**

The Victoria Cross is the highest honour which can be received for conduct in action. It was instituted in 1856 by Queen Victoria at the end of the Crimean War. At that time, awards for gallantry could only be made to officers and normally to those within the commander in chief's staff. While the Distinguished Conduct Medal had been instituted to allow for recognition of non-commissioned officers and privates, the need for an award open to all, regardless of rank, was recognized by Queen Victoria. In 1855, the Duke of Newcastle wrote that "it does not seem to me right or politic that such deeds of heroism as the war has produced should go unrewarded by an distinctive mark of honour because they are done by privates or officers below the rank of major." The final words in the Royal Warrant specified that the medal was to be awarded "to those officers or men who have served Us in

---

* The Awards Source: Captain H. Taprell Dorling, *Ribbons and Medals* (London: George Philip & Son Ltd. 1974.); Evans Kerrigan, *American War Medals and Decorations* (New York: The Viking Press, 1964).

** John Percival, *The Victoria Cross* (London: Thomas Methuen, 1985) pp. 714.

the presence of the Enemy and shall then have performed some signal act of valour or devotion to their country."

The Victoria Cross is a bronze cross pattée, one-and-a-half inches across, with a lion statant gardant on the Royal Crown on the obverse side. Below the Crown are the words "FOR VALOUR." The original medals were cast from bronze obtained from two eighteen-pounder Russian guns captured in the Crimea.

In 1867, the award of the decoration was extended to officers and men of the Colonial Forces. In 1902, King Edward declared that, for soldiers or sailors killed before receiving their medal, the Victoria Cross would be sent to their relatives. Prior to the Second World War, sixty-six Canadian soldiers and sailors had received the Victoria Cross, twenty-two of these posthumously.

Distinguished Service Order

This medal was established in 1886 for rewarding individual instances of meritorious or distinguished service in war by commissioned officers. Persons nominated had to be marked by the special mention of his name in despatches for "distinguished service under fire, or under conditions equivalent to services in actual combat with the enemy." The recipient may use the letters DSO after his name and bars may be awarded for further acts.

The DSO ranks immediately after the Order of the Companions of Honour, and Companions of the DSO take precedence after Commanders of the British Empire (CBE).

The Military Cross

This decoration was instituted in 1914. It is an army decoration and no person is eligible to receive it unless he is a captain, a commissioned officer of lower grade, or a warrant officer in the army. Recipients are entitled to use the letters MC after their names and bars may be awarded for further acts. The original warrant provided for the award of the MC "in recognition of distinguished and meritorious services in the time of war." An amendment in 1931 laid down that it should be awarded to officers not above the rank of major "for gallant and distinguished services in action."

Distinguished Conduct Medal

This decoration was instituted in 1845 for "meritorious service," to be awarded on the recommendation of the Commander-in-Chief only to sergeants. The DCM for non-commissioned officers and men was sanctioned in 1854 to replace the old "Meritorious Service Medal" for gallantry in action. Recipients may use the letters DCM after their name and bars may be awarded for further acts.

The Military Medal

This medal was instituted in 1916 for award to non-commissioned officers and men of the army for individual or associated acts of bravery brought to notice by the recommendation of a Commander-in-Chief in the field.

Mention in Despatches

This is an emblem denoting brave conduct granted under the authority of the Commander-in-Chief. It is represented in the form of a bronze oak leaf to be worn on the ribbon of the War Medal, 1939-45. No citation was required for those recommended for this award.

B. Special Awards

Netherlands

Militaire Willems-Ordre (Military Order of William)

Named after King William I, this Order was instituted in 1815 and is the highest military decoration in the Netherlands, corresponding to the Victoria Cross. It can be awarded to all ranks for "most conspicuous acts of bravery, leadership and extreme devotion to duty in the presence of the enemy."

Bronzen Leeuw (Bronze Lion)

This decoration is awarded for military acts of gallantry and leadership in the presence of the enemy which are of a very high standard, but do not merit the Military Order of William. The emblem is a bronze cross with a circular shield in the centre bearing the crowned lion of the Netherlands.

Bronzen Kruis (Bronze Cross)

This decoration, instituted in June 1940, was designed to be awarded to all ranks of the Netherlands armed forces or civilians, or to foreigners, who distinguish themselves by acts of gallantry or leadership in the presence of the enemy. It corresponds to the British Military Cross and Military Medal.

United States

Silver Star Medal

This decoration was instituted on July 9, 1918 for "gallantry in action, published in orders issued from headquarters of a general officer, not warranting the award of a Medal of Honor or Distinguished Service Cross."

Bronze Star Medal

This decoration was instituted on February 4, 1944 to be awarded to any person in the military forces of the United States on or after December 7, 1941 who has distinguished himself by heroic or meritorious achievement or service in operations against an armed enemy. The award is designed to recognize acts of heroism of a lesser degree than for the Silver Star.

D. Immediate versus Periodic Awards

Immediate Awards

The powers to confer awards of the DSO, MC, DCM and MM was delegated by His Majesty to certain General Officers for particular acts in a military operation. The Commander-in-Chief was to notify the War Office which, directly upon receipt of this notification, prepared a submission for the King's approval.

Periodic Awards

General officers could accompany their Despatches with a list of recommendations for awards for services rendered during the period covered by the Despatch. Recommendations for Periodic Awards covered recommendations for gallantry in the field which, for various reasons, had not been conferred as Immediate Awards or in saving life other than in actual fighting with the enemy.

E. Awards Made Posthumously

In the system of British honours and awards in effect in 1939, the only military awards which could be made posthumously were the Victoria Cross and Mentions-in-Despatches. A soldier, sailor or airman recommended for any other decoration would not be eligible to receive that award if he were reported killed, missing or prisoner of war before the recommendation was put forward.

ORDERS OF BATTLE
THE 3RD CANADIAN INFANTRY DIVISION

ARMOURED

7th Canadian Reconnaissance Regiment

ARTILLERY

12th Canadian Field Regiment
13th Canadian Field Regiment
14th Canadian Field Regiment
3rd Canadian Anti-Tank Regiment
4th Canadian Light Anti-Aircraft Regiment

ENGINEERS

3rd Canadian Field Park
6th Canadian Field Company
16th Canadian Field Company
18th Canadian Field Company

SIGNALS

Signals 3rd Canadian Division

INFANTRY

The Cameron Highlanders of Ottawa (M.G.)

7th Infantry Brigade

The Royal Winnipeg Rifles
The Regina Rifles
1st Battalion, The Canadian Scottish Regiment

8th Infantry Brigade

The Queen's Own Rifles of Canada
Le Régiment de la Chaudière
The North Shore (New Brunswick) Regiment

9th Infantry Brigade

The Highland Light Infantry of Canada
The Stormont, Dundas and Glengarry Highlanders
The North Nova Scotia Highlanders

SUPPLY AND TRANSPORT

Royal Canadian Army Service Corps 3 Can Div

MEDICAL

14 Canadian Field Ambulance
22 Canadian Field Ambulance
23 Canadian Field Ambulance

ORDNANCE

3 Canadian Infantry Division Ordnance Field Park

ELECTRICAL AND MECHANICAL ENGINEERS

PROVOST

4 Canadian Provost Company

INTELLIGENCE

3 Canadian Field Security Section

2ND CANADIAN ARMOURED BRIGADE (INDEPENDENT)

6th Canadian Armoured Regiment (1st Hussars)
10th Canadian Armoured Regiment (The Fort Garry Horse)
27th Canadian Armoured Regiment (Sherbrooke Fusiliers)

LIST OF AWARDS*

Rank	Name	Unit	Award
	The Victoria Cross		
Sergeant	Aubrey Cosens	QOR	
	Distinguished Service Order		
Lt-Col	Charles Alexander Baerman	7Recce	
Major	James Wallace Braden	SDG	
Capt (A/Major)	Gordon Emmerson Clarke	SDG	
Capt (A/Major)	Latimer Hugh Denison	RWR	
Capt (A/Major)	Benjamin Dunkelman	QOR	
Major	Earl Grey English	1CScot	
Lt-Col	Allan Stuart Gregory	Regina	
Major	Joseph Charles King	HLI	
Capt (A/Major)	Lesmere Forrest Kirkpatrick	12FA	
Major	Erwin Frank Klugman	HLI	
Major	Charles Roch Lamoureux	Chaud	
Major	Hardy Lawrence Main	16FCoy	
Major	Leonard Vincent McGurran	Regina	
Capt (A/Major)	Allan Kerr McTaggart	HLI	
Major	Richard Dillon Medland	QOR	
Major	Orson Allen Nickson	QOR	
Major	John Wilson Powell	6CAR	
A/Brig	John Meredith Rockingham	9HQ	Bar/DSO
Major	Joseph Armand Ross	Chaud	
Maj (A/Lt-Col)	John William H. Rowley	NSR	
Lt-Col	Gustave Olivier Taschereau	Chaud	
A/Major	Kenneth Nelson Webber	NNova	
Major	Lloyd Christian Winhold	NNova	

---

* This Appendix lists only those decorations mentioned in this book.

Military Cross

Lt	George Galt Aldous	RWR	
H/Capt	John MacMorran Anderson	HLI	Bar/MC
Lt (A/Capt)	William Atkinson	Chaud	
Lt	Harry Haultain Badger	RWR	
Capt	Thomas Johnston Bell	12FA	
Capt	John Paul Brennan	27CAR	
Lt (A/Capt)	William Cameron	14FA	
Lt (A/Capt)	Stewart Leslie Chambers	1CScot	
A/Capt	John Douglas Crowe	12FA	
Capt	John Alexander Dure	SDG	
Lt	David Eggo	6CAR	
Capt	Arthur Fairweather	RWR	
A/Major	John Alexander Ferguson	HLI	
Lt	George Douglas Goodwin	27CAR	
Capt	William Patrick Hair	12FA	
Lt (A/Capt)	Harry Lorne Hamley	NSR	
Lt	John Leslie Hancock	QOR	
Lt	Gerard Jean	Chaud	
Lt	Warren Lincoln Keating	Regina	
Lt	Owen Kevin Hugh Kierans	NSR	
Capt	Roger Nelson LeBaron	14FA	
Lt	George Oxley Macdonald	HLI	
Lt (A/Capt)	John Douglas MacFarlane	14FA	
Lt	Donald Charles MacKenzie	RWR	
Lt	Neville Whitney Davis Mann	6FdCoy	
Lt (A/Capt)	Peter Ferguson McDonnell	1CScot	
Lt	Lloyd Carlton McKay	QOR	
Lt	William Myers	NNova	
Capt	John Ivan Nicholson	Regina	
Lt (A/Capt)	Donald Albert Pearce	HLI	
Capt	Herbert Sinclair Roberts	Regina	
Capt	Robert Lionel Rochon	Chaud	
Lt	Merrill Asal Ruiter	CHO	
Lt	Alexander Harry L. Stephen	SDG	
Capt (A/Major)	John Gerald Stevens	7HQ	
Lt (A/Capt)	Donald Charles Stewart	SDG	
Lt	Robert Alfred Warriner	27CAR	

Distinguished Conduct Medal

Sgt	Austin Bennett	NSR
A/CSM	Joseph E. Bernard	NSR

Sgt	Roger Chartrand	Chaud
Sgt	George Etienne Deschenes	Chaud
Sgt	Darrow Gomez	3AT
Sgt	Frederick Howarth	SDG
L/Cpl (A/Cpl)	Philip Peter Katchanoski	1CScot
Pte	Leo Major	Chaud
Pte	Chesley Roy Mathews	SDG
Sgt	James Ivor McIvor	RWR
CSM	Guy Nadeau	Chaud
WO II (CSM)	James Little Nimmo	1CScot

Military Medal

Gnr	William Clifford Ace	12FA
Cpl	Milton Eugene Adolph	Regina
Cpl	Hugh Charles Atchison	SDG
Cpl	Ernest William Baker	SDG
CSM	Harry Jardine Bishop	NNova
Sgt	Lorne George Sandy Blue	RWR
Sgt	Horace Boulay	NSR
Spr	Hakon Ingeman Bredeson	20FCoy
Sgt	Wilfred Francis Bunda	3AT
Sgt	John Sterling Cameron	QOR
L/Sgt	Donald Gustave Campbell	6CAR
Pte	Gerald Robert Campbell	SDG
Sgt	Lewis John Campbell	6CAR
L/Cpl	Walter Bruce Carstairs	RWR
Cpl	Kenneth Amos Chapman	7Recce
Rfn	William Chapman	RWR
Cpl (A/Sgt)	William Edward Coburn	CHO
Sgt	Walter Arthur Cochrane	3AT
L/Sgt	Armond Thomas P. Connell	27CAR
Sgt	Edward Joseph Corbett	3AT
Cpl	Melvin Louis Coulas	SDG
Pte	Waldo James Cousins	NNova
A/Sgt	Ernest Crain	QOR
Sgt	Lloyd Cummings	1CScot
Rfn	Bernard Cyr	RWR
L/Cpl	Milton David Davis	27CAR
L/Cpl	Emile Desjardins	Chaud
Cpl (A/Sgt)	Israel Maurice Deslippe	Chaud
L/Sgt	Alvin Clifford Dolan	SDG
Cpl	Sherman Walter Erison	HLI

Sgt	Elmer Milton Evoy	Regina	
Rfn	John Gingras	RWR	
L/Bdr	Roy William Hammond	14FA	
Cpl	Clifford John Handley	SDG	
Pte	Wallace Malcolm Hazlewood	1CScot	
Sgt	Joseph Lawrence Hennigar	NSR	
A/Cpl	Frank Hole	RWR	
Sgt	Thomas Alexander Hopkins	HLI	
Rfn	James Donald Innes	Regina	
A/Sgt	George Hughes Jackson	1CScot	
A/Sgt	Frederick James Jarman	HLI	
A/Cpl	Frank Reginald Jull	HLI	
L/Cpl	Albin James Kellerman	1CScot	
L/Bdr	Robert Donald Kerr	13FA	
Cpl	William Knowles	1CScot	
Cpl (L/Sgt)	Gerald Royce Langton	Regina	
Sgt	Norman Joseph Lowe	RWR	
Pte	Peter Alexander MacLean	SDG	
L/Cpl	Allen Plumb MacMaster	HLI	
CSM	Charles Cromwell Martin	QOR	
CSM	Maxwell Aitken Martin	CHO	
Gnr	William John Maynes	13FA	
Spr	Alexander McCullagh	16FCoy	
L/Bdr	John Russell Millar	14FA	
Pte	Ernest Morris Miller	SDG	
Rfn	Mervyn Frank Milson	RWR	
Rfn	Mervyn Frank Milson	RWR	Bar/MM
Cpl (A/Sgt)	Alfred Robertson Minnis	1CScot	
Pte	Russell Georald Munro	NSR	
Rfn	Charles Nahwegezhik	QOR	
Bdr	James Ninnes	12FA	
A/Sgt	Charles Abbott Post	SDG	
A/Cpl	John Charles Pritchard	6CAR	
Sgt	Joseph Prokopchuk	NNova	
L/Sgt	Cornelius Jerom Reidel	HLI	
Sgt	Arthur Rigby	27CAR	
Rfn	John James Robertson	QOR	
Sgt	Francis Jeremia Ryan	RWR	
Gnr	Benjamin Satten	14FA	
Pte	Edward Davis Scott	SDG	
Pte	Gordon Francis Scott	NNova	
Pte	Daniel Isaac Shanks	NNova	
Sgt	William James Shaw	Regina	

A/Cpl	Reginald Alastar Shepherd	NSR
L/Cpl	Arthur Charles Smith	20FCoy
Pte	David Harold Snyder	SDG
Cpl	Ernest Augustine Stanley	3DSigs
Sgt	George Stewart	SDG
Gnr (A/Bdr)	John Riley Stromquist	13FA
Sgt	Edward Stanley Tenklei	Regina
Sigmn	George Edward Thomas	3DSigs
Sgt	Thomas William Todd	12FA
Sgt	John Alexander Tree	NSR
Gnr	Floyd Marshall Tufts	4LAA
Pte	Florian Victor Veilleux	Chaud
Pte	Ernest Fowlie Watling	NSR
Rfn	James Matthew Watson	QQOR
Rfn	George Henry Webster	RWR
Pte	James Allan W. Whitacre	SDG
Sgt	Cedric Godfrey Whittall	7Recce
L/Cpl	Raymond Wickens	4PCo
L/Cpl	John James Wighton	HLI
Gnr	Donald Wright	12FA

MENTION IN DESPATCHES

L/Cpl	Roy Wilfred Conrad	1CScot

NETHERLAND

Militaire Willems-Ordre

A/Cpl	Joseph William Campbell	NNova

Bronzen Leeuw

Cpl	Wilfrid Arseneault	Chaud
Maj	Donald Gordon Brown	Regina
L/Sgt	James William Bryan	6FdCoy
Lt-Col	Desmond Gerald Crofton	1CScot
A/Cpl	Edwin Garfield Harvey	27CAR
Rfn	John Wilfred Johnston	QOR
Pte	Maurice Lacasse	Chaud
Pte	James Benedict Lynch	NSR
Sgt	William Lemuel MacKay	NNova
Capt	Robert Bryant Menzies	HLI
Cpl	Frederick James Nicol	1CScot
Sgt	Joseph Antoine Ouellet	NNova

Cpl	Wilfred Paradis	1CScot
Capt (A/Major)	John Douglas Pickup	QOR
A/Cpl	Allan Sheppard	7Recce
Sgt	Peter Joseph Steinman	HLI

Bronzen Kruis

Sgt	Howard Edward Bird	CHO
Sgt	Cecil James Brown	RWR
L/Cpl	Hector John Edwards	SDG
Pte	Norman Edward Fisher	NSR
Cpl	William Lawrence	1CScot
Sgt	Alexander Lawton	SDG
L/Sgt (A/Sgt)	Nicholas John Perry	QOR
Lt	Kenneth Frederick Prueter	CHO
Cpl	Alfred Harold Stroud	CHO
Cpl	Floyd Edison Webb	CHO

UNITED STATES

Silver Star

Sgt	Alfred Francis Richardson	RWR

Bronze Star

H/Major	Jean Robert A. J. Dalcourt	Chaud

ABBREVIATIONS

UNITS

Chaud	- Le Régiment de la Chaudière
CHO	- The Cameron Highlanders of Ottawa (MG)
HLI	- The Highland Light Infantry of Canada
NNova	- The North Nova Scotia Highlanders
NSR	- The North Shore (New Brunswick) Regiment
QOR	- The Queen's Own Rifles of Canada
Regina	- The Regina Rifles
RWR	- The Royal Winnipeg Rifles
SDG	- The Stormont, Dundas and Glengarry Highlanders
1 CScot	- 1 Battalion, The Canadian Scottish Regiment
3AT	- 3rd Anti-Tank Regiment
3DSigs	- 3rd Canadian Infantry Division Signals
4LAA	- 4th Canadian Light Anti-Aircraft Regiment
6 CAR	- 6th Canadian Armoured Regiment

6 F Coy	- 6th Canadian Field Company RCE
7 Recce	- 7th Reconnaissance Regiment
7HQ	- 7th Canadian Infantry Brigade Headquarters
8HQ	- 8th Canadian Infantry Brigade Headquarters
9HQ	- 9th Canadian Infantry Brigade Headquarters
10 CAR	- 10th Canadian Armoured Regiment
12 FA	- 12th Canadian Field Artillery Regiment RCA
13 FA	- 13th Canadian Field Artillery Regiment RCA
14 FA	- 14th Canadian Field Artillery Regiment RCA
16 F Coy	- 16th Field Company RCE
18 F Coy	- 18th Field Company RCE
20 FCoy	- 20th Canadian Field Company RCE
27 CAR	- 27th Canadian Armoured Regiment

RANKS

A/Sergeant	- Acting Sergeant
A/Capt	- Acting Captain
Capt	- Captain
Bdr	- Bombardier
Cpl	- Corporal
CSM	- Company Sergeant Major
Gnr	- Gunner
H/Capt	- Honourary Captain
L/Bdr	- Lance Bombardier
L/Cpl	- Lance Corporal
L/Sgt	- Lance Sergeant
Lt	- Lieutenant
Lt-Col	- Lieutenant-Colonel
Pte	- Private
RCA	- Royal Canadian Artillery
RCE	- Royal Canadian Engineers
Rfn	- Rifleman
RSM	- Regimental Sergeant-Major
Sigmn	- Signalman
Spr	- Sapper
Sgt	- Sergeant
Tpr	- Trooper

BIBLIOGRAPHY

Barnard, Lt Col. W. T. *The Queen's Own Rifles of Canada 1860-1960*. Don Mills: The Ontario Publishing Co. Ltd., 1960.

Bartlett, Jack Fortune. *1st Battalion, the Highland Light Infantry of Canada, 1940-1945*. Galt: The Highland Light Infantry Association, 1951.

Bird, Will. R. *No Retreating Footsteps: The Story of the North Nova Scotia Highlanders*. Kentville. Kentville Publishing Co., n.d.

————. *North Shore (New Brunswick) Regiment*. Fredricton: Brunswick Press, 1963.

Boss, W. *The Stormont, Dundas and Glengarry Highlanders: 1783-1951*. Ottawa: Runge Press, 1952.

Castonguay, Jacques et Armand Ross. *Le Régiment de la Chaudière*. Lévis, Le Régiment de la Chaudière, 1983.

Conron, Col. A. Brandon. *A History of the First Hussars Regiment 1856-1980*.

Copp, Terry and Robert Vogel. *Maple Leaf Route: Victory*. Alma, Ontario: Maple Leaf Route, 1988.

Dunkelman, Ben. *Dual Allegiance*. Toronto: MacMillan of Canada, 1976.

Essame, H. *The Battle for Germany*. New York: Charles Scribner's Sons, 1969.

Hickey, Rev. R. Myles. *The Scarlet Dawn*. Fredericton: Unipress, 1980.

Jackson, Lt Col H. M. *The Sherbrooke Regiment (12th Armoured Regiment)*. privately published, 1958.

Luxton, Captain Eric. *1st Battalion the Regina Rifle Regiment 1939-1946*. Regina: The Regina Rifles Association, 1946.

Martin, Charles Cromwell. *Battle Diary: From D-Day and Normandy to the Zuider Zee and VE*. Toronto: Dundurn Press, 1994.

Pavey, Capt W.G. *An Historical Account of the 7th Canadian Reconnaissance Regiment in the World War 1939-1945*. Montreal: privately published, 1948.

Ross, Lt-Col. R.M. *The History of the 1st Battalion Cameron Highlanders of Ottawa (MG)*. Ottawa: privately published.

Roy, Reginald H. *Ready for the Fray: The History of the Canadian Scottish Regiment (Princess Mary's) 1920-1955*. Vancouver: The Canadian Scottish Regiment, 1958.

Stacey, Colonel C. P. *The Victory Campaign*. Ottawa: The Queen's Printer, 1966.

Tascona, Bruce and Eric Wells. *Little Black Devils: A History of the Royal Winnipeg Rifles*. Winnipeg: Fry Publishing, 1983.

Thompson, R.W. *Battle for the Rhine*. New York: Ballantine Books, 1959.

Whitaker, W. Denis and Shelagh Whitaker. *Rhineland*. Toronto: Stoddart Publishing Co. Ltd., 1989.

Williams, Jeffery. *The Long Left Flank: The Hard Fought Way to the Reich 1944-1945*. Toronto: Stoddart Publishing Co. Ltd., 1988.

NAME INDEX

Stromquist, A/Bdr John R. 49
Stroud, Cpl Alfred H. 29
Taschereau, A/Lt-Col Gustave O. 85
Tenklei, Sgt Edward S. 37
Thomas, Sigmn George E. 209
Todd, Sgt Thomas W. 35
Tree, Sgt John A. 70
Tufts, Gnr Floyd M. 78
Veilleux, Pte Florian V. 86
Warriner, Lt Robert A. 132
Watling, Pte Ernest F. 149
Watson, Rfn James M. 60
Webb, Cpl Floyd E. 171
Webber, A/Maj Kenneth N. 200
Webster, Rfn George H. 156
Whitacre, Pte James A. 124
Whittall, Sgt Cedric G. 144
Wickens, L/Cpl Raymond 143
Wighton, L/Cpl John J. 207
Winhold, Maj Lloyd C. 115
Wright, Gnr Donald. 184

ACKNOWLEDGEMENTS

Grateful acknowledgement is make for permission to quote from the following copyright sources: from *The Battle for Germany* by H. Essame, Copyright (c) 1969 E. Essame by permission of Macmillan Publishing Copany and also of B. T. Batsford Ltd; from *Dual Allegiance* by Ben Dunkelman (c) 1976 by permission of Macmillan of Canada; from *Battle Diary* by Charles Cromwell Martin (c) 1994 by permission of Dundurn Press; from *Battle for the Rhine* by R. W. Thompson (c) 1959 by permission from Random House Inc.; from *North Shore (New Brunswick) Regiment* by Will R. Bird (c) 1963 from University Press of New Brunswick; from *Maple Leaf Route; Victory* by Terry Copp and Robert Vogel (c) 1988 by permission form Terry Copp.